# JOURNAL OF FRANCIS BUCHANAN

# JOURNAL OF FRANCIS BUCHANAN

**(AFTERWARDS HAMILTON)**

## KEPT DURING THE SURVEY OF THE DISTRICTS OF PATNA AND GAYA

**IN**

**1811-1812**

**Edited with Notes and Introduction**

**By**


## V. H. Jackson



GYAN

*Published by*

GYAN

Gyan Publishing House
5, Ansari Road
Daryaganj, New Delhi-110002
Phone: 011-47034999, 9811692060
E-mail: books@gyanbooks.com

*Distribution Network*
gyanbooks.com
India, USA, Canada, UK, Australia, France



ISBN : 978-81-212-3645-4 (PB)
First Published, 1925

2nd Impression 2020

*Printed at:* Gyan Press, Delhi.

# JOURNAL

OF

# FRANCIS BUCHANAN

(AFTERWARDS HAMILTON)

KEPT DURING THE SURVEY OF THE DISTRICTS

OF

## PATNA AND GAYA

IN

1811-1812

---

Edited with Notes and Introduction

BY

V. H. JACKSON

PATNA
SUPERINTENDENT, GOVERNMENT PRINTING, BIHAR AND ORISSA
1925

# JOURNAL

OF

# FRANCIS BUCHANAN

KEPT DURING THE SURVEY OF THE DISTRICTS

OF

# PATNA AND GAYA

IN

# 1811-1812.

---

## Introduction.

### The Buchanan Journal and Maps.

PRACTICALLY the whole of the information which is now available concerning the life and work of the author of this Journal, including an account of the circumstances under which his great statistical Survey of Bengal was undertaken, and the subsequent history of the manuscripts connected therewith, is to be found in Sir David Prain's admirable Memoir published in Calcutta in 1905, entitled "A Sketch of the life of Francis Hamilton (once Buchanan), sometime Superintendent of the Honourable Company's Botanic Garden, Calcutta". It is therefore unnecessary to attempt a summary here, particularly as Sir D. Prain himself has been good enough to promise a contribution to the Journal of the Bihar and Orissa Research Society on the subject.

The Journal, which is now published for the first time, forms only a small part of the manuscripts relating to the Survey, on which Dr. Buchanan—as he may still be called for present purposes since he did not assume the name of Hamilton until three years after his retirement from India—was employed between the years 1807 and 1815. It is the official daily Journal which he kept during his tour of the districts of Patna and Gaya in the cold-weather months of 1811-12, i.e., the fifth season of his work on the Survey. The original manuscript is in his own handwriting and extends over 224 pages, bound up with other papers in the last of those three volumes of the Buchanan Manuscripts in the Library of the India Office which are concerned with Patna and Gaya. As regards other districts of Bihar included in the Survey, similar Journals kept during the cold-weather tours of Bhagalpur, etc., in 1810-11 and Shahabad in 1812-13 are also in existence in the Library, and occupy 250 and 175 pages respectively in the corresponding volumes of the series, but the Journal of the tour in Purnea undertaken in the season 1809-10 cannot now be traced, and apparently has never been in the Library's possession. There also appear to be no Journals in existence relating to the Bengal Districts of Dinajpur and Rangpur, and the United Provinces District of Gorakhpur.*

The three Journals which still remain are quite distinct from Buchanan's Reports on the corresponding districts, and are only to be regarded as supplementary to the latter. It is necessary to lay emphasis on this difference in order to avoid any possibility of misunderstanding, especially because on page xxxviii of his Memoir Sir D. Prain refers to the Reports themselves as "a journal of the utmost value, which has never been completely published or properly edited", while in later pages when describing the attempts which have been made to publish the Reports, he continues to refer to them as a "journal". It seems possible that when he wrote he was under the impression that Buchanan had drawn up his Reports in the Bengal Survey in the same form as that adopted in his "Journey from Madras, through the countries of

* I am indebted to Mr. C. E. A. W. Oldham, I.C.S., retired, for this information.

Mysore, Canara and Malabar" which was undertaken in 1800-01. This was a daily Journal, which was published in London in 1807 in the form in which it was written, although in the preface Buchanan explained that he had intended to abridge it and alter its arrangement before publication, but could not do so, as the printing had commenced before his arrival in England on leave in the previous year. Taking warning by this experience and by the criticisms of the form in which the work appeared, his methods were altered when he undertook the Survey of Bengal. His study of each district which he then surveyed was arranged so as to occupy a whole year. After an extended cold-weather tour, during which he and his assistants collected a very large amount of information additional to that actually recorded in his daily journal, he established his headquarters at some town in or near the district concerned, and spent the following hot-weather and rainy seasons in completing his enquiries and in writing his Report. Each of these Reports is therefore a self-contained and carefully finished work which was clearly intended for publication. Not only was it drawn up in strict accordance with the detailed instructions issued to Buchanan by the Government at Calcutta in September 1807, as recorded in pages viii to x of the Introduction to "Eastern India", but in its arrangement it followed the actual order of these instructions. The Journals, on the other hand, were evidently not intended for publication, and unfortunately were not maintained during the period spent at headquarters. Much of the information recorded in them has been included in the Reports, and has often been transferred without any substantial modification, but in all cases it has been rearranged under the appropriate sections.

Of the Reports and their various Appendices, with the sole exception of the Journals, two copies are known to be in existence, one of which is in the India Office Library, as already mentioned, and the other in the Library of the Royal Asiatic Society. The original manuscript cannot be traced and appears to have been destroyed, as neither of the sets is in

Buchanan's own handwriting, but both have been written in a beautifully clear hand by the same copyist. There is some uncertainty about the identity of a set of the Reports which was in the possession of the Indian Government at Calcutta about 1833 and, as Beveridge suggested, it is possible that a third copy may still be in India, even though the efforts to trace it made by Sir W. W. Hunter, Sir D. Prain and others have been unsuccessful. It seems much more probable, however, that not more than two copies were ever made, and that the volumes now in the possession of the Royal Asiatic Society are in fact the set of the records which were formerly kept in Calcutta, and referred to in the following extract from the preface to the Report on Dinajpur, published at Calcutta in 1833 :—

> "The original records, occupying twenty-five folio volumes in manuscript, were transmitted by the Indian Government to the Honourable Court of Directors, a copy of the whole having been previously made and deposited in the office of the Chief Secretary at Calcutta. Duplicates of the drawings and maps were unfortunately not preserved with the rest, probably from the difficulty at that time of getting them executed in India."

This duplicate copy was made after Buchanan had left India in February 1815, and the originals sent to London were received there in the following year. As regards the copy then retained in Calcutta, it is known that in 1831 the M. S. Report on Dinajpur was made over by Mr. G. Swinton, who was then Chief Secretary, to Captain Herbert, the editor of *Gleanings in Science*, in order that it might be published by instalments in that Journal : and three years later James Prinsep, the first editor of its still living successor—the *Journal of the Asiatic Society of Bengal*—in the preface to Volume II, while announcing with regret that the publication of the remaining Reports would have to be discontinued owing to lack of support, mentioned that on completion of publication of that on Dinajpur :—

> "The Government meantime placed the remaining volumes of Buchanan in the Editor's hands, with an intimation of its desire that the printing of these records should be continued."

It seems not unreasonable to suppose, therefore, that this set of the Reports reached the Royal Asiatic Society after passing out of Prinsep's possession; and further that no copy of the Journals, as well as of the drawings and maps, was made before the originals were forwarded to the Court of Directors, since no such copy is included in these volumes. This fact was probably not realised in 1871, when permission was given to Sir W. W. Hunter to bring the India Office collection of the manuscripts temporarily back to India, as the original Journals, of which no copy had been retained, were thus exposed twice again to the risk of total loss at sea.

These Journals of Buchanan's tours in the Districts of South Bihar seem to have attracted very little attention hitherto, probably owing to their close resemblance to portions of the corresponding Reports, and to the greater importance of the latter. The following extract from Mr. H. Beveridge's article on "The Buchanan Records" in the *Calcutta Review* for July 1894 is the only published reference to them which I have been able to trace :—

> "There is a good deal of repetition in Buchanan, and some portions of his folios are taken up with his Journal, e.g., his Bhagalpur and Shahabad Journal, which does not contain anything material that is not also in his report."

This statement is not strictly correct, as will be indicated later, and even if it were, it appears that the publication of the Journals, especially the Patna-Gaya Journal, can serve a useful purpose at the present time, because much of the material included both in the Journals and in the Reports has never yet been published. Montgomery Martin's methods as editor of "Eastern India", the three-volume abridgment of the Reports published in 1838, have been justly condemned by everyone who has examined the original manuscripts. In deciding what portions of the Reports should be omitted, he followed no consistent plan, but merely, as Sir W. W. Hunter observed, left out "the parts which he did not understand or which did not interest him". Matters of topographical and antiquarian interest are the principal feature of the Journals, and in these respects the Reports, and particularly the Report on the districts of Patna and Gaya, have greatly suffered at his hands. On this point Beveridge says:—

> "On the whole I have not found that Mr. Martin has suppressed much of value in the historical or antiquarian chapters. For instance, there are no suppressions in the account of Gaur, which, by the way, is to be found in the Purniah volumes. The most serious omissions are in the accounts of Patna and Shahabad. There Mr. Martin has drawn his pencil through much interesting matter, though in not a few cases he has afterwards repented and written "stet". In all the volumes he has omitted a good deal of the descriptive matter, and he has greatly abridged the elaborate account of castes which occurs in the first of the three volumes relating to Purniah."

During his tour of the districts of Patna and Gaya, Buchanan naturally came across antiquities considerably more extensive and important than those contained in the districts which he had previously surveyed, and his description of them may be regarded as the special feature of the Patna Report. Unfortunately, though fifth in natural sequence, it was the first on which Martin began his work of abridgment, and he carried it out with special severity, as may be judged by the fact that approximately 167 out of the 370 pages in the M. S. Report, which form the chapter on topography and antiquities, have been omitted from the corresponding Chapter III of Eastern India, Volume I. This represents about sixty of the pages as printed in that volume, and the omissions include the whole of the account of Maner, as well as important portions of the descriptions of Patna, Gaya, Bodh Gaya, Rajgir and Baragaon. With the exception of Patna itself, Buchanan's observations at each of these places are adequately recorded in the Journal.

Notwithstanding Mr. Beveridge's unfavourable opinion, which was probably based on a somewhat cursory examination of the manuscripts, there are several respects in which the Journals are an extremely useful supplement to the Reports, even in places where the latter have not been abridged. They principally differ from the Reports in giving a detailed description of the route which Buchanan actually followed, without which it is at the present day very difficult to identify some of the places described in the Reports, particularly the various hills and the mines, quarries, caves or springs associated with them. Many examples of this which have come within my own observation could be quoted, but the following will suffice :—In the Bhagalpur Report (East. Ind., Vol. II, pp. 184-85) Buchanan describes "a calcareous matter in mass, called Asurhar, or Giant's bones", which was used for making lime, and says that "the greatest quantity is found at a place, in the centre of the (Kharagpur) hills, called Asurni, or the female Giant". The manufacture of lime from this source has long been discontinued, and as the existence of the place appears to be unknown to the Koras and Naiyas who now live in the vicinity, it would be almost impossible to find it without reference to the Journal. This gives not only the route taken on March 22nd, 1811, from Bharari along the valley of the Anjan (Azan), but also a rough sketch showing the position of the quarry itself at the head of a side valley near Karahara, by means of which the remains of the kilns, etc., can be found without the least difficulty, although they are concealed by thick jungle. Similarly, in the Patna Report (Vol. I, pp. 254-56) the interesting description of the cave "at a place called Hangriyo" in the southern range of the Rajgir Hills from which *silajit* was procured, was not sufficient to enable me to identify this cave without reference to the Journal for January 11th, 1812. This showed that the cave was not the Rajpind Cave in the Jethian valley, as I had been inclined to suppose, but one in the southern face of the Hanria Hill, the existence of which is kept as secret as possible owing to the value of the *silajit* still obtained from it; and an examination of this cave has served to clear up several difficulties connected with Hiuen Tsang's route between Bodh Gaya and Rajgir, and has shown that the Hanria Hill itself was Hiuen Tsang's Buddhavana Mountain.

Another feature of the Journals is that they frequently contain minor details which Buchanan did not consider of sufficient importance to include in the Reports, but which are of value in unexpected ways. For instance, in measuring the temperature of a hot spring in order to ascertain the nature of its seasonal or secular variation, a problem in which I have been interested for the last fourteen years, it is of particular importance that the thermometer should be placed, if possible, in exactly the same part of the spring as that observed on previous occasions. In the Bhagalpur Report (Vol. II, page 200) when describing the hot springs near Bharari in the Kharagpur Hills, Buchanan says :—

> " The thermometer on being placed in a crevice of the rock, from whence the water issued accompanied by air bubbles, rose to 150°."

There usually are at these springs four or five places which might answer to this description, at none of which is the temperature either identical or constant, but the corresponding passage in the Journal removes all uncertainty, since it can only refer to one particular place :—

> " Where the finest spring is, and the water issues immediately from the foot of the hill, without running any way under the stones, and is accompanied by many air bubbles, the thermometer arises to 150°."

No other hot spring in Bihar, issuing in its natural state directly from the earth instead of rising, as it usually is made to do, into the water already contained in a tank or kund, can be identified with such absolute certainty as this. Since 1909, I have measured its temperature on several occasions, at different seasons of the year ; and as the maximum temperature noticed, after allowing for all necessary corrections, has never exceeded 149°, and as there is no reason to suppose that there has been in this case any measurable change of a secular nature even in the last hundred years, the inference is that the thermometer which Buchanan used in his measurements on hot springs read at least one degree Fahr. too high. This is confirmed by similar though less reliable comparisons elsewhere, such as at Bhimbandh, Sitakund near Monghyr, and Rajgir; and in any case is likely enough, since the discovery that all ordinary mercury-in-glass thermometers, even if correctly graduated when first made, read too high as they grow older was not made until 1822, so that Buchanan was not aware that any correction of his own thermometer was necessary. It may be mentioned that one of the thermometers which I have used for making these comparisons shows this effect plainly enough, in spite of the precautions now taken by the instrument-makers, as it reads 0·5 degree Fahr. higher than it did when it was graduated by them, and 0·1 degree higher than when it was first compared in October 1912.

In these Journals it is interesting to notice the care with which Buchanan tested the truth of any statements made to him, whenever opportunities occurred later; as well as, in general, the thoroughness with which he had adopted the principles of modern scientific research. A good example of his methods is shown in the present Journal, in the endeavours which he made, though without much success, to obtain a criterion by which Buddhist and Jain images could be distinguished from one another. The hot springs of Bihar, which he was the first to describe, have been examined by several later observers, such as Kittoe, Sherwill and Waddell, but their own accounts are in no case so detailed or precise, and in fact possess very little scientific value.

Buchanan had practically no works of reference to assist him in identifying the antiquities of Bihar, such as the Travels of the Chinese pilgrims which have revealed so much to later archæologists, and it is not surprising that at times he rejected information which now appears very significant. For instance, on the grounds that his informant was "a stupid fellow, and no other person has heard of such a tradition", he did not think it worth while to refer in his Report to the names "Hangsa Nagar" and "Hangsapur" mentioned to him in connection with Giriak. Fifty years later, the remains which still exist on the hill above Giriak were conclusively identified by Cunningham with the Goose Stupa and Monastery described by Hiuen Tsang. Similarly, the jungle-covered valley of Old Rajagriha seemed to him obviously so unfitted for the site of a city, being "surrounded on every side by arid rocks, which would render the heat intolerable" and the situation "to the last degree insalubrious", that he did not trouble to investigate for himself the truth of the local belief that it was the site of the old city of Jarasandha. There can be little doubt that Old Rajagriha was actually proved to be an unpleasant dwelling-place, partly owing to the reasons mentioned by Buchanan and perhaps still more to lack of water at the hottest season of the year : and that its abandonment and the establishment of New Rajagriha outside the hills were due to the comparative advantages of the latter site, rather than to the legendary reason as related by Hiuen Tsang. But that Old Rajagriha was at one time inhabited by a large population is a fact which cannot but be evident to anyone who examines the site even now ;* and the Journal shows that the reasons why Buchanan never noticed even so much as its massive walls were, first, that he did not ascend either Baibhargiri or Vipulagiri sufficiently far to get a proper view of the valley within the hills, and second, that when he did enter the valley in order to examine the Sonbhandar Cave, his path went past a part of the old city where its wall has been almost completely cut away by the western branch of the Saraswati stream.

The Journals of South Bihar show that during his tour in each district Buchanan kept up the practice

---

* Notes on Old Rajagriha, A. S. R., 1913-14, pages 265-271.

adopted during the Mysore survey, which was, in the words of Sir D. Prain:

> "To make a stated daily march, and in the morning before leaving camp to gather round him the leading people of the neighbourhood whom he questioned on the various points enumerated in his instructions. During his march and at the places where he halted, his own observations were carefully noted, and extensive botanical and geological collections were made."

Much of the material recorded in the Journal of Mysore, especially the observations on agriculture and botany, finds no corresponding place in these Journals, but has been incorporated direct into the Reports. There is one feature, however, which shows a marked development in this later series of Journals. This is the care with which the distance is estimated between each successive village, river or other notable feature of the country passed over during each day's march. Buchanan had discovered that the existing maps of the districts included in the Bengal Survey were all more or less unreliable, and the details of distance which he sets down in his Journals were evidently intended for use in preparing the revised map of each district which he himself drew. This task, which he set himself for it formed no part of his instructions, must have involved much labour, especially as no trained surveyor was attached to his party; and practically the whole of the work which he carried out in this manner—both as an independent geographer and as the direct successor of Rennell--has escaped notice hitherto, owing to the fact that his manuscript maps, still preserved in the Map Department of the India Office Library, have never been published except in a very incomplete and unsatisfactory form. For this reason, a detailed account of those which relate to South Bihar may appropriately be set down here.

All internal evidence points to the conclusion that Buchanan had no maps of Bihar to consult during his Survey other than those contained in the second edition of Rennell's Bengal Atlas, published in 1781. The first edition of this Atlas, which was published in 1779-80, contained only Plates I to XII, but there are references in the Bhagalpur Journal (January 2nd, 1811) to Rennell's plans of Mir Kasim's fortifications at Udhua Nullah near Rajmahal, and in the Patna Report to his plan of Patna City, which are included only in the later and more complete edition, as Plates XXI and XV respectively.

There is no indication that Buchanan knew anything about the series of larger maps (on the scale of five British miles to the inch) drawn by Rennell in 1773 and published quite recently by Major F. C. Hirst, Director of Surveys, Bengal, from the originals in the India Office collection. As Hirst points out in his accompanying Memoir,* these maps must have been used by Rennell in preparing the Atlas, but they differ considerably from the latter in certain important details which Buchanan would undoubtedly have noticed, if he had had access to them.

So far at least as the Districts of Monghyr, Bhagalpur and the Santal Parganas are concerned, the existence of any maps later than those in the Bengal Atlas is conclusively disproved in the first paragraph of the following passage, which Martin omitted from page 2 of the Bhagalpur Report as published in Eastern India, Volume II :—

> "The turbulent state of the inhabitants, and the difficulty of access into the country, when Major Rennell made his survey, opposed obstacles which have rendered his map of this district less valuable than most part of his excellent work, and I have to regret that a copy of a more recent survey, which had been deposited in the office of the Collector, has been lost. Owing to these circumstances, to the very uncommon manner in which many of the subordinate jurisdictions have been intermixed, not only with each other, but with other districts, and to the disputed and undetermined nature of the

* The Surveys of Bengal, by Major James Rennell, F.R.S. 1764—77, Calcutta, 1917

boundaries, I have not been able to trace these in a manner that can be at all satisfactory, and in almost every case I have been under the necessity of proceeding by conjecture, and that in many cases of a very vague nature.

"In calculating the proportion of various kinds of land and the extent of cultivation, I found the proprietors so evidently departing from the truth that I have in great measure been obliged to trust entirely to what I and my native assistants could actually observe, on which account we traversed the district in many directions and with much pains. Notwithstanding this labour, I am much less satisfied with the result than with those which I procured in the districts formerly surveyed. The conduct of my enquiries owing to this circumstance has in this district been rather disagreeable. The managers of the estates showed much alarm, a want of veracity that could only be equalled by their total indifference about its being discovered, and a degree of intellect vastly inferior to the people of Bengal. No general statement could be procured from the most intelligent, and the details which they gave were in such diametrical opposition according to the nature of the questions proposed that no reliance whatever could be placed on their assertions. If for instance a man was asked, why so much land was waste, he would assert that seven-eighths of his estate were cultivated; but in explaining the heaviness of his burthens he would show an account in which, with an extent of ten or twelve miles square, he had not above one or two thousand bighas in cultivation."

In addition to the passage just quoted, there is ample evidence throughout the Journals and Reports that Buchanan was by no means satisfied with the accuracy of Rennell's maps. Though he himself does not say so, it is interesting to note that the plan which he formed was to prepare a revised edition of the maps in the Bengal Atlas itself, so far as they related to his Survey. His own maps have been drawn on exactly the same scale as the somewhat inconvenient one employed by Rennell in Plates I to VIII of the Atlas, which are common to both editions. This scale was one of ten geographical or nautical miles to an inch, Rennell's marked preference for nautical units being explained by Hirst in the memoir already cited as being due to his training as a Marine Surveyor. Rennell assumed that a nautical mile was 6,090 feet (6,080 feet is more correct), so that this scale should correspond to 11·53 statute or British miles to an inch. In the copies of his maps which I possess, the real scales are slightly smaller than this, owing doubtless to a certain amount of shrinkage in mounting, and the actual values are approximately 11·8 and 11·6 miles to an inch in Plates II[1] and III[2] respectively. Small though this difference may appear, it is not altogether negligible, as it corresponds to a discrepancy of about three miles between the extreme limits of the map which shows the boundaries of Monghyr, Bhagalpur, and the Santal Parganas.

Altogether, there are eight of these manuscript maps in the India Office Library, and very careful tracings of the three which refer to South Bihar have been made for me by Miss Anstey. The description of these is as follows:—

(A) "M. S. maps of Districts by Dr. Buchanan Hamilton. Drawn in about 1814. No. 1. Bhagalpur. Size 11 inches by 14."

Title on Map, in Buchanan's handwriting, "Bhagalpur". No scale of miles is drawn on this map, but comparing selected points on the tracing with Rennell's map, the scale is 11·67 miles to one inch.

(B) "Map of Zila Behar, including the City of Patna, drawn by Dr. Buchanan Hamilton about 1814. Scale about 11½ miles to 1 inch; size 8 inches by 11."

Title on Map, in Buchanan's handwriting, as given above. Scale of miles drawn on map. On the tracing, 60 miles = 5·11 inches, or 11·74 miles to one inch.

---

(1) "The Jungleterry District and the adjacent Provinces of Birboomi, Rajemal, Boglipour, etc., comprehending the Countries situated between Moorshedabad and Bahar."

(2) "A Map of South Bahar, including the course of the Ganges to Chunargur."

(C) "Manuscript map by Dr. Buchanan Hamilton. Drawn in about 1814. No. 4. District of Shahabad. Scale about 11½ miles to 1 inch; size 12 inches by 11."

Title on Map, in Buchanan's handwriting, "Sketch of the district of Shahabad". Scale of miles drawn on map. On the tracing, 60 miles = 5·18 inches, or 11·58 miles to one inch.

The small variations in scale can likewise be explained by unequal shrinkage of these tracings, and the original maps were evidently superimposable on Rennell's own. It is hardly likely that all of these maps were drawn in or about 1814, as stated, for Buchanan was busy on the survey of Gorakhpur during that year, and left India early in February 1815. It is much more probable that each map was drawn at his headquarters immediately after finishing the tour of the district concerned, and that it was used for the general geographical description contained in the Report, such as the courses of the various rivers, etc., much of which has been omitted in Martin's abridgment. If so, the Bhagalpur map must have been drawn at Monghyr in 1811, the Patna-Gaya map at Patna in 1812, and the Shahabad map at Chunar in 1813.

Buchanan's opinion of the ordinary roads in Bihar was by no means high, as numerous entries in his Journals indicate; and his maps show none of those between various places which are given by Rennell, but in all other respects the details which they contain are fuller as well as more accurate. The only names written on the maps themselves are those of the rivers and their tributaries, every one of which is thus distinguished. In order to avoid the confusion which would have been caused by attempting to add further lettering to maps drawn on so small a scale, the method which he adopted as regards other particulars is the following:—

Hills are shown in their proper position and approximate outlines. Their names, so far as the

Bhagalpur and Patna maps are concerned, can be ascertained by reference to separate maps of the Hills drawn on a larger scale (about two miles to an inch). The corresponding map of the Hills of Shahabad cannot now be traced, if it ever existed. Thana boundaries are drawn on the maps, and distinguished from one another by coloured fringes, while the Thanas themselves are indicated by roman numerals. Within each Thana the position of the chief villages or market places is shown by small circles and arabic numerals. These numbers refer to an "Index to the Map" of each district which forms one of the (unpublished) Appendices to the corresponding Report. Each Index further contains under every Thana and market place a list of merchants and petty dealers, as shown in the following extract from the Index to the Map of Bhagalpur :—

*IX.—Division under Thanah Mallepur* :

50 Dealers in grain, salt, catechu and cotton wool, etc. (Bepari or Mahajan), 2 have capitals of Rs. 100 each, 48 have from Rs. 100 to Rs. 200.

10 Persons who import cotton, wool and cloths and retail themselves, capitals from Rs. 50 to Rs. 200.

5 Dealers in grain, salt, drugs and tobacco (Baniya), capitals from Rs. 100 to Rs. 200.

11 Baldiya Beparis who keep cattle and deal in grain, etc.

125 Retailers of provisions and drugs (Modi or Baniya, Bepari or Pasari), capitals from Rs. 10 to Rs. 50.

1 Person who exports timber, fuel, wooden posts and bamboos, etc. (Kathaiya Mahajan), capitals Rs. 150.

200 Farmers who deal in same, capitals from Rs. 5 to Rs. 20.

50 Strange Dealers (Baldiya-Beparis) who come in the dry season from Behar and Mungger and reside here about 8 months when they export grain by their cattle, capitals from Rs. 100 to Rs. 300.

4 Retailers of betel-leaf (Tambuli), capitals from Rs. 4 to Rs. 5.

1 Retailer of Capsicum, etc. (Khattik), capital Rs. 5.

1 Retailer of vegetables (Kungjra), capital Rs. 5.

1 Retailer of Hemp Buds (Gangjawaleh).

MARKET PLACES.

1. *Mallepur.*

11 Dealers in salt, grain, cotton cloths, etc. (Bepari or Goldar).

11 Baldiya Beparis who keep cattle and deal in grain, etc.

8 Retailers of provisions and drugs (Khichri furosh).

3 Retailers of sweetmeats (Halwai).

3 Retailers of oil (Taili).

2 Retailers of betel-leaf (Tambuli).

2 Retailers of potters ware (Kumar).

15 Goyalas, who retail curdled milk, etc.

1 Tailor.

1 Mali, or seller of garlands and flowers.

1 Worker in lac (Laheri).

4 Goldsmiths.

1 Distiller of spirituous liquors (Kulal).

2. *Jamui.*

2 Hats in the week (with similar details).

3. *Sono.*

2 Hats in the week (with similar details).

4. *Panchrukhi,* ditto.

5. *Kharma,* ditto.

X.—*Division under Thanah Tarapur* :—

And so on.

Martin has extracted the names of Thanas and market places from the Indexes to the Maps of Bhagalpur and Patna (Vol. II, Appendix, page 8, and Vol. I, Appendix, page 54), but has omitted the corresponding list referring to the Map of Shahabad. He has also summarised in a separate Appendix (Vol. I, Appendix, pages 35-38) the statistics regarding the number of "artists" and the nature of their occupations in the city of Patna and in the various districts of Bihar, but has only given the distribution by thanas, and not by individual towns or *hats*. He has omitted the corresponding lists of traders and the nature of their trades.

The value of Buchanan's maps would have been considerably enhanced if they had been reproduced on a somewhat larger scale, such as that of eight miles to an inch adopted in the most recent Gazetteers; because it would then have been possible not only to retain all the information which they include, but also to add the names of the hills, and to substitute the actual names of Thanas and market places for numerals, thus rendering the maps independent of their indexes. Had this course been adopted in 1838, when they were copied by J. & C. Walker for Martin's Eastern India, the extent of Buchanan's contributions to geographical knowledge, as compared with the Bengal Atlas, would have been clearly recognized; but unfortunately a different course was adopted. In order to conform to the size of the printed pages in these volumes, the scale of the maps was reduced to one of about 25½ miles to the inch in that of Bhagalpur, and 21¼ miles to the inch in those of Patna and Shahabad. The omissions thus rendered inevitable have greatly impaired their value. The only features which have been reproduced just as Buchanan drew them are the boundaries of the thanas and the courses of the rivers and tributaries. None of the hills have been shown, and nearly all the names of rivers, etc., have been omitted. The names of thanas, and of some of the market places in each thana, have been transferred to the maps by using the key given in the Indexes, but in choosing place-names, the space available for their insertion rather than the relative importance of the places themselves has been the dominant consideration. The Bhagalpur map, over which Buchanan had taken special pains as the extract already quoted shows, is the one which has suffered most—not only by the reduction of its scale, but also by the absence of proper editing. No less than 163 out of 186 names of rivers and tributaries and 104 out of 181 names of places have been left out. The town of Bhagalpur itself is shown merely as "Kotwali", Monghyr as "Barabazar", and Rajmahal as "Neyamutullah Khan", these being the names of the bazars in each of the towns which occur first in the lists given in the Index. The map of Patna in "Eastern India" is on the whole less unsatisfactory, although 60 out of 79 names of rivers, etc., and

155 out of 236 names of places have been left out. Even amongst those inserted there are several mistakes, such as "Rasisa" instead of Buchanan's Bahadurganj (one mile east of Ghosrawan), while his "Kazi Fatehchuk" (Kazi Chak, six miles north of Sheikhpura) has been inserted twice over, once in its proper place though spelt "Hazefutechuk", and once as "Hazi Futehchuk" instead of his "Chauyari", (Chewara, six miles south-east of Sheikhpura).

Notwithstanding the absence of any reliable maps, it will be noticed that all the distances recorded in the Journal are set down with scrupulous accuracy, as even fractions of a mile are not omitted. It is quite clear that during each day's journey Buchanan only walked when his road became too bad for any other means of transport, or when the nature of the locality required close examination. Though he seldom specifies his actual means of conveyance, he usually travelled either on an elephant or in a palanquin. His method of estimating distances is not stated anywhere in so many words, and the only indications of it which occur in the Patna-Gaya Journal are the following :—

> "My watch having stopt by the way, I cannot judge of the distance, which is called four coses." (November 19th, 1811.)

> "My watch now goes so ill that I cannot rely in computing distances by it." (November 30th, 1811.)

The necessary clues are however contained in the Bhagalpur Journal of the previous year. On the 6th December 1810, at the end of his account of a march from Gunpura to Narayanpur, a distance of "about eight coses by the direct road, that I came through the copse", and in which the total of the individual distances recorded comes to between 15 and 16 miles, he says — "I took four hours to go it on a good elephant". On the 5th and 6th March 1811, when he was on a particularly bad road and was almost certainly travelling by palanquin, against each of the distances recorded in the body of the Journal he has inserted a marginal entry showing the number of minutes taken. These clearly show that his practice in all such cases was to allow an average of fifteen minutes to each mile. On the 5th March, in fact, he has himself added up in the marginal notes the total number of minutes, namely 225, and has divided by 15, getting the quotient of 15 miles which corresponds to 14¾ miles as approximately recorded item by item in the Journal, and similarly on the 6th March he has allowed 10¼ miles to 154 minutes, the time actually taken.

A Supplement consisting of 18 pages of "Observations" is attached to the M. S. Journal for Shahabad, an examination of which brings out the interesting fact that Buchanan carried this method of estimating approximate distances much further. The Observations themselves are chiefly concerned with the state of agriculture as noticed on each day's march from November 3rd, 1812, when he started his tour of the district from Koilwar on the river Sone, until February 24th, 1813, when he left the district to enter that of Mirzapur, on his way to Chunar, his headquarters for that year. Day by day, except on December 17th when "watch stopt" is recorded, or during his tour of the hilly districts of Rohtas, Shergarh, etc., a series of figures is set down in columns headed "Rivers (or Water)"; "Hills"; "Occupied Land"; and "Waste Land"; the totals of which are as follows :—

| | |
|---|---|
| Rivers (or water) ... ... ... | 53 |
| Hills ... ... ... ... | 241 |
| Occupied land ... ... ... | 4,301½ |
| Waste land ... ... ... ... | 3,077 |
| Total ... | 7,672½ |

Comparing the individual entries as well as the totals for each day's march with the corresponding distances recorded in the Shahabad Journal, it becomes clear that *these figures represent in every case the time taken, to the nearest half minute, in travelling over the types of country thus specified.* As the corresponding total of approximate distances given in the Journal is 490 miles, the average rate allowed works out as 15⅔ minutes to each mile.

In the daily notes contained in the Shahabad Observations, the "waste land" is as a general rule still further sub-classified in the same way, as the following summary shows :—

| | |
|---|---|
| Broken corners ... ... ... | 243 |
| Land covered with woods ... ... | 945½ |
| " " " bushes ... ... | 308½ |
| " " " long grass ... ... | 429 |
| " clear, but never cultivated ... ... | 400½ |
| " deserted, formerly cultivated... ... | 377 |
| " uneven, near hills ... ... ... | 15½ |
| " covered with Soda (Reh) ... ... | 1 |
| " marshy ... ... ... ... | 1 |
| Total | 2,721 |

In all probability Buchanan kept a similar record in each of the districts which he surveyed, and made use of it in preparing his elaborate statistical table showing the soil, situation and manner of occupation of the land in each district, as given for Patna and Shahabad on pages 2 and 44 of the Appendix to Eastern India, Volume I. It is significant at least that, in the Table referring to Shahabad, he estimated that of the "level waste land exempt from floods and of good soil", 343 square miles were taken up with "woods, bushes and deserted villages", and 327 square miles consisted of "reeds, pastures or deserted fields"; a relative proportion which agrees very closely with the corresponding figures of 1,254 and 1,206½ minutes shown in the summary just given.

It is not so easy to check the accuracy of Buchanan's method of estimating distances by comparison with modern large-scale maps as might be supposed, because there is usually a certain amount of uncertainty regarding the track which he actually followed. The general indications are, however, that for journeys across country or on bad roads the method was accurate enough, but that it led on decent roads to an under-estimate of distances, amounting at times to as much as 15 or 20 per cent. For instance, in travelling from Mekra to Patna between October 26th and November 4th, 1811, it seems certain that the old military road which Buchanan used hardly differed from the present road close to the south bank of the Ganges, and that it was in fairly good condition. The exact distance along the present road from Mekra to the site of the eastern gate of Patna City is 43 miles, but according to his estimate it was only just over 36 miles. On the 30th November his route from Gaya to the foot of the Gurpa Hill clearly followed the present District Board road as far as Fatehpur, which is now marked by mile-stones but was then probably only a rough cross-country track. The correct distance from the "small hill about a mile from the south end of Sahebgunge" (at Salimpur on the east bank of the Phalgu) to Fatehpur is eighteen miles. Adding up the distances recorded in the Journal, Buchanan's own estimate comes to "at least" $16\frac{1}{24}$ miles, considerably nearer the truth,[*] although he suspected the reliability of his watch on that day. Another instance of close agreement is shown on the 3rd December, when he made the sum of the distances from the small hummock at Kewali to Koch to be rather more than 13 miles, whereas this distance by milestones on the District Board road from Gaya to Koch is exactly 14 miles.

The references to Patna and Bankipore in the Journal are extremely brief, and I have therefore added in full the account which Buchanan incorporated in his Report. Some of the most interesting passages omitted by Montgomery Martin from this have previously been published by Beveridge in the *Calcutta Review*, amongst which in recent years attention has been particularly directed to the story of the recovery of the two remarkable statues which are now in the Calcutta Museum.* Amongst others which have not been previously published may be mentioned the estimates showing the great strength of Sikhism at Patna about 1812, from which it would appear that the number of adherents of both sects, including their families, was well over 50,000; the clear statement that the building on the river bank at Gulzarbagh now occupied by the Government Press was the old English Factory, and not a Dutch building as is generally supposed ; and Buchanan's characteristic comment on the Golah at Bankipore. The compiler of the Statistical Account of Patna District, misled as so many others have been by Montgomery Martin's methods of editorship, regarded the omission of any reference to this building in the account of Patna which appears in Eastern India, Volume I, as a sign that Buchanan's work was defective :—

> " Dr. Buchanan Hamilton was clearly so disgusted with the dust and disorder of the place that he was unable to see any good in it whatever. He has even omitted to describe the Gola, a high dome-like store-house, which is certainly the most striking building in the whole extent included by him in his account of the city." (Volume XI, 1877, page 69.)

This criticism is all the more unjustifiable because the full Report was available at Simla while Hunter's Statistical Account of Bengal was being compiled.

The Journal of Patna and Gaya has been printed from a copy of the original manuscript in the India Office Library which I was permitted by the Secretary of State in Council to make, while on leave in 1911, on the usual conditions as regards publication. I took special precautions to ensure not only that this copy should be verbally accurate, but also that as regards punctuation, orthography, etc., it should be a faithful reproduction

*K. P. Jayaswal, Statues of two Saisunaka Emperors (483-409 B.C.), J. B. O. R. S., Volume V, Part I, March 1919.

Sherghati or other parts of the country traversed by the Grand Trunk Road. When this is taken into consideration it will be seen that very little of importance in the districts of Patna and Gaya, except in the neighbourhood of Rajgir and Jethian, escaped his notice.

PATNA,
*September* 1923.

V. H. JACKSON.

# ERRATA.

On page 2, paragraph dated 25th October, *for* " Chuhusari " *read* " **Chakwars** ".

On page 9 among the footnotes *after* (2) *insert* " (3) **Belkhara** ".

On page 31 and the fourth line of paragraph 2 *for* " Tilhetais " *read* " Tilheta is ".

In the statement on pages 190-195 in the fourth column of Reference *for* the page numbers *read* one figure in excess with the exception of items 1, 11, 16, 18, 27, 38, 44A, 44B, 76, 81, 89, 95, 96, 100, 101, 104, 105, 108, 109, 111 and on page 196 one figure in excess with the exception of items 2, 3, 4.

On page 196 under Minerals of the Plains *read* item 4 thus : " Yellow clay, called Rapura or Gori Mati, from the Ganges at Fatuha ".

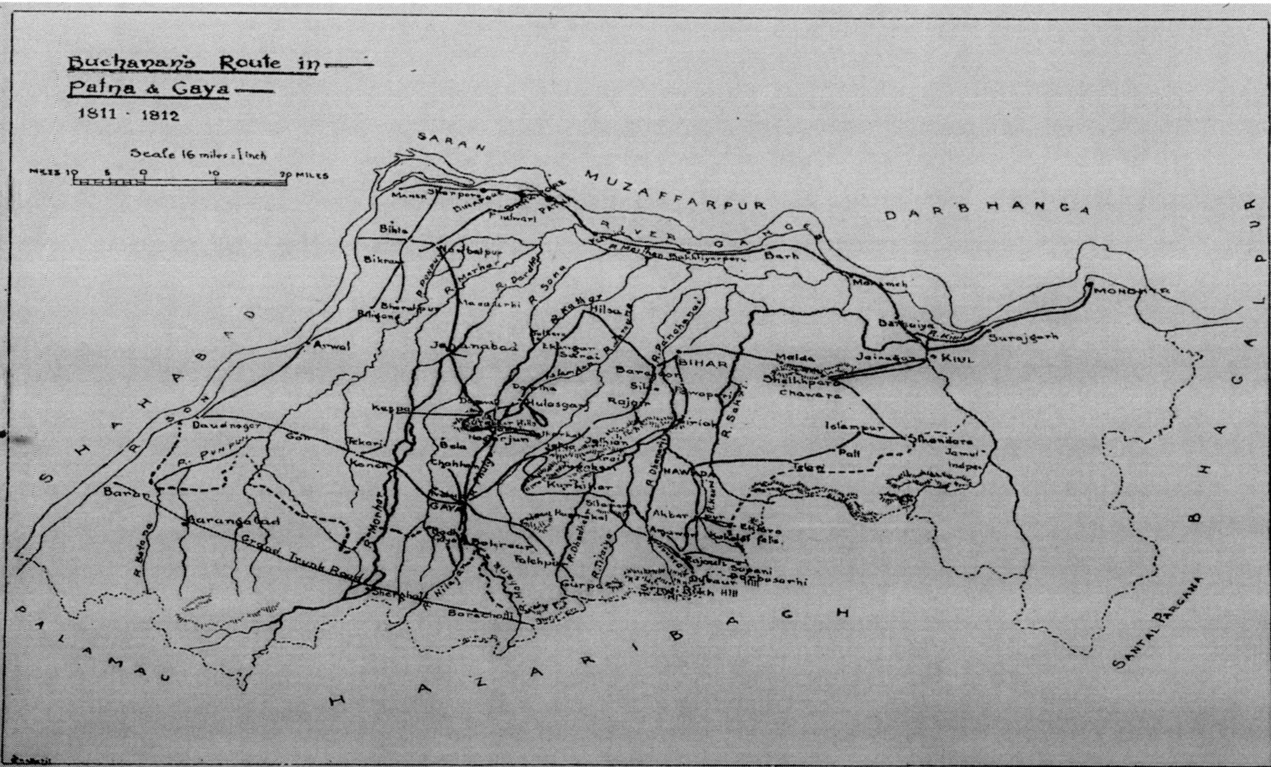
Buchanan's Route in
Patna & Gaya
1811 · 1812
Scale 16 miles = 1 inch
MILES 10 5 0 10 20 MILES
SARAN
MUZAFFARPUR
DARBHANGA
RIVER GANGES
BHAGALPUR
SHAHABAD
PALAMAU
HAZARIBAGH
SANTAL PARGANA
MONGHYR
Surajgarh
KIUL
Jainagar
Barh
Bihta
Bikram
Arwal
Jahanabad
Hilsa
BIHAR
Islampur
Sheikhpura
Chawara
Malda
Hulasganj
Bela
GAYA
Daudnagar
Goh
Tekari
Konch
Barun
Aurangabad
Grand Trunk Road
Sherghati
Barachatti
Fatehpur
Akbarpur
Nawada
Rajauli
Pali
Kurkihar
Bharatpur
Masaurhi
R. Punpun
R. Sakri
Zincographed in the B & O.D O. Gulzarbagh

# Gyah Journal.

16*th October* 1811.—I left Mungger [1] and went to Baha.

17*th October*.—I went to Suryagarha.[2]

18*th October*.—I went to Bolguzor [3] in Gyah. About 1½ miles from the custom house at Suryagarha, came to the Gundri nullah which at this season is very wide and deep, although almost stagnant. Immediately below the ferry it sends a small branch to the west, which is also called the Gundri. I proceeded along its southern bank most of the way that I had formerly come.[4] About 3¼ miles beyond the great Gundri I crossed a small torrent called the Hoel, which is inconsiderable but rapid. It forms the western boundary of Perganah Suryagarha, and its banks seem to have been fortified. Rather more than five miles farther, through a rice country and very bad roads indeed, I came to the Kiyol,[5] which now contains a great stream, but not knee deep and very dirty. The channel may be half filled and 400 yards wide. From thence to the riverside at Bolguzor is rather more than three miles. The country is well wooded and tolerably occupied, but at this season looks very ill, the villages being uncommonly slovenly and the fields being mostly either new-ploughed or too soft yet for that operation, but when the winter crops spring it will probably look well. The huts mostly mud.

I had been led to expect that the roads from Mungger to Suryagarha were almost impassable, and,

---

(1) Monghir, R. and B.A.; **Monghyr.**
(2) Suragegurra, R.; Surajegurra, B.A.; **Surajgarh.**
(3) Balgudar, R.; Balguda, B.A.; **Balgudar.**
(4) On 25th March, 1811; *see* Bhagalpur Journal.
(5) Kewle N., B.A.; **Kiul N.**

from Suryagarha to Dariyapur that they were good, and accordingly made arrangements to obviate difficulties, but this care was vain, as I found that the very reverse of the account given was the case.

Bolguzor is a large village chiefly inhabited by Dusads and Doms. It is situated at a little distance from the river which passes Gyah; but here it is not called the Fulgo, its name changes to Hulwan.[1] It is navigable seven or eight coses up, and at Bolguzor is never fordable, although it does not seem to be above 100 yards wide. It has little current and is very dirty.

19*th October.*—Having crossed the Phulgo, I passed through a very fully occupied and populous country to Dariyapur.[2] The country finely wooded, and many new plantations forming. The villages are very slovenly and not shaded, but many of the huts are good and their yards surrounded by mud walls. I passed through Protappur[3], Jyetpur[4], Indupur, Boraiya[5], Horija, Damna[6], Marah[7], and Hadda[8], all large villages with shops. The fourth and seventh are Invalid Thanas. The women do not conceal themselves so much as in Bhagalpur. They are as dirty.

25*th October.*—I was detained until this day at Dariyapur by the backwardness of the people to give information. I believe that they were in part withheld by the Muharir of the Thana, who it is said advised them to be very cautious. The Daroga, a decent man, appeared to do all that he could. Threats, it is said, were used against one of the zemindars who first came forward. I saw only the people of Giaspur. Those of Milki the Chuhusari, and those of Selimabad, kept at a distance. In the morning I went about five coses to Makra[9], an invalid station. Dariyapur is a large

---

(1) **Harohar** N.
(2) Derryapour, R.; Derriapour, B.A.; **Darlapur.**
(3) **Partappur.**
(4) Jaintpour, R. and B.A.; **Jaitpur.**
(5) **Barhia.**
(6) Doomarah, R.; Doomarra, B.A.; **Dumra.**
(7) **Maranchl.**
(8) Hattedaw, R.; **Hathidah.**
(9) Macrah, R.; **Mokra.**

village with many shops and a very large inn. It is poorly built, the houses huddled together. There is one regular street, but very narrow.

The country very beautiful, well planted and cultivated. Passed several large villages, all containing shops. No gardens, very slovenly huts mostly built of clay but very rough. The ruinous walls in many parts have raised little eminences on which the villages stand, new clay being chosen for rebuilding the walls. Many gourds, etc., partly on the roofs, partly on arbours. A few Ricinuses occasionally as a shade for the yard, road narrow, much neglected.

At Mekra the invalids complain much. They say that after having been at the expense of clearing the Bita, of which each had five or six bighas, the whole has been taken from them and Tal given in its stead. The Tal produces about 2 mans and lets at 3 annas. Mekra, that is, the invalids' station is a large village with a wide street. A bungalow has as usual been built at it by Colonel Hutchinson. It consists of one very large room, rather ruinous. A fine camping ground in front for a small detachment. At the other two stages in this district where I have been, there was no place fit for a dozen tents.

*26th October.*—I went about four coses to Bar[1] through a similar country. The road in most part very narrow, about eight feet [wide] and not much beaten. Many pilgrims, very few other passengers.

*1st November.*—Remained at Bar until this day. Bar is a very large place, the Kazi says that it contains 5,000 houses (Varis). The streets very narrow. The brick houses of the worst Hindustani fashion, and the thatched roofs and mud walls inconceivably rude. Several Muhammadan families in respectable circumstances and good manners reside at it. They seem to prefer towns, as they have all landed estates but seldom visit these.

---

(1) Bar, R. and B.A.; Barh.

In the morning went about five coses to Bukhtiyarpur.[1] The road part of the way led by the side of a nalah, a branch of the Ganges, which becomes dry in spring. The river there seems to be gaining although the people complained that a whole Tapah had been carried away. A good many large villages with shops, thatch in particular exceedingly rude. Bukhtiyarpur a small village with some shops, as usual in this country.

*2nd November.*—I went about 8½ miles to Vaikanthpur,[2] through a country much the same as that seen for some days past. Vaikanthpur is a large serayi. The village has once been large, but all except the Brahmans have left the place. The reason assigned by the zemindar is that they were very much subject to be seized as porters. The zemindar, who pays 8000 Rs. a year, is a decent peasant, exceedingly civil.

*3rd November.*—I went rather more than eight miles and halted a little west from Jaffier Khan's garden. About two miles from Vaikanthpur I came to an old garden of Setab Rai's, now grown quite wild. It is surrounded by a square wall of brick with a kind of turret at the corner. It is not of any considerable size. About two miles farther came to Futwa,[3] for this country a large town. Most of the houses clay, a great many much neater than [at] Bar. It is close built, but the streets very narrow. In the town I crossed the river Punpun,[4] of considerable size. There had been a wooden bridge with very massy piers of bricks, but some of them have given way and the Company defrays the expense of an excellent ferry. In the time of Major Rennell Futwah would appear to have been on the west side of the Punpun. A part is still so, but by far the largest part is now on the east side. The great Punpun of that geographer is now quite dry, but a small bridge marks where a small stream passes in the rainy season. From the size of the two bridges, both old, what Rennell calls

---

(1) **Bakhtiarpur.**
(2) Bycontpour, R.; Bykontpour, B.A.; **Baikatpur.**
(3) Futwah, R.; Futwa, B.A.; **Fatuha.**
(4) Pompon, R. and B.A.; **Punpun N.**

the small Punpun must always have been the larger. Without the town towards the west is a large Sangot of brick. Near Jafier Khan's garden has been another probably dependent, nothing however remains except four turrets surmounted by cupolas at the corners. The whole is cultivated. Near it, towards the east of it, a native merchant of Patna has a very handsome country seat. A shut up zenana, and an open house for entertaining company at some distance, with a neat garden between. There is besides a stone temple of Siv in a garden on the opposite side of the road, the handsomest Hindu building that I have seen, although it is small. It seems to have been built on a European plan, and consists of a pyramid with a portico towards one side. Between this garden wall and the road is a terrace covered with plaster and shaded with trees for the refreshment of passengers. A merchant has also dug a tank near Jafier Khan's garden and lined it on four sides with brick, but it is a very poor rude work, the steps on the descent being about two feet high and the banks quite rough. Jafier Khan's garden has been a kind of fortification, surrounded by a wall strengthened by turrets and some buildings, part of which remain. In the centre has been erected the chief Songot of the Sik sect. I was admitted only into the garden in front, which is surrounded by a mud wall with a gate towards the north daubed with wretched paintings of Hindu Gods and Heroes. I could not be admitted into the brick buildings south from the garden with my shoes, and as the Mahant and his chief disciples were absent at the Mela, I did not think this worth while.

*4th November.*—I went to Patna. All the way from Jaffier Khan's garden to the eastern gate, about 1½ miles, is a kind of suburb very meanly built. But there is one very handsome house belonging to some native, entirely in their own style but built with much taste. From the east gate I went through narrow lanes, but with many tolerable houses, to the western; which I should have taken to be a distance of three miles, but Major Rennell makes it only 1½ miles.

From the western gate and to the west end of the town of Bankupur is not quite two miles. Bankupur is in general very poorly built, but contains many of the European houses and that of Rajah Koliyan Singh, a very great building in the Anglo-Indian style. Beyond it is a plain round which many of the European houses are situated, and terminated to the west by the Golgarh.

*6th November.*—I went to Phulvariya,[1] having remained a day at Patna in order to procure orders for the agents of different officers of Government. Phulvariya is a large village with many shops and a few brick houses, one of which is a respectable-looking village. About four miles from the Golgarh, I passed a tank dug by Balaichand, a merchant of Patna. It is lined with brick, but from the rude state of the bank is a very unsightly work. Phulvari was said to be four coses from Patna, but I do [not] think it can be so much as six miles. The country high and well cultivated. Few plantations except those of Palmiras. The road fully as good as the great road to Calcutta.

Phulvariya is a large close-built village inhabited chiefly by Muhammadans, among whom are several respectable families. One of them, Kazi of the Perganah, has a respectable house of brick. The others live in very large houses of mud, tiled, which on the outside at least are very slovenly. These three families keep Madrisahs, one of which is in a Mosque fronted with stone and in a very different style of architecture from any that I have seen. The roof is flat, supported by stone pillars along which large stones are laid, and these again support the flags which cover the roof. The pillars are four-sided but flat and with few or no mouldings. In place of the domes there are three cupolas over the three niches in the back wall. The structure of these very clumsy. Part of the ornaments of the gate are of a red stone said to have been brought ready carved from Dilli or Agra. The carving very neat and the stone singular.

---

(1) Fulwarry, R. and B.A.; Phulwari.

*7th November.*—I went not quite eight miles to Nobutpur.[1] I was assured at Patna that the distance was at least sixteen miles or eight coses, which made me divide the journey into two stages, but in fact the road does not seem to be above thirteen miles.

*9th November.*—I went above three miles south-west to see the old fort of the Cheruyan Raja.[2] It has no traces of a ditch, and is an elevated square terrace of about thirty yards each side, without any cavity in the middle. The people say that it was surrounded by a thick brick wall, and the space within filled up with earth, but what purpose such a building could serve except as a place of worship I cannot say. At the north-east corner is a ruined very small temple, in which are several fragments of images carved in relievo on stone. One is a female. The whole is called Goriya, or the deity of the fort, and sacrifices are still offered. At a little distance from the temple is lying another stone carved with images in relievo. It is said to represent the doorkeeper of the deity. The ruin appears to me to be of the highest Indian antiquity, while the princes lived in castles rather than forts.

*11th November.*—I went west to the Son[3] river, to see the manner in which the pebbles are found. It is an immense channel, filled with sand. The water at this season is about one hundred yards wide, not very deep nor rapid and rather muddy, but it is not fordable. The channel is however filled with shallows, so that only very small boats pass up and down. In spring it is fordable and canoes pass with difficulty. Small stones are thinly scattered among the sand or in a few places form small beds, and I understand are found everywhere from Moner[4] to Rotasgar[5] or higher, but more and more plenty the farther up. They are fragments of various silicious stones, none of them

(1) **Naubatpur.**
(2) Baliyadihi in Report. About two miles south of **Arap?**
(3) Soane R.; R. and B.A.; **Sone R.**
(4) Moneah, R. and B.A.; **Maner.**
(5) Rotasgur, R. and B.A.; **Rohtas.**

aggregate, some are quite opaque fat white quartz, or quartz tinged red, yellow, or various colours. Others are diaphanous glassy quartz, and what are called the Son pebbles. These are pretty common, so that in a few minutes I found eight or ten, but none of them fine. This was about three coses from the mouth of the river.

I passed two old channels of the Son called by that name, besides the one near the Thanah. I do not know which it is that is laid down by Major Rennell. At present they contain no stream, and in most places are dry. Near the second is a ridge running some way east and west and containing many fragments of brick. This place is called Raph,[1] and is said to have belonged to a Cheruyan Raja. I presume that the ridge is in some measure natural, being too large for a ruin, although the ruin may have added very considerably to the size, the fragments being very numerous. No appearance of any fortification.

12*th November*.—It was said that Thanah Jehanabad was twelve coses distant, and that half way was Bagwangunj,[2] a village of Shahabad. There is a more direct route, but the road at present is impassable for loaded cattle. I found that Bagwangunj is about sixteen miles from Nuhubutpur instead of six coses, and in many places there was no other road except the small banks confining the water on rice fields. About eight miles from Nuhubutpur I came to the Pompon at a village called Pituangs[3] (Fetwas, Rennell). It is perhaps 150 yards wide, half covered with a dirty stream, but is fordable, being only about two feet deep. About 1½ miles farther on, came to the boundary of the two zilas.

Nuhubutpur is a close-built village with many shops as usual in this country. A hat was held while we were there. Many petty traders came with Jira

(1) **Arap.**
(2) **Bhagwanganj.**
(3) Fetvass, R.; Fetwas, B.A.; **Pitwans.**

and Turmeric on oxen, but there was not that hubbub usual in Bengal, and few women attended, nor were small wares sold.

Bagwangunj is a close-built village with many shops, belonging to Masaur [1] Pergana, which together with Arval[2] is the property of the Rani of Jeswont Sing, whose name it is not decent to mention. She resides at Belkari,[3] eleven coses from Bagwangunj which is on the west side of the Murahar [4] river. The people say that near Pollay [5] was the abode of another Cheruyan Raja, none of the caste remain.

13*th November*.—My people are now beginning to become sickly, for a long time they have been remarkably healthy. I first went south for about two-thirds of a mile parallel to the Murahar, which I then crossed. It is a small channel, perhaps 20 yards wide, with some dirty water pretty deep in pools, but little stream. Bottom muddy. About half a mile farther I came to the boundary of Behar, from whence to Jehanabad[6] is about nine miles, but there is no road and the path lies chiefly along the banks of reservoirs, and therefore is exceedingly circuitous. With a little pains they might be made to serve for roads sufficient to admit loaded cattle. The road not so bad as yesterday. About two miles from Jehanabad is a very large marsh.

Jehanabad is a large country town, close-built with narrow crooked streets, many of the houses tiled, all with mud walls. Those that have two stories have at a distance a good effect, the roof being somewhat in the Italian style. The walls in general on near approach exceedingly slovenly. A very little pains in smoothing them would make neat houses, especially if whitewashed. The windows above all very rude. At the junction of the rivers a merchant has built a temple, where he has

(1) Massora, R. and B.A.; **Masaurhi.**
(2) Arval, R. and B.A.; **Arwal.**
(4) Murahar N., R.; Little Pompon R., B.A.; **Morhar N.**
(5) Pollay, R. and B.A.; **Pali.**
(6) Jehonabad, R. and B.A.; **Jahanabad.**

placed the grave of a Sanyasi (a Somadi) and the ashes of a faithful spouse who burned with her husband's body, and images of Krishna, Ram Chanda, etc., and has appointed a Sannyasi as Pujari. This person has no hesitation in declaring the place to have been sacred for many years, but has not had impudence to dream nor to contrive a miracle. The temple is therefore neglected; although the junction of the rivers is holy. The situation is fine, and the square area in which the different small temples are placed is surrounded by a wall, at the corners of which are small buildings for the accommodation of holy travellers. Behind is a flower-garden, very slovenly.

16*th November*.—I went almost three miles easterly to Dumaula, to see the Cheruyan Rajah's house. I crossed the river just below the junction. It is a channel about 100 yards wide with a small stream in each branch. It will soon probably be dry.

The Cheruyan Rajah's house is an oblong heap, not near so long as that I saw at Raph, but it must have been a very considerable building. The villagers say that the merchant who built the temple at Jehanabad opened it, and took out the stones and bricks with which he erected that work. So far as opened, it consisted of many small chambers filled with rubbish. The people at Jehanabad say that only a few stones and bricks were brought. One of the steps has evidently been a rude pillar of rough granite. North from the heap is a small tank. There is no trace of a town or of fortifications.

19*th November*.—I went to the vicinity of Dora[1] and Kurta,[2] in order to see the place where soda was collected. My watch having stopt by the way I cannot judge of the distance, which is called four coses, south-east. The cose here I understand is about three miles. I crossed the river just below the junction and continued near the east bank of the [Jamuna] most of the way

(1) Dhourha.
(2) Kurtha.

*20th November*.—I went about ten miles, but by a very circuitous route, to Keyoa Dol.[1] I proceeded first south-east about three miles until I left to my right a village and old mud fort named Duraut.[2] I then inclined more to the south about 2⅜ miles, until I came to the east end of Beyok,[3] a detached part of an exceedingly rugged ridge of granite among which are only some stunted bushes and climbers. A great many turtle doves breed in the crevices. It does not consist of great rocks but of immense irregular blocks. It is a middle-sized grain of a grey colour very slightly tinged with red. The felspar occupies much space. The micaceous matter black minute grains, in a pretty considerable proportion. The quartz granular. It is a very perfect granite.[4] North from this hill are two detached smaller hills of a similar rock. I went west along the south side of this ridge for about one and a quarter miles, and it continues some way farther, but is exceedingly irregular. I saw one round mass detached a little way south from its west end. I then proceeded south through a fine plain for about one and a half miles when I came to the west corner of a low ridge adjoining to [the] west end of Burabur pahar,[5] the highest and largest of this cluster, and I passed between this low ridge and another detached hill farther west. The north face of Burabur is not near so rugged as the northern ridge, but is only covered by stunted bushes, but on the south it is exceedingly rough and contains some immense precipitous rocks. Its west end, Dihiri, consists of a fine-grained perfect grey granite, much black granular micaceous matter. The felspar small and not in a great proportion. The quartz granular. This forms the boundary between Hulasgunj and Sahebgunj. From thence to Mukdumpur[6] at the foot of Keya Dol is about one and a half-miles along a fine plain. The plains adjacent to these hills are free of stones. The granite rises like rocks from the sea.

---

(1) **Kawa Dol.**
(2) **Dharaut.**
(3) **Bhekh.**
(4) Appendix, No. 16.
(5) Caramshaw Hills, R. and B.A.; **Barabar Hills.**
(6) **Makhdumpur.**

Keoyadol is an immense very naked rock of perfect middle-sized-grained white and black granite. The people at a distance pretend that its name is derived from a rocking stone that was on its top, so nicely balanced as to be moveable by the weight of a crow. This they say fell down about 50 years ago, but the most respectable people of Mukdumpur say that their fathers never remembered such a stone, nor do they believe that it ever existed. They say that no blocks have fallen within their memory, and although some of the top would appear to be in a very tottering state, it would seem in fact that no considerable mass has fallen for ages, as on almost all the large blocks towards the plain are engraved figures of great antiquity, and these blocks are undoubtedly the latest that have fallen. All along the north side and east end of the hill these carvings in relief are very numerous, and represent various deities or persons remarkable in Hindu mythology, all exceedingly rude and many of them much worn by the action of the weather, although as I have said they are engraved in a very perfect granite. The figures are therefore of a very great antiquity. The only figures almost about which any two persons are agreed are those of Ganese and the Linga, which cannot be mistaken, but the most common represents a female with four arms, killing what is probably meant to represent a buffalo. This is called by the people of the neighbourhood merely Devi, that is, the Goddess, but among my followers no two agreed, that is to say, the image differs in some points from any that they know, having several attributes common to different deities but others by which it may be distinguished from any one of them. Among these images are several of Bhouddhs or Jains, I will not take upon myself to say which, although the former is most probable, because the chief temple near the place contains an image called Bouddh Sen.

I shall now mention the most remarkable places about the hill. At Makdumpur, towards the north-west side of the hill, are several large heaps of brick, which are with probability supposed to have been dwelling houses of some prince; but the people are not agreed whether he was a Cheruyan or a Bundawut, both of which races are said to have governed the country before the Muhammadan invasion. The images are most usually attributed to the former. Farther east, proceeding along the north face of the hill, are two large blocks forming an angle, and on each of them is a row of figures. One of the rows consists chiefly of an repetition of the female figure destroying the buffalo. Of these I have directed a drawing to be taken.

Near this is the monument of Husa Mudin Sahei, much frequented. It is a large tree surrounded by a terrace constructed of pillars, capitals, doors, windows, etc., and probably taken from the chief temple of the place, which is situated a little farther east. It is totally ruined, but the image remains entire in its place in a recess at the east end of the temple. It is called Bouddh Sen and is of the usual form, made of black indurated potstone, and the recess has been ornamented with the same and covered with figures of the Hindu Mythology, of which many fragments are lying round to a great distance. The temple has been about 44 yards from east to west by 30 from north to south and has been of brick, but has been supported by pillars of granite, and the doors and windows have probably been of the same material, as many fragments are scattered round. The pillars are exceedingly rude, ten or twelve are still erect and entire. The roof has been very low, probably not above 8 or 10 feet. Near the temple has been a small building of brick perched on the top of an immense block of granite, which it has covered, and has probably been the den of some ascetic. Some way farther forward, a small block of granite has been cut square and on each face has been engraved an image. This on the whole although exceedingly rude is the most elegant work of the whole. I have therefore directed drawings to be taken of it. At the east end of the hill are the foundations of a small stone building, near which on the face of a rock is a Boudh with a row of disciples sitting on his right and a Ganesa on his left. Of this also I have directed a drawing to be taken. On the south face of the hill, a little west from its east end, is the most perfect relief of the most common female deity with the buffalo, which also I have directed to be drawn.

It is said that a Srotri Brahman who lives about a cose off is Pujari for all the idols on the hill, and makes offerings to Bouddh Sen as well as the others. The Pandit can find no tradition concerning the place, except that Jara Sandha stood with one foot on Keoya Dol and the other on Burabur. The Pujari is a most ignorant creature, says his ancestors have for 7 or 8 generations enjoyed the place, which has no endowment. He is of the sect of Saiva, and being asked why he worships Buddh Sen, he says that the image was made by Buddh Sen, but represents Bhairov. The Pandit seems to think that the ancestor of the Panda finding the people still afraid of the image, took upon himself the worship, and called the image of Buddha a Bhairov merely as an excuse, as it has not the smallest affinity to the representations of that destructive power.

21st November.—I went rather less than four miles to the foot of the hill called Nagarjun,[1] which is a very rugged peak of granite at the east end of Barabur. I had given the most positive orders to have my tents pitched at Karn' Chaupar about one mile farther west, but as there was a well at Nagarjuni and none at Karn' Chaupar this was totally neglected. I however found at Nagarjuni a fine cave of which I perhaps might not have heard had I not gone to the place, for the people here are so stupid, and have so little curiosity, that you can scarcely find out any antiquity except by chance. An exceeding rude stair of granite and mortar winds up the hill for about 150 yards among detached blocks of granite,[2] until it reaches a solid convex rock running east and west. On a little level at the bottom of the rock has been built an Idgai of brick and mortar which points out the direction of Medina, towards which

(1) Nagarjuni.
(2) Appendix, No. 63.

the faithful turn when they pray. This Idgai and the stair have every appearance of being very modern, although the keeper, who has 25 bigas of land, says that they are above a hundred years old. Behind the place of prayer, a small door in the solid rock leads into an oval cave, 43 feet long and 18 feet 10 inches wide, the door being in the centre of one of the sides. The walls rise about six feet perpendicular and the roof is arched, 10½ feet high. The whole has a marble polish but not neat, as the chisels employed in excavating the rock have in a vast many parts penetrated deeper than the surface that has been polished. There is not the slightest ornament nor moulding, and the roof being covered with soot, the whole is very dismal even when lighted. It has no aperture except one small door, and is therefore hot and noisome, although perfectly dry. A small platform of brick and mortar is placed against the wall near the west [1] end, and is called the Chilla of Mukdum Saha Minhajuddin,[2] who according to the keeper came here at the same time [as] Sherifuddin came to Behar. The Chilla is the place where the saint sat two years without moving, to pray and meditate on divine things. He had 360 Chillas in this district. On the rocks above the door is a small inscription very much defaced. On the left side of the door, entering, is a long inscription in an old Nagri character pretty entire. On the right hand is one line more like the Pali. The Muzuir says that when the saint came the place was in possession of Nagarjuni Deo, a holy man who was destroyed by the saint. This saint afterwards went to Busora where he was buried. His son was buried at Behar. My informant is a descendant, there are many others near Behar, at Baliyari, and at Soho, and at Kotbunpur Jaffra[3] near Nagarjuni where a grandson Kotbun Haji is buried. My informant says he is the seventh of eight in descent from this person. All the descendants of the Saint are Pirzadas. The Edga was built [by] Nahar

(1) Should be "East."
(2) Haji Hurmayen; in Report.
(3) Jafra.

Khan Newati an Amil, Mitirjit Singh repaired or built the stair. It was formerly of earth only.

After breakfast I went to visit what is called the Satgar, or seven houses, situated towards the east end of Burabur hill. I passed the easternmost point and went into a recess between it and the next projection, where I ascended a crooked bad path a little way towards the west. I there came to an old wall of rude stones going across the gap between two rocky peaks, but the wall is now mostly fallen. There had been a gate here, as a pillar remains erect and the stones which formed the door are scattered about. Advancing west a little way, with an old tank and a small level on my right and a ridge of solid granite on my left, I soon came to a door in the latter facing the north, where a high peak crowned by a temple of Mahadeva bounds the plain in that direction. The rock at this door has been cut perpendicular, leaving a small projection at each side some way from the door. Before this door have been some small buildings of brick. The door leads into a chamber, polished like that of Nagarjuni and equally devoid of ornament. It is about 16 feet from east to west and 40 from north to south, and about seven high to the spring of the arch. At its west end is a platform about a foot high and three feet broad. On the projection west from the door are three images in relief, very much defaced. One is evidently a linga. The others seem to have been males with two arms and standing. It is impossible to say what these represent. Some Brahmans call them Gauri Sankur, but this is very doubtful. On either side of the door is some writing. This cave is called Karn Chaupar or the house of Karna. This Karna is supposed to be the brother of Yudishtir, who passed some time here as a hermit.

Passing round the west end of this ridge to its south side, you come to two doors. The first or most western is plain, and has on each side a few words engraved. It leads into a chamber of about the same size with that called Karna Chaupar. At its east side is a small niche. At its west end is a door in the wall, which is convex, and over the door is a kind of cornice. The door leads into a circular chamber, arched above like the others and polished in the same manner. The floor of these chambers contained about a foot of dirty water and mud. This cave is properly called Satgar and is supposed to have been built by Sudama, brother of Krishna. The other door east from the above has been somewhat [but][1] very rudely ornamented, as will appear from the drawing. Under the arch above the door is an inscription of considerable length. It seems to have been intended to have formed two chambers similar to those of Satgar, but although both have been excavated, neither has been completed nor polished except in a few parts. This is supposed to have been the abode of Lomus Rishi, pronounced Momus Rikhi, or Muni, a hairy saint of these remote times.

Having visited these places I returned to the tank, and ascending a ridge of granite I looked down upon a torrent called Patel Ganga, which in the rainy season contains many pools, near which in the Chaterdesi of Bhadur about 50,000 people assemble, and next day they bathe in the pools, besides that during the whole of Bhadur perhaps 500 people bath daily. The virtues of this were discovered by Ban Raja who founded the temple of Siva on the adjacent hill, and who had a house at Sonpur about three coses west from Karna Chaupar.

Descending to the west side of [the] ridge from which I had viewed Patal Ganga, I found a cavity in the rock about 7 feet high, as much wide, and 9 feet deep. In its far end is a door, and it seems to have been intended to have made a chamber there, but the workmen have abandoned it after excavating a few feet in diameter. This excavation has an inscription, and is said to be the Morai or small house of Viswamitri,

---

(1) "by" in MS.

one of the Munis. The passage between [the] ridge in which it is dug and that on the right of the path by which I ascended, has also been closed by a strong rude wall of stone. On all other sides the small hollow in which these cells are [is] surrounded by the most rugged rocks and precipices. These cells, however, could have only been intended as habitations for ascetics, and why they should have been fortified would be difficult to say. Karna may have been an ascetic by force, and it may have been necessary for his brother to have access shut up. The whole is supposed to have been dug by Karna, and no doubt the cutting and polishing such chambers must have been a costly work, although nothing can be more destitute of convenience, elegance or taste. Although polished they are so sombre that two torches and a lantern with two wax candles served only to make the darkness visible and to see the wall close to where any of the lights was held, but the form could only be ascertained by groping. Our eyes were no doubt dazzled by the sun and lights, and a stay of some time might have rendered the parts more distinct, but the noisome stifling of the air rendered any stay exceedingly disagreeable, and I was satisfied with going round the walls to ascertain whether they contained any passages, ornaments, images, or writing; but the interior of all the chambers is destitute of such. The writing is confined to the sides of the doors, where alone indeed it could be visible.

The granite of these rocks is grey white felspar and glassy quartz in middle-sized grains, with a good deal of black micaceous matter.[1] In some places that have been polished the felspar is reddish, but I did not see any detached blocks of that colour.

I sent a man to the temple of Mahadev on the hill called Surjiruk,[2] said to have been originally founded by Ban Raja, but there is nothing of antiquity remaining except the images. The linga is generally

(1) Appendix, No. 38.
(2) The Gorathagiri Hill; *see* J.B.O.R.S., Vol. I. Part II, Dec. 1915.

admitted to have been placed there by Ban Asur, but is broken. There are two female figures carved on stone in relief and called Bhairav, Bhairavi, but both are female. One of them has over it an inscription in Deva Nagri, on which account they are probably modern. The present buildings were erected by a Gulal Baruti, a Dosnami Sanniyasi of great virtue and chastity, about 80 years ago. He built several other small temples of Siva in various places. This is called Siddheswar. The temple has been lately repaired by Jevonath, another Dosnami, who built a small chamber near the temple, for the residence of a Sannyasi, but he only stays there at night. The owner, Siva Baruti, of the land attached to the temple lives at Lahagunj[1] near Tikari, where he is Mahant of an akhara. About five begahs below the temple towards the east is a natural cave called Yogiasna, or the seat of the Yogi. In this it is said that Goruknath passed some time in prayer, sitting on an asna or seat used in prayer, which remains. The bottom of the cave, which is merely a cavity under an overhanging rock, is said to be always covered with ashes, which many use for putting the mark on their foreheads. A man that I sent says the cave is not deep and contains ashes. All those that bathe in Patalganga make offerings to the Siva, and a few go to Yogi Asna. At the bottom of the hill are to be found scattered many masses of fine iron ore, called Losinghana.[2]

*23rd November.*—My people being employed on the inscriptions, it was necessary to halt some days at Nagarjuni. I went therefore to visit the neighbourhood. Passing east along the south face of Nagarjuni, I found that from the stair leading up to the Dorga there had run a wall of stone parallel to the hill, and terminating on the Bunbuni[3] where the hill also terminates. The Bunbuni has here on its opposite bank a small granite ridge called Rawa. The Bunbuni a little way

(1) Lashkarganj ?
(2) Appendix, No. 105.
(3) Bhurbhuri, in Report.

below joins the [west][1] branch of the Fulgo called San,[2] and on their west side is a fine plain called Ram Gaya, about a mile from north to south, bounded on the former by the hill called Soleya and on the south by Nagarjuni, which is a very narrow ridge through the immense blocks of which are many openings that admit the light to pass. The plain from east to west is very irregular, a small hill named Murli rising in its middle and an arm of Nagarjuni passing from its west end far through the plain towards the east. There are many heaps of bricks and stones throughout the plain, and an old road leads up to the top of Murli, where there appears to have been some building; but the most remarkable antiquity is in the recess between the two arms of Nagarjuni. On entering the recess you first find a heap of brick. Then you come to the foundation of a wall of stone forming with the northern arm of the hill an oblong area, in which there is a heap of brick and a well. The west end of the area has been shut up by [a] building of brick, which may have been 50 by 30 feet. It has contained many stones, some of a fine hornblende with very large crystals, but not polished. In the rock immediately adjoining to the east front of the building, is a door leading into a small chamber about 10 feet by 15, arched above and polished, but the arch is not above 9 feet high. There is an inscription on the sides of the door. It is said to be the Mirza mandin or house of a Moslem noble; but the inscription is Hindu. At the north end of the brick building has been a stone door leading out to a small angular recess formed by the meeting of two great blocks of granite. In the face of the western of these blocks is another door with an inscription, leading to another [a] similar cave, but a wall of brick has been built across towards its far end, leaving a small chamber behind, the only access to which is through a kind of window through which a slender man may creep. This is called the abode of Haji Hermain. The house is said to have

(1) "East" in MS.

(2) Suar, R.; Sungr, in Buchanan's Map. Phalgo N. or Sunr N.

been [built] by a Naudiya[1] Seyud. It is possible that a Moslem may have built his house in the place, and made use of the Hindu cave as a concealment for treasure, and the brick wall countenances this opinion, but no doubt the plain from the number of ruins has been a town, and probably the residence of the Hindu prince of whom so many works remain in the neighbourhood. The neighbouring Brahmans say that Ram performed his ceremony on Gaya here, and still about 20,000 people assemble on the plain on the Viswa or end of Chaitra. The Brahmans of Gaya have found it convenient to have a Ram Gaya nearer themselves : but many of the Goyali Brahmans come to the Mela and employ the Srotriya Brahmans of the place to perform some ceremonies for them. The only temple remaining is a small ruinous temple of Siva.

*23rd November.*—I went above five coses, called three, to visit the quarries near Kukuri.[2] I crossed the Munmuni at the end of Nagarjuni, and about $1\frac{1}{3}$ mile from the tents. I came to the bank of the Fulgo, up which I proceeded about half a mile to Sultanpur.[3] Where I crossed it the channel is above a quarter of a mile in width, but is even now mere sand with a few shallow pools of water and a very trifling stream indeed, but plenty of good water may at all seasons be procured by digging a very little way into the sand. I continued to go south for about $1\frac{1}{3}$ miles until I had the little hill Keni on my right and Lodi on my left, both appear to be small heaps of granite. I then turned east $\frac{1}{5}$ of a mile and passed close by the south side of Lodi. About $1\frac{1}{2}$ miles farther east came to Rauniya,[4] a village with a kind of wretched mud castle with loopholes and rather ruinous. About four miles farther on, came to Laili,[5] another village with an old mud castle, and about four miles farther I came to another called Katari.[6] Near this are several images

---

(1) Nawdyah, R.; Nawdia, B.A.; **Naudiha.**
(2) **Khukhari.**
(3) **Sultanpur.**
(4) **Rauniyan.**
(5) **Haili.**
(6) **Katari.**

carved on detached stones of hornblende, and such as are carved on the rock at Keoyadol. The female figure killing a buffalo is much larger than any of the others and differs a good deal from those at Keoya Dol, having eight hands, and the head of the buffalo is separated from the body which a lion is tearing, while the female is killing a man seated on the neck of the buffalo. This figure is called Jagadumba and the others were called her children, although two of them represented Har with Gauri his spouse sitting on his knee. These villages with castles belong to Mitrjit, and were fortified by his grandfather, who had predatory habits.

From thence I went about half a mile to the quarry on the hill called Baluya [1] from the number of bears that it shelters. It consists of several small heaps and peaks of granite,[2] about a mile in length and a quarter of a mile wide. Towards its south-west corner are three quarries of very heavy blackish potstone, called by the workmen Song Musa. About 12 years ago being in want of work they found this stone projecting in a small mass at three places, two on the hill and one near it. They followed the stone, which is in veins running with a great inclination from the perpendicular and covered by a very curious granular white calcareous marl[3] to a considerable thickness, perhaps in some places 10 or 12 feet. Among the marl is found scattered large rounded blocks of a rude white jasper[4] with large irregular greenish marks. The blocks are often four or five feet in diameter but it seems analogous to the flint found in chalk rocks. The Song Musa or Stone of Moses [5] is found in small masses never larger than a cubit in diameter and of very irregular form, covered with a decaying grey crust and disposed in veins, which are covered above and on both sides with the marl. One of the quarries is now above

(1) Baijla.
(2) Appendix, Nos. 76, 82.
(3) „ No. 100?
(4) „ No. 109.
(5) „ No. 96.

20 feet deep, and the sides falling in have killed one man and disabled two. Another is filled with water, so that stones are procured with difficulty, the workmen being as unskilled in quarrying as usual with their countymen. There is little or no demand for the marl although it makes very good lime. It has therefore to be thrown out, and the masses of jasper (Baru বাড়ু) must be pulled up with ropes, for they have not had sense to make a sloping road. The granite (Urdiya উড়দিয়া) is above and around the whole, and most of it does not differ materially from that of Nagarjuni, but some seems to be composed of small grains of white felspar and mica intermixed with granular hornblende.[1] About a quarter of a mile north from Baluya is a large heap of granite, a quarry of the Marl (Chunapatar),[2] not quite so harsh as that on Baluya, has been opened. It is said that the bridge of Futwah was constructed with this lime, and the excavation is pretty considerable and quite superficial, surrounded on all sides, however, with granite. The silicious masses [3] found intermixed with this marl seem very different, as it is of an uniform grey colour but seems to contain many disseminated masses of felspar. This little heap is called Chuniya. It is said that Mr. Thomas Law took it as a substance for making chinaware, but this is probably a mistake. We can scarcely suppose any European to have been so ill informed. I saw not the smallest trace of animal exuviæ among this marl.

Between the heap called Chunea pahar and the quarry on the hill Baliya, is a small smooth heap which seems to contain a mine of iron, as all round its bottom is covered with little bits of ore [4] which is entirely neglected.

Having examined these I visited the quarry on the hill called Jerra or Paterkati,[5] situated about a mile

(1) Appendix, Nos. 82, 76.
(2) ,, No. 101.
(3) ,, No. 1.
(4) ,, No. 89.
(5) Jarha or Patharkatl.

south-westerly from Baliya. It is also very rugged, and consists in a great measure of granite, but its southern end is chiefly of the hornblende kind. The greater part is black potstone with a fine grain, and is so much inpregnated with silicious hornstone that it has a conchoidal fracture.[1] It is very hard and [is] used for making pestles and mortars. It is called merely Kalaputur or black stone. There is however a very fine quarry of [hornblende][2] consisting of large crystals,[3] which is called Vishnupodi, because it was employed to erect the temple of that name at Gaya, and the workmen were brought from Jaynagar on purpose. There is no demand for this stone now, and the workmen are reduced to live by making cups, plates, etc. of the potstone, and mortar and pestles of that impregnated with silicious matter. Very fine masses of the pure hornblende may be procured, the silicious potstone is more intersected by fissures.

The tradition at the quarry is that it was first wrought by Harchand Rajah, who built Rotas and dug the caves of Burabur, etc., and who finding the materials too hard desisted and sent his workmen to Alura (Ellora) in the south, where he dug very great works in the rocks.

In the evening I returned to Nagarjuni by a route further north, leaving Tatariya[4] and Dunmoa,[5] two small hills, on my left and Niyera[6] on my right. These hills are low and smooth and therefore probably of a different structure from the rugged granitic masses of the neighbourhood (consist). Near the Fulgo I had on my right a very rugged ridge named [Jibhiya] on which there is a small temple of Siva, and I passed close to a granitic heap which is [south] from the above mentioned ridge. The Fulgo here divides into two. The western

---

(1) Appendix, No. 10.
(2) "Hornstone" in MS., but *see* later, and also East India Vol. I, p. 262.
(3) Append x No. 113.
(4) **Tetarlya.**
(5) **Dhanmahua.**
(6) **Nadira.**

branch called Sanr passes on one side of the ridge, and the eastern branch retains the name and passes on its other side.[1]

24*th November*.—I went a little way east to Ibrahimpur[2] in the fork between the Sanr and Fulgo rivers. To the former from Nagarjuni is about ⅔ of a mile. The river is about ⅓ of a mile [wide]. Immediately in the fork has been a small fort with round bastions at the corner, but the buildings within have left several heaps, one round and pretty considerable. The walls of a small brick building are still remaining. The village extends about half a mile from the fort to the mosque, which is small and covered with three domes, but is not destitute of taste. It stands on a terrace raised on short thick pillars, which support flags under which some holy men have made hovels. There is a gate and place for a crier on the east side of the terrace, opposite to the mosque which occupies the western. South from the mosque has been the house of Ibrahim the conqueror of the vicinity, who with the spoils of the infidels seems to [have] erected a large abode of brick and stone. Two parts of the walls only are now standing, but the size of the heaps of ruins shew that the building has possessed considerable dimensions. This Ibrahim was a great saint, and is buried at Behar.

25*th November*.—I went to Aima Choki[3], and by the way visited Kenipahar, where it was said there were some remains of antiquity. Rather less than two miles from Nagarjuni I came to the boundary of Sahebgunj, and followed it a little way south, having that division on my right and Holasgunj on my left for about a quarter of a mile. About one mile from the boundary I came to the Fulgo, which I crossed obliquely for half a mile to Keni, which is washed by the river. It is a great heap of very large

(1) Westernmost branch now called Phalgo N. and easternmost branch Mohane N. The former divides again about eight miles further north, and its eastern branch is called Sunr N.

(2) Ibrahimpur or Jaru.

(3) Alwan.

masses of perfect granite, where very fine stones might be procured. I went a little way along its south side, where I found a small temple. The Pujari said that the only thing remarkable was a cave where a hermit had passed his time in devotion. With great difficulty I scrambled up the rock and found the hermitage to be a den under a shelving rock not above three feet high, but wide and long enough to shelter several people, and quite dry. The priest then shewed me at the foot of the hill a large block of granite under a tamarind tree, where he said the great man (Mahapurus) was wont to play (Kelna). What play the holy person used I cannot say. There were two holes on the stone such as those in which the people here often beat rice. From the east end of Keni I proceeded about $1\frac{1}{2}$ miles east to join the great road between Patna and Gaya, which is miserable. I followed it south-west for about three miles to Aima Choki, so that my route was exceedingly circuitous.

26*th November*.—I went to Sahebgunj. The road until near that place leads near the Fulgo, and is very bad. About a mile from Ram Sil are two ruined small mud forts called Alepi. They seem of modern Hindustani structure, being square with bastions at the corner. South from them I crossed the Fulgo, which is very wide and contains some small islands. Rather more water than at Nagarjuni, and several fine canals go from it for irrigation. The water clear. In the rainy season it rises and falls with great suddenness. I crossed at Ramsil. The Gunj begins a little way south from thence and is not large; but the streets are straight and tolerably wide, with a row of trees on each side. Almost all the houses are tiled, but in general small and poor. Some however are decent, and some are built of brick or rough stone. The Jail is large, and consists of several ranges of tiled buildings surrounded by a strong wall of rough stone and brick. South from the Jail are two gateways with a street between, one is like a triumphal arch built after the European style with brick. It never seems to have been finished. These gates seem to have been intended to have formed the entrance into a serai, which has never been finished. They are attributed to Mr. Seton, one when Register and the other when Judge. The town may be rather more than half a mile from north to south and somewhat less from east to west.

29*th November*.—I went to visit Ramsil, which is about a mile from the south end of the town. At its south side is a tank dug a few years ago by a Krishna Chond Bose of Calcutta. Immediately above this is an European bungalow, beyond which, passing to the north with the hill on the left, you come to the Imamvari, a small building. Beyond this, where the hill comes to the edge of the Fulgo, is a small but neat temple of Siva built after the Moslem style with a dome, and adjacent to it is a small tank surrounded by a wall of stone with turrets on the corners. The stone of the temple and tank is in rough masses covered with plaster. Two inscriptions in white marble, one in Songskrit the other in Persian. It was lately (about 20 years ago) built by Trikait Rai, Dewan of the Nawab Vazir.

From the temple of Siva to the top of the hill the above mentioned Krishna Chond has constructed a way, where the hill is steep in the form of a stair, and where the declivity is small in [the] form of a sloping pavement. Both are constructed chiefly of rude stone found on the hill, united with lime, and are inconceivably rude. In the rainy season the stones are so slippery that many of the pilgrims have been severely hurt, and if the ascent has been rendered more easy, the descent has become much more dangerous. On the left at the top of this stair is a small temple of rude stones, said to be that of Ram and Sita. The images shown as such and as Hanuman appear to be totally different from such as I have before seen. That of Sita has been broken, and the larger portion thrown out. Above this has been constructed a terrace of stone, mostly of granite which must have been brought from a distance. On this is a small mundir of cut granite which contains a Linga. The Pandas have no tradition by whom it was built, they know that the image came to the place of itself (Prakas). The same Krishna Chand has erected a small and rude Nat Mandir in front of this temple. It seems evident to me that the temple has been built of the ruins of another, which has been much larger and probably occupied its present site, or rather the whole summit of the hill. For a great many of the stones of which the terrace consists, from the ornaments carved on them being broken through the middle and placed without symmetry, show that they have been taken from a ruin; and those which contain no ornaments are exactly of the same granite with them which are carved and with the temple. The mass contained in the terrace is vastly larger than that of the temple, and a great many stones of the same kind have been employed in the structure of the stair. From this I judge that the old temple has been much larger than the present, and the present temple also contains many stones ornamented with carvings that could not have been intended for their present situation. Raja Mitirjit indeed alleges that no one of the present temples at Gaya is above 90 or 100 years old. What the God was which occupied the old temple, I cannot say. Among the ornaments built into the new temple or terrace I observed nothing in the human form, but on the terrace are lying several images, and by the sides of the stair are placed a good many, some of which are still objects of worship and most of which are exactly in the same style with those called Ram, Sita, and Hanuman. Most of them are standing, which is here considered as a sign of their gods worshipped by orthodox (Astik), but some are sitting, which Raja Mittrejit contends is a proof of their having been made by heretics (Nastik). Among them is one evidently of a Buddh in the usual sitting posture, but it is at present worshipped as Brahma. This image is however said to be a stranger. A Brahman two or three years ago found it among the ruins of Kurkihar, about six coses east from Ram Sil, and established it on the hill with a small endowment for a priest. There are however other images in a sitting posture, especially some said to represent Bhairob, but quite different from such as I have seen of that deity. I have seen the same, however, both in the ruins of Peruya and Mungger, and it seems to me to represent a man sitting in a boat, but so very rude that I may readily be mistaken. The priests were very sturdy beggars.

The view from Ram Sil is exceedingly fine—an immense rich plain like a map under your feet, studded with little rocks, and terminating towards the south and east by mountains. The hill is very rocky, barren, and parched, but not so rugged as those of proper granite. It has more the appearance of those of petrosilex, and the stone [1] certainly approaches nearly to that, being divided by numerous fissures, horizontal and vertical, into cuboidal masses, and being exceedingly hard. It is however an aggregate, consisting of black, ash-coloured, and some glassy particles, concerning the nature of which I cannot pretend to decide, but they may be of the three natures usually found in granite, somewhat changed from their usual appearance.

*30th November* 1811.—I went south-east in order to view that part of this overgrown division.

Crossing the Fulgo obliquely, I went up its east bank to a small hill about a mile from the south end of Sahebgunj. The country near the river very poor and sandy, but planted with mangos and palms, which grow well enough. At this hill I turned easterly, and for about a cose went along high poor land, very badly occupied but clear. I however crossed two fine canals conveying water from the Fulgo, and even now containing streams. About a mile from the river [I] had on my left a small cluster of low bare hills, named Gunhar. [2] On the eastern edge of the high land towards my right was a low smooth bare hill.

---

(1) Appendix, No. 11.
(2) Gandhar.

Beyond this for about $2\frac{1}{2}$ miles I went through very fine rice lands belonging to Sohipur,[1] where there is a pretty large tank quite choked with weeds. Beyond this rice ground I went about a mile over high poor land, covered with bushes, and passing through an opening in a long bare broken ridge extending from south-west to north-east for a considerable way, I first came to a small hill on my right, consisting of arid white quartz. The low hills forming the left of the passage consist of quartz or rude jasper, in some places stained red. The north end of the south part of the ridge,[2] which is by far the highest, consists also of a white silicious stone with neither the fracture of flint nor of quartz, and stained of a dirty red in irregular specks. On passing this ridge I had in full view the Moher[3] hills, leaving on my left a high conical peak with a chain of low hills running to the south. The Moher hills are smoother than the last-mentioned ridge and covered with stunted trees. I passed between the large hill and a small hill Tilheta[4] beyond its southern end ; but saw no rock near. The fragments are of silicious stone, white and reddish, with a foliated texture in decay. The Moher ridge is at least four miles from that of Sohipur. The country between very much neglected, perhaps one-third of it waste. There is however much rice and some dry field, but I saw no irrigation by machinery except at Moher, where there are some gardens. Near the Sohipur hills is a small river in a narrow deep channel of clay called the Kewar.[5] It contains however a fine little stream, and I passed a canal (another river)[5a] taken from it for irrigation. In the middle of the plain I came to a large heap on the south side of a large tank. Both are called Badan,[6] and the peasants at work near it had no tradition concerning the place. It seems to me to have been a large temple. At its side are lying three broken images, one

---

(1) Sohaipur.
(2) Bandhuwa.
(3) Mahar (Maher).
(4) Telheta.
(5) Paimar N.
(5a) Written afterwards.
(6) Bhadan.

in a standing posture, with two arms resting on the heads of two dwarf attendants, has a resemblance to one of the figures in the Elephanta. At Koch I observed two such, one called Surja has in both of the hinder hands a wheel or Chakra. The other has such in his left hand and a mace or some such instrument in his right. This was there called Vishnu. The other two are the common representations of Buddhs in a sitting posture.

. Between Badan and Moher is the Bangsi, [1] a fine little river in a narrow channel of clay, which sends off several canals for irrigation. Immediately beyond Tilhetais a fine tank in good repair. From Moher to Futtehpur [2] is about $3\frac{1}{2}$ coses. The first $1\frac{1}{2}$ cose to Dibor[3] is mostly waste, with stunted Palas trees. Dibor is a good village with some sugarcane. About a cose beyond Dibor is a large brick Math belonging to the Sannyasis, where about 20 reside. Near it is a large Grange or farm. The building large but clumsy. The country west from thence waste, east from it to Futehpur well cultivated. Rice chiefly, some sugar. Futehpur is the residence of Bahadur Sing, a Kutteri, who purchased it. Komgar Khan the original proprietor. Bahadur Sing very kindly invited me into his house, but I could not stay. He made his fortune of a Major Crawford who took Bijaigur. Futtehpur is a large village with a mud fort in tolerable condition, which now serves as a zanana.

About a mile from Futtehpur I came to the Darhar,[4] a wide sandy and rocky channel with a little clear stream, and affording canals for irrigation. The rock in its channel is a fine-grained grey granite with silver mica, but much decayed. On the east side of the Bangsi is Dunaiya [5] belonging to Mahummad Husayn of Shakhpur, who takes the title of Nawab. He is building a neat brick house at this place and his

(1) **Bansi N.**
(2) **Fatehpur.**
(3) **Dhibar.**
(4) Dahder R.; R. and B.A.; **Dhadhar N.**
(5) **Dunaiya.**

residence there will perhaps tend to improve the country, for all beyond Dunaiya to near Katautiya [1] three coses east is a forest, stunted near Dunaiya but containing large trees towards the hills. The most common trees the Boswellia which I see notched for extracting the rosin ; the Catechu from whence some drug is prepared; and the Asan and Emblica. At Katautiya some Tasar is reared by the Ghatwars, who occupy that village and cultivate much in the same style as in the jungles of Banka. Maize and Orrhor with probably Maruya seem to be their chief crops, but they also raise Bhut, Sirsu, Kurti, and Cotton. Mr. Christian has induced them to sow indigo merely for the seed, and it has thriven amazingly. The second cutting five feet high. The Ghatwars have exactly the same countenances with the hill tribes. They speak only the Hindi dialect, and say that they are different from the Bhungiyas. I went about a mile south from the village to the foot of Gauripa [2], the highest peak of a granitic ridge extending east and west about four coses. Gauripa is about one cose from the west end of the ridge, and consists of a large-grained granite, white quartz and felspar, and black foliated mica. On its top is said to be an image of Gurupasin carved in the human form. The peak was so high and rugged that I could not ascend. All the neighbouring castes when afraid offer sacrifices. There is no priest, and if one is required the votary brings a Purohit with him. I returned, and at Dunaiya found that the Nawab's people, it being evening, had prepared a dinner for me, and I was sorry that I could not accept of the kind offer, but as it was I did not reach my tents until two in the morning. My watch now goes so ill that I cannot rely in computing distances by it.

1*st December*.—I went to Preth Sila, distant three coses by a fine road with a row of trees on each side, made by Monun Dotto Bose[3] a Bengalese, about twenty

(1) Kathawtiya.
(2) Gurpa.
(3) Madanmohan Datta, in Report.

years ago. Pret Sila is the most considerable peak of a cluster of rocks either granitic or approaching to granite in their nature, but having also a nature approaching to hornstone like the neighbouring rock of Ramsila. The lower peaks are the most rugged, and are of the more clearly defined granite, while Prethsil is not so much broken and its stone is smaller-grained and more flinty in its fracture.[1] At the bottom of the hill is a small tank and some buildings for the accommodation of pilgrims, constructed by the same Modon Dotto. A small spring, very dirty and swarming with frogs, runs from the bottom of the hill into the tank. The ascent of the hill is by a stair constructed by the same Modon Dotto, as rude as that of Ramsil and much steeper, but not so long. Most of the stones are rude fragments taken from the hill, but many are squared perfect granite brought, I suppose, from Burabur, as the stone is of the same nature. The people say that these squared stones are those of a former stair which had become ruinous and was too narrow; but had been entirely constructed of such stones. Modon Dotto has carved his name on several steps of the stair in different places. Several small images are lying by the side of the stair in different places. One only is I believe an object of worship. It is called Brahmapod or the feet of Brahma, and represents the impression of two feet cut on a square stone. Near it are some broken images, one of which seems to me to represent a Boudh sitting and supported on a globe held by [a] figure kneeling below. A Brahman called it Lakshmi although it is male, but I soon found that these images were viewed with no interest, and were called by each person by whatever name first occurred to the person's memory. The buildings on the hill, partly by Modon Dotto partly by Ahila Bai, are very petty and quite modern. Tradition relates that there was an old temple on the place, and I observed one pillar built into the stair; but there are no traces to show that this old temple has ever een of considerable size.

---

(1) Appendix, No. 8.

The original object seems to have been a projecting rock called Prethsil, or the devil's stone, and part of the ceremonies is still performed before this emblem of terror. A priest attends, directs in a very careless manner and with no affectation of devotion the manner in which the offerings are to be made, and concludes by asking a Paisa from each votary, who has previously paid fully as much as he could afford. The Paisa was probably the whole originally demanded, and the ceremony of asking for it is continued after such an offering would be received with contempt. In fact, the words were mere matters of course, as no Paisah was given. Another fat dirty ill-dressed priest leaned very carelessly against the rock, and the votaries after having made their offering according to their rank either stooped down and touched his body or threw themselves before him and kissed his feet.

Near the rock and covered with dirt was lying a small image carved on stone, which represented Gauri sitting on the knee of Sankar in the usual manner, but was called Preth Bhawani. The other object of worship in the temple is a mark on a rock supposed to have been made by Brahma. It is an octagonal space about two feet in diameter, very uneven in the surface and surrounded by a notch. The angles are so sharp that it appears to me very modern. The inequalities of the surface are attributed to the feet of the deity who has, it is said, left on the stone three marks of gold. The place was covered with dirt, but although washed I could not from the distance of 8 or 10 feet see any such marks with the assistance of a glass, but being short-sighted some yellow marks may exist.

The number of votaries is very great. At the Devil's Stone, during 8 or 10 minutes I looked on, one succeeded another as fast as the priest could repeat the forms, which did not take half a minute. He said merely—Pour water there—Throw your pots there—Give me a Paisa—or some such words. The whole worship is totally destitute of splendour, neither priest nor votaries being either clean or well dressed, nor is there any order or imposing procession; all is done in a hurry with much noise and tumult. The priests are quite ignorant, nor do they affect any extraordinary devotion. They live at Gaya and resort daily to the temple, where they go through the ceremony with as much indifference as a huckster retailing petty wares; but are to the last degree clamorous for money. The case with the votaries is very different. They seem strongly impressed with devotion and the remembrance of their deceased parents, to whom they were performing their duties. Many of them were old and infirm, and required the assistance of friends or servants to enable them to ascend and descend the stairs, which they did on their bare feet. Some of them from distant parts bestowed blessings on me for the protection and safety with which under the British Government they enjoyed their religion, while two of them made bitter complaints of the rapacity of the priests. One from Malwa alleged that he had been stript of every thing that [he] had; another that the demands were so exorbitant that he could not afford to perform the ceremony. For such evils I had no remedy to offer.

3*rd December*.—I went west about 16½ miles to view the country in that direction. Not quite four miles from my tents I came to a small hummock at the south end of Kewali,[1] the southern peak of the cluster of hills in which Prethsila is placed. This hummock consists of a stone exceedingly difficult to break, and consists of small grains, some patches are a grey consisting of black and white grains.[2] Other patches consist of black and rust-coloured grains. In some places the black grains are pretty equally diffused, in others they are conglomerated into irregular spots. Its fracture is somewhat conchoidal, and it is vastly more difficult to break than granite. It has no appearance of stratification. About 1½ miles farther I came to the Yomuna,[3] a small river

(1) Kewali.
(2) Appendix. No. 15.
(3) Jumnah N., R., Pomna N., B.A.; Jamuna N.

in a deep channel of clay, but it contains a fine little stream and affords several fine canals for irrigation. One of the best bridges that I have yet seen in the course of this survey is on this river. It consists of three small arches of brick in the gothic form, but is wide and the road good, with very neat parapets and a stair at each end to facilitate the descent to the river; just beyond it is a neat small temple of Siva. Both built by Raja Mitrejit. From the Jomuna to a small hill named Dhermsala[1] is not quite $1\frac{1}{2}$ miles. This hill has at its north end a small hummock, both are of a smooth surface, and I saw no rock within reach to give me an idea of their structure. Near Dhermsala I found people employed in making lime from Ganggot.

From Dhermsala to Pochananpur[2], a market place is rather more than $3\frac{1}{2}$ miles. Pochananpur is a little west from the Morhar[3], a river which has a sandy channel perhaps $\frac{1}{8}$ of a mile wide. The stream is very small but exceedingly clear, and contains many small fishes, so that it probably is perennial. Several fine canals taken from it. So far the road is good, with many bridges and in many places an avenue of trees. All made by Raja Mitirjit. Rather more than two miles from Pochananpur at a village named Pali,[4] I observed three heaps of brick, and all are said to have been temples of Siva, which would appear in some measure to have been the case. The heaps are also attributed to the Kol, once the lords of the country. The largest is by the side of a tank, by the side of which is lying a large Linga. The heap of bricks and stones is very considerable. On its summit has been erected a small temple of granite, a few of the stones of which are still in their places. Within these is standing up the end of a stone of hornblende, probably a lintel. On one end of this is carved a Buddh. On the heap next to this is placed a square block of hornblende, the top of which is carved into a Linga; but

(1) **Dharampur.**
(2) Pachainpour, R., Pacianpour, B.A.; **Panchanpur.**
(3) Muthar N., R., Moorhur R. or Little Pompon R., B.A.; **Morhar N.**
(4) **Pali.**

this obscene object of worship is evidently placed upon the heap after it had become a ruin. Near it is lying a long stone of hornblende much carved. It contains four figures sitting, with many others in a posture of adoration. The four figures are in the usual posture of Buddhs, and resemble them in every respect except in having four arms. The third has no images, but it is said that it contained a Linga which has been removed.[1]

From Pali to Koch[2] is rather more than 4½ miles. From the Morhar to Koch the road has as yet been only marked out by two rows of young trees, and in the rainy season must be impassable as the country there is low. There are several fine wells (Inderas) built by Raja Mitrijit, who seems to be an attentive Landlord. Koch is a very large village, mostly tiled as indeed is the case with a great many houses on the way. A few are neat, being smoothed and painted, and a very little pains might make such houses very pretty, but in general they are very rough and slovenly. From entering the town I went about half a mile north to an old temple of Siva, which is a little beyond the town. The north end of the town stands on some large heaps of bricks and stones, usually said to be the remains of the Kol. Beyond these heaps and a mud fort recently gone to ruin, is a tank, and on the west side of this is a large heap of bricks and granite, among which are some pillars of a curious structure but not exceeding four feet in length.

The whole of these ruins are supposed to have belonged to the temple of Siva, and the vulgar allege that they are the work of the Kol, but the priest says that he knows nothing of the Kol, and that the temple was built by Raja Bairu Indra, but the priest knows nothing of what country he governed, where he dwelt, to what caste he belonged, nor when he lived. I am inclined to think that the temple is of very modern date, as so much of the plaster by which it was encrusted

(1) "*See* Journal from Jehanabad". (Note by Dr. B.).
(2) Cowch, R., Couch, B.A.; Koch.

remains entire that it cannot well be above four or five centuries old. It further seems to me to have been built on the ruins of a former temple. Before it are lying many images carved in relievo on hornblende. These were probably among the ornaments of the former temple. Among them are many of Surja, Vishnu, Devi, Ganesa, Hurgauri, Krishna and Rada, etc.; and two remarkable groups, one representing the Avatars of Vishnu, among which Budh is omitted and Rada put in to supply his place. The other I have nowhere else observed. It represents eight females sitting in a row on an equal number of animals, but it is called Naugraha so that one figure has probably been broken away. Among the others were two of Buddh, the only ones which contained inscriptions. They were broken, and the head of the one and legs of the other have been lost, but the whole figure may be made out from the two. Their hands are in a posture different from the common, but over the head of one is placed a smaller Bouddh in the usual posture. I could hear of no other inscription at the place. I was here met by the Moslem son of Raja Mitterjit, a very obliging young man, who has European instruments for drawing and has made a little progress in the art. He gave me two drawings of waterfowl which I had not before seen, and was employed taking a drawing of the temple for my use. Had he masters I have no doubt that he would make much proficience.

Sorujugiri, a learned Dasnami of Buddh Gya, says that the account of the actions of Sankara Acharya is contained in the Sankar Dig Vijayi. He established four principal muts—Sringagiri, Jaisi near Rameswor, Sarada in Kashmir and Goverdon at Jugannat. He gives the following account of the origin of the Dosnamis—Sankara came to Kasi destroying the Nastik. The Raja was a Buddh, and in order to make Sankara love his caste, confined all the Brahmans and dressed up some people like them. These people entertained Sankara and he ate their food and drank their liquor, afterwards some of his disciples did the same and scandal arose. The disciples having been accused of eating and drinking with low people by their master alleged his example in their defence. He reprimanded them severely for their impudence in pretending to imitate him, who had license to do everything, and heating a piece of iron red hot ate it up. As they could not venture to do the same they were degraded. They are now mostly of the Virbhav and Sakti sect, and have deserted the doctrines of the Smart in the South. The Mahants and Chelas take the same Upades. None ought to be admitted as Sannyasis but Brahmans, Kshatriyas and Vaisyas. In this district no Sudras are admitted. Rajputs and Kateri are both admitted to be Kshatriyas. The Kateri are very common in the Punjab, and cannot pronounce the Ksh. The Dosnamis give Upades to all castes. Those of them who are Saivi or Vaishnavas give Upades only to those of their own sect, but those of the Sakti sect give Upades to any one. When they came to Gya, the whole people had left the place, which was a forest. They consider the image as representing Budh Avatar. The whole of [the] bricks and stones in the present Math of the Sannyasis [were] taken from the temple of Boudh. This contained many images of the ordinary Hindu gods, but a little different from those used by the Astik. On being shown the drawings of Keya Dol he says that they are all Nastik, and that [they have taken] vast numbers of such from the old temple and have placed them in the new temple. The Nastik as usual were persecutors, and long stopped the worship of the orthodox at Gya. He says that the Nastik and Astik always existed, but that sometimes the one sometimes the other have prevailed. Formerly Vishnu, taking into consideration that mankind offered innumerable sacrifices and put many animals to death, took upon himself the form of Budh Avatar and prohibited sacrifices : but afterwards considering that this was contrary to the Vedas he disappeared and sent Sankara and Udayan to destroy the Boudhs. He says that he never heard of Amara Singh having built Bouddh Gya, but such a story is current, and he says that Amara was no doubt a Nastik because in the introduction to the Amarkosh he used none of the invocations which if an orthodox Hindu he certainly would have done.

*4th December.*—I went to Chakun[1] to see a place where Soda is found. Passing north not quite a mile, I came to Ramsil, a hill already mentioned, which extends along the bank of the Fulgo for about $\frac{1}{3}$ of a mile. I then went north about seven miles to Chakun, where there is an old mud castle still inhabited by an Amildar of Rajah Mitrijit. Similar castles have been at most of the villages by the way, but they have become ruinous. At a distance they have had a picturesque effect, but on near approach look very mean. They usually consist of four square towers with pent roofs, joined by lower buildings. Turning west from Chakun about a mile, I found the saline earth scattered among the fields, for the greater part is cultivated. The quantity of soda that I saw was small, but a good deal had been scraped away, and I could find no intelligent man to show me the extent. The people said that it is found where the soil is Rerh, that is, a poor light earth in a thin stratum over sand. When scraped off by the washermen, those alone who take it away, new soda effloresces again in the same place in from 8 to 30 days according to circumstances. It is never found in Kebal or clay, nor in every place where the soil is called Rerh.

*7th December.*—I went to visit some of the most remarkable places in the town of Gaya. This town is large and built mostly of brick and stone, but the stones are not squared except such as have been taken from ruins, and the whole building whether brick or stone is often covered with plaster. The town stands on a rocky eminence on the bank of the Fulgo, and as many of the houses are large looks tolerably well at a distance, but a near approach fills with disgust. Some with round turrets and open galleries have a very picturesque effect. The streets are narrow (6 to 10 feet) dirty and crooked. The galleries

(1) Chakan.

which serve for shops are mostly very slovenly, and even of those which are neat and gaily painted some corner or other is usually defiled by smoke or dust and cobwebs. The very best houses are rendered slovenly by cakes of cowdung for fuel patched on their walls, and the jealousy of the men prevents any reasonable number or size for the apertures intended to intromit air or light, while the small ones that are tolerated are secured by rude wooden shutters without paint or polish. In walking through the town, precautions are necessary as formerly in Edinburgh. The passenger must call out to prevent inundation from above.

It may be observed of all the buildings about the place except the Vishnupad itself, that in a great measure they are composed evidently of ruins, and consist partly of stone, partly of brick. The pillars of course are of various lengths, thicknesses and form, as found in various buildings, but are all of granite and bear all the marks of a rude antiquity, while many pillars have [been] built into the walls. A vast number of stones of a small-grained black potstone containing images carved in relievo, inscriptions, or the sides and lintels of doors, are built into the walls, and the carvings and writings are often turned outwards as an ornament; but placed without the least regard to symmetry. And unfortunately some of the inscriptions have been half built into the walls or cut half away, in order to suit the stone for the place it now occupies. Some of the inscriptions and carvings are on granite, but potstone is the more usual material. In fact the people say that the Buddhs had destroyed all the old temples, and that the place had lain waste and was unfrequented until about four or five centuries ago, when the Gyalis again began to recover and pilgrims to return, but it is farther acknowledged that the place did not recover any considerable celebrity until about 200 years ago.

None of the Gyalis would have communication with me, each being afraid that his companions would blame him, but I was accompanied by the most learned Sannyasi of Buddh Gaya, by a learned Pandit from

Draveda, by an intelligent Purohit, as well as by the Pandit of the mission.[1] Some of the inscriptions which I have had explained are by the Pal Rajahs, well known to have been Buddhs, and among the images carved in relievo a great many of them represent Buddh. Many more however represent various deities of the Hindu Theogony, but these are common to all the sects of Hindus, and some sects of the Buddhs admit of their worship although others reject this practice, but these images seem merely intended as ornament and as such would have been admitted even by Gautama. In fact by far the greater part of these images, although evidently representing personages now worshipped by the Orthodox, such as Ganesa, Naroyon, Kali, are said by the skilful to be represented with emblems which clearly show them to have been the work of the heterodox. Others it is alleged are represented in an orthodox manner, and it may be alleged that the Buddhs took these from previous orthodox buildings and placing them in their new temples associated them with others of their own heterodox invention. Similar images, orthodox and heterodox, are scattered intermixed through every part of the vicinity for 8 or 10 coses round, and in Keyoa Dol are carved intermixed on the same rocks and all in the same style of art. I suspect therefore that the whole are the work of the Buddhs, and that some of the images which these used resemble exactly what the orthodox employ, but there are evidently two periods in the buildings. The figures on the Burabor hill, owing indeed perhaps to a difference of material, are vastly ruder than those of Gaya, and the inscriptions are in a very old Nagari still used in some parts of the South of India, and legible by the Pandit of Mailcotay, while the inscriptions of Gaya are mostly in a bad Deva Nagari intermixed with Tirahuti, and vastly more modern.

(1) The following is crossed out by Buchanan : "It seems to me that if Gaya has in times of antiquity been a place of orthodox worship and has been destroyed by the Buddhs, it did not lie waste in the interval. The Buddhs have evidently erected buildings on the place, and it is from their ruins that the present temples have been constructed."

I first visited the Vishnupad with the numerous small places by which it is surrounded. The entrance is by a very small door at the end of a lane. Over it is built a Nohobut Khana of brick and stone, very rude and mis-shapen. In a narrow court between the first and second door is a small temple dedicated to Gayeswori, a female riding on a lion and killing a buffalo, with eight arms. The image is one of those supposed to have been formed by Brahma. No one knows who built the temple, for the Gayalis have no sort of learning nor give themselves the smallest trouble about their benefactors or building. The second door is scarcely five feet high and not above two feet wide. It leads into a long court paved with stone, and confined by buildings. On the right is first placed a building called a Chatur. A vile stair leads up to a court surrounded by cloisters, intended for the entertainment of Brahmans. Some of the apartments are neat were they tolerably clean, but they are to the last degree slovenly. In one are placed three images of white marble, not so large as human size and clothed in dirty yellow cotton cloth. Two are standing, and represent Narayan and Lakshmi. The third is sitting, and represents Ahila Bai, by whom the building and Vishnupad were erected. The statuaries from Jainagar[1] exceedingly rude. Farther on to the right of the same court is another building erected by a contribution of the Gayalis for giving entertainment to Brahmans, and called a Dhermsala. On the left of the court is first an Akara or convent of Sannyasis, said to have been built when the orthodox worship was first restored. Then there is a rude pillar of granite called Gyaguj, which is taken as a witness by the pilgrims of their filial duty.

Behind this is the temple of Godadhor, the next in size to the Vishnupad of all the temples about Gaya. All those of any considerable dimensions consist of two parts, a kind of pyramid called Mondir and placed over the image. These mondirs much resemble the pyramids that in Draveda are placed over the gateways of the

---

(1) Jaipur; in Report.

great temples built by Krishna of Vigayanagar. Before the pyramid, and connected with it, is a building usually supported by several rows of columns, and to which infidels may be admitted. This is called Natmondir or Soba Mundup. The Mondir of Godadhor is very lofty, and rudely constructed of granite. The Soba Mundip is very long and flat-roofed. Both were built a considerable time ago, probably on the restoration of worship, but having become ruinous have been lately in a great measure rebuilt. In front of the Soba Mundup is [a] Nohobut Khana, with a door leading to a stair of granite descending the bank of the Fulgo, which would be a good work were not the stair vastly too steep. It has been just finished, but the Pandit from the South when he arrived, just before the work commenced, saw in the old building a stone containing an inscription which attributed the old stair and a temple of the Sun to be afterwards mentioned to Pritapa Rudra, a well-known prince of Warangkol. In the gateway leading from the temple to the stair is now placed a stone containing a small defaced female figure with an inscription over it. Whether or not the same with the above I have not learned. South from this stair is a Dharmsaleh built by Rai Dulobh, father of Rajbulobh, well known in the English history of Bengal. In its wall is built a stone containing a defaced female image with an inscription. North from Godadhor is a Sannyasi's math in which are two loose inscriptions of some length. South from that Dhermsaleh, and adjacent to it, is the residence of a disciple [1] of Madhava Acharya, who is Guru of all the Gayali Brahmans. On my approach his people shut the door.

From this court surrounding Godadhor there is a narrow winding passage into that surrounding the Vishnupada. This passage is surrounded by little rude buildings. In one of these is an image, not worshipped. On a rude pillar of granite at its door is an inscription, but it has a modern appearance and was probably cut

(1) Dandi Swami; in Report.

after the pillar was taken from the ruins to occupy its present situation. On entering the area of the Vishnupada you have on your right the front of the Natmondir, but so near that you can form no judgment of the effect which the building ought to have, and can only judge of its merit by a lateral view and a consideration of the parts. Although it would make only a small parish church, this building possesses very considerable merit, and was erected entirely by Ahiliya Bai with stone brought from a quarry already mentioned by workmen from Jainagar. The stone is only roughly cut, although soft and easily cut smooth, but the design of the Natmondir far exceeds in elegance any Hindu work that I have seen. The ground plan and elevation of the work will give some idea of the structure. My painters failed in an attempt at placing the whole building in perspective. The Mondir is exceedingly clumsy, after the fashion of the great gateways of the south, but built entirely of stone. The Natmundir is a light building and the outside of the dome is peculiarly graceful. Its inside is not so light, but still is highly pleasing to the eye. The most singular thing is that although constructed entirely of stone it is not an arch. The stones are built in horizontal rows gradually diminishing in diameter until they meet at the summit. The chief workman says that the dome might have been constructed on the same plan of double the size, and required no centre or support when building. This is I believe a species of masonry totally unknown in Europe. The stones are $1\frac{3}{4}$ cubits in width from the outer to the inner side of the dome, and each row forming a circle round the dome, the sides are parts of the radii of the circle, so that the stones are wedged into the row. Every joining is secured by three iron clamps. The outer and inner superficial; the former in form of a dovetail, the inner a plain parallelepiped. The middle one is also a parallelepiped but descends to the bottom of the joining. The keystone is above, wider than the aperture left by the last row, but its lower part fits the aperture exactly. On the south side of this temple there is an open area sufficiently ample to give a good view of the whole, on all other sides it is shut up by wretched buildings, and it is kept in a miserable state of slovenliness. At the south side of the temple is an elevated terrace of stone, brick, and plaster. It is called Sworga Dewari, and on it are several Lingas, one of which is exceedingly indecent. Into its perpendicular sides are built many old images, on one of which representing Ganesa is an inscription. Near this is lying a broken pillar. In a wall is built a stone representing the nine planets (Naugraha) exactly as [at] Koch, but it is Nastik, each planet being a female sitting on some animal. In the ruins are other Naugrahas, partly of the same form, partly Astick.

The great temple, besides the impression of Vishnu's feet, contains a Siva placed there by Ban Raja. Ahiliya Bai has added a bull or Nandi of white marble, very rude. Close to the east front of the great temple Ahiliya Bai at her death was erecting another temple over a rock called Sorusbedi. The first order of columns had only been erected when her death put a stop to the work, which is much to be regretted as it would in all probability have been very fine. The rock is very rough, and the eye of Hindu faith, assisted by a strong imagination, can discover on it the impressions of the feet of eighteen deities.

On some of the stones of the pavement between Vishnupad and Sorosbedi are short inscriptions, but such as are legible, not yet having been worn by the treading of feet, merely mention the names of pilgrims.

East from the Surusbedi is a small rude temple of Narasingha, surrounded by small irregular buildings. Before it, in particular on the left of the inner door leading into the area of the Vishnupad, is an image of Goraknath. The door of the temple of Narasingha, which is very small, is constructed of a fine black stone richly carved. The lintel contains a Bouddh with an inscription on the back of the stone, written transversely with respect to the image. Above the lintel on a separate stone is a short inscription. On the wall at the left hand of the God is also a long inscription in Devanagri. In one of the small buildings north from Narasingha are heaped many images, Astik and Nastik, and there is an inscription. Within this is a Siva Linga in a small apartment. The door is of fine-grained black stone, much ornamented, with four Buddhs on the lintel. Over the door is an inscription on an old pillar, half built into the wall, and another inscription still legible is built into the wall of the inside of the apartment.

North a little way from the Vishnupad is a small tank, very deep sunk but containing only a little dirty water. The walls covered with plaster are exceedingly high, and at three corners are places where offerings (Pindi) are made by pilgrims. The walls were erected by Rajah Mitrijit, and the tank is called Surja Talau from an old temple of Surja or the Sun, which according to the inscription formerly mentioned was built by Pritapa Rudra.

A short way west from Surja Talau is a place of worship called Krishna Dwarika, where there are several little ruinous temples, with a cloister surrounding a small court, lately built by the Gywalis for their entertainment. In the wall of one of the temples is built an inscription and one of the numerous images similar to the Surya of Koch has a short inscription.

I went from thence south-west to the outside of the gate of the town, where there is a poor tank without any building. It is called Boiturni, and many pilgrims here offer cows to the Brahmans, but it is not one of the 45 Tirthas. On the east end of the hill beyond this tank is a very small rude temple, flat roofed, open at the sides and supported by six pillars. It stands on a rock of granite similar to that used in the buildings of Gya, and in this is a very large irregular cavity supposed to have been formed by the knee of Bhim Sen when he performed his devotions. This place is therefore called Bhim Gaya. Higher up this hill, which is called Basmakut, is a brick temple called Jenabdun. It consists of a small pyramid with a porch in front. No one knows who built them. On a loose stone lying in front is an inscription much defaced. South from thence, on the descent of the hill, is a similar small temple to that over the impression of Bhim Sen's knee. This is over a rock of very unequal surface and covered with little cavities supposed to be the marks of cows' feet, on which account this place is called Gauprochar.

At the foot of the hill on the south side is a temple of some size, called Prapita Maha. The lower part of the building is of stone. Over the image is a Mundir of brick, over the porch or Soda Mundip are five small pyramids of the same material. A small stone inserted into the north side of the temple near a door contains an inscription in impure Sangskrit dated in the [year] 1277 of the Vikrama Sombot, and relative to this temple built by a Raja Deva, son of Rama Deva, son of.........[1]Pal.. Immediately adjoining to this on the south are some Dhermsalehs, and contiguous to these [is] the Oksha Bot supposed to have been planted by Brahma. It stands on a very large elevated terrace, composed of ruins and having every appearance of a very recent work. Under the tree is a small temple of Siva. In its wall has been built an old inscription. South from the temple is a choked tank called Goda Lal. In it is shown a stone supposed to be the mace with which Vishnu killed Hetnama Rakshus. I had with me the most learned persons that could be procured, but they differed very widely in their accounts of this personage. It was agreed however that like Ravana he was the son of a Brahman, by a female Rakshasa who were a very ugly black race of people, who ate everything and obeyed no law, but were very strong and violent.

West from the Okhyabot is a small ruinous tank called Rukmikund, which has been lined with brick.

A little east from the Okhyabot is a small tank called Brahma Sarawar, lined with stone at its north end

(1) Left blank. (Probably Ajaya.)

where there is a small temple built over a hole dug into the rock. In the bottom of this hole is a figure, beyond all description rude, of Jom the judge of the infernal regions.

A little north from thence is a temple and porch of brick, dedicated to the Markanda Siva, which came there of its own accord. It is situated at the west side of the Baiturni tank, which I have mentioned as being situated without the southern gate of Gya, and immediately under the temple of Jenabdun.

North from thence, between the two eastern arms of the ridge of hills, is a dirty pool called Gadaveri, on its north side are two small places of worship, one dedicated to Pap Muchun alone; the other to Pap Muchun and Rhin Muchu. Near them is a well of very modern structure called Girdukup, and a Banyan tree called Girdu Bot. This shades a terrace with many old images. Opposite to the tree is a small temple of Girdeswor Siva. East from that is a neat small temple lately built by Mitrejit over a Siva that was found by Mr. Seton when forming a road.

Akas Gunga is a spring coming from a recess in the hills west from these last-mentioned places. North from them is the ruin of a tank called Vasishta Khund, through which Mr. Seton made a road, on which account the Tirtha has been deserted.

*8th December*.—I went to view the range of hills south and west from the city of Gaya. Proceeding along the city I came to its north-east end, called Muruli or Girdkut, beyond which is a lower part of the hill, called Singrik. At its west end, where there are some small modern buildings on the plain, is held a great Mela. Beyond this is a small hummock, and a long ridge called Mandam in the language of men and Udyant in that of the Gods. At the west end of Udyant is a small plain surrounded by some small hills. On the plain are the ruins of a small temple. By them is the image of a cow giving suck to a calf, I believe an emblem of the Jain worship. It is called Dhenukaruna.

From this plain I went west between Mondain and a ridge to the south of it, descending on a recess between that ridge and the hill of Brahmajoni. Passing round the south side of this, at its east end I came to a dirty pool lined with rough stone, called Sabitrikund. On the top of the hill which is a very rugged peak, is a small temple of Sabitri Devi with a delan near it, both built by Balaji Pondit, a Marattah. Near them is a hole in the rock called Brahma Joni, through which sinners creep. A little north from Sabitrikund is a larger and cleaner tank named Radakund.

I had now surrounded the hill, which consists of several different hummocks and peaks, of various rocks very strangely intermixed. The greater part consists of an imperfect granite [1] like that of Ramsila but in various parts approaching to hornstone, and this in some parts seems as if impregnated with hornblende,[2] becoming black and tough, and in others contains black dots. In others again, both the imperfect granite and hornstone have degenerated into a white granular stone,[3] in some places retaining black dots from the mica.[4] At the east end of the hill is a portion of very perfect granite,[5] and immediately above Bhim Gaya there is imbedded in this a large mass of the hornstone,[6] the two rocks being perfectly contiguous. In other places there are large rocks of quartz, white, glassy, etc., etc.[7] The most remarkable is a hummock west from Brahmajoni, the masses decaying on which have a vertical appearance. They are partly red, partly white with a few greenish portions, and it is said may be cut into seals. Perhaps they approach to cornelian, having a very greasy fracture.[8] West from thence the imperfect granite[9] and hornstone[10]

(1) Appendix, Nos. 34, 22.
(2) ,, No. 78.
(3) ,, No. 23.
(4) ,, No. 22.
(5) ,, No. 41.
(6) ,, No. 27.
(7) ,, No. 44.
(8) ,, No. 95.
(9) ,, No. 22.
(10) ,, No. 81.

is decaying in vertical schistose masses, but where the rock is entire there is nowhere the slightest appearance of stratification.

I then went into the town to visit some places south from Vishnupad. I went first to Gyakup, where an octagon well has been lately constructed by Nara Pant of Burahunpur, a petty work for so great a personage. Between this and Vishnupad is a hole in a rock with a rude image carved in its bottom, exactly like that of Jom near Brahma Sarowar, but called Gaya Sir. It has over it a rude temple. A little west from thence, through hilly narrow lanes, is Minduprista, a small temple of a Sakti. A little south-west from thence is a rock where Pindi is offered to Godadhor. There is no mark on the rock except some Pilgrims' names, but it is covered by a small temple like that over Bhim Gaya. Behind it is the temple, with some good accommodations for the priest.

*9th December.*—I went to Buddh Gaya, distant from the south end of (the) Sahebganj near six miles, and situated on the west side of the Fulgo. The houses and gardens of Gaya extend about 1¼ miles south from Sahibgunj. The country through which I passed, overloaded with plantations.. I here was visited by and visited the Mahant, who received me very civilly, and his principal chelas, who have been very great travellers, were fond of talking on the subject, and had here laid aside the habit of begging ; on the contrary they are here exceedingly charitable or hospitable. The convent is surrounded by a high brick wall containing a very considerable space on the banks of the west branch of the Fulgo, between it and the great temple of Buddh Gya. The wall has turrets in the corners and some at the sides, and has two great gates, the handsomest part of the building. Towards the river is a Dharmsaleh, consisting of a long cloister, but not quite finished. The principal building is a large square, with towers at the corners like a castle, and very few windows outwards. It contains several courts and many apartments totally destitute of neatness, elegance, or convenience. Within the wall is also a garden, a plantation of turmeric, and a burial ground where several Sannyasis are deposited in temples of Siva. The buildings have been erected at very different times, each Mahant having made various additions, so that there is no uniformity nor symmetry of parts. The materials have been taken almost entirely from the ruins, and the Mahants seem to have been at particular pains to have rescued the images although all Nastik, and to have placed them where they might be saved from injury. In a small building is an image of Gautoma and Mannat, near it in a wall have been built images of Sakimuni and Chandamuni. These three Munis are three of those admitted to have been lawgivers among the Buddhs. Under one of the sides of the western gate is a flag containing a long inscription partly visible. In the wall of one of the courts has been built an inscription in the Pali character of the Burmas. In the wall of the south-east turret of the outer wall fronting the river, is built an image of the Sakti, but having a necklace of Buddhs in place of human heads, with which she is represented in orthodox images. A short inscription partly defaced under her feet. Immediately north from the Dharmsaleh on a tower is a Buddh, with an inscription at his shoulders and another at his feet. In the wall south from the gate facing the river is a large female figure with many heads and arms. It is allowed to be Nastik and to have been taken from the ruins. In a small chamber on the north side of the same gate is an image standing with a short inscription. The number of Munis built into the wall is very great.

The Gosaigns say that there is a place of worship as celebrated among the Hindus as Mecca is among the Muhammadans. It is situated nine days journey beyond Tata on the sea side, and is named Hingulad, where there is a temple of Parbuti. The pilgrims go from Tata to Rambag in three days, from thence to Soonmeane three days, from thence to Hingulad three days. The inhabitants of the vicinity are Muhammadans, and are called Lumri.

West from the north end of the Convent of the Gosaigns, on the ruins of the old palace of Asoka Dherma, has been erected a large building, constructed lately but at different periods and containing two temples, one of Jagannath the other of Ram, built according to an inscription by Ganga Bai. In the wall of the temple of Jagannath is also built an inscription but it has been taken from the ruins, Jagannath having been built by the present occupant's father. The building on the whole respectable in size. It has no endowment. The ruin of the palace very large. It has had a ditch, but no cavity is to be observed within.

*9th December*.--I went to visit some places east from Buddh Gaya. I crossed the western branch of the Fulgo just above the convent. The river here is very wide, but is divided into two channels by a low sandy island. The western channel is called Kanoksor in the Hindi and Sobornasor in the Pali language. The eastern or larger branch in the Hindi is named Nilajun and in the Pali Nirinchiya.[1] Both contain a stream, but very trifling. The channel fully as large as at Gaya. About half a mile beyond the Fulgo is a pretty large tank called Matungabapi, but it has become dry, although a dirty stagnant creek (Ralim nalah) passes through it. At its north end are two small temples with many images from Buddh Gaya, and a small tank lined with brick. The plain is acknowledged to be Astik and to have been established by Markanda Rishi. About ¼ of a mile beyond that, I crossed a small nulah called Dherma Rond, and about an equal distance farther I came to a considerable heap of bricks on which four small buildings of brick have been erected. One is over [a] deep pit like a well, where Dherma Rajah, the son of Pandu, performed yug. Of course this is the Astik story, as the Buddhs perform no yug. One is a temple containing an image of that personage. Another is a temple of Parswanath, which is frequented by the pilgrims of the Srau Jain who come from the west of India to visit

(1) Garee R., R.; Ammanat R., B.A.; Lilajan N.

their holy places. I am told that most of the inhabitants of Jainagar are still Jain, and that it is only a few years since the present Raja was converted by a Mithila Brahman and became of the sect of Sakti. The last temple is that of Brahma, but I am persuaded that all the images are Nastik. That of Parswanath is placed on a throne evidently intended for the place it occupies. It is standing and clothed. The others appear to have been brought from Gya, and many are built into the walls.

A very little beyond Dherma Rond is the eastern branch of the Fulgo, not such a wide channel but containing a larger stream than the western branch. In the Hindi dialect it is called Mohane [1] and in the Pali Mahanada. I descended this river, passing two brick akaras belonging to the Mahant of Buddh Gya, for about a mile and a quarter, to a small new temple called Singbahini, near it have been buried many of the Gosains, each has over his grave a very small monument terminated by a Linga or more commonly by an ornamental stone brought from the ruins and shaped like a beehive, but containing images of Munis on four sides.

I then went down about 1¼ miles to Saraswoti, where many pilgrims bathe and where there is a small temple surrounded by buildings of brick with a tiled roof. In the court are many graves [of] Gosaiyns similar to those just now described. I returned from thence to Matunga Bapi, crossing Dherma Rond nalah alone, Rata nala having joined it higher up. Immediately west from Dherma Rond nalah a heap of red and white rude jasper rises above the surface.

From Matunga Bapi I proceeded west to a large heap opposite to Buddh Gya, and near the river. I at first took it for a small hill, but was told that it was an old temple of the Buddhs, and I found that it was composed of bricks covered with a little earth. The people say they remember it as entire as the temple of

(1) Mahonah R., R. and B.A.; Mohana.

Mahamuni now is, but that it was round and solid. Mr. Boddam removed many bricks for his buildings at Gya, which reduced it to a mere heap. In digging for the bricks he is said to have found a stone chest containing bones and many small images of Lak. He also removed a stone pillar which has been erected in Sahibgunj. A large image like that of Bhairab has also been found, but it has lately been covered with earth, so that I could not see it. Round this central temple are several pretty large heaps of brick, which have no doubt been accompanying buildings. On the whole this has been a pretty considerable temple, although not quite so large as that of Buddh Gya. It is said that when Gautoma Muni came here to perform penance, accompanied by a vast many other Munis, that one of these distinguished persons died and was buried in the temple, which is called Koteni Bakraur.[1] This is the account of the Mahant, who calls Gautoma indiscriminately a Muni and a Bagawan. Mr. Sisson[2] says that Mr. Boddam procured from this a small stone image of very great beauty, which he saw. Some of the Astik attribute this work to Amara Singha, but they do the same with the palace of Asoka Dharma, Amara Singha being the only Buddhist with whom they are acquainted.

I then took a view of Buddh Gya, accompanied by a Rajput who has been converted to the doctrines of the Buddhs by two officers dispatched by the King of Ava to visit the holy places of this vicinity and to bring him an account of their state. He says that the sect so far as he knows has become perfectly extinct, and that no books relating to it are now procurable in the country. The messengers from Ava taught him much in the Pali or Sanskrit language, and from their books were able to discover the old places of worship, which are numerous in this vicinity, as being the native country of Gautama. They said on the authority of their books

(1) Bakraur.

(2) "Acting Magistrate of Behar"; in Report.

that [1] the temple' was built by Asoka Dharma, King of Magades, who resided in the palace immediately adjacent about 5,000 years ago. The Rajput calls the Burmas Brahmas. It must be observed that some families of Rajputs still continue to act as priests of the temple of the Buddhs or rather of Mahamuni, for the image represents that lawgiver, but he was worshipped by the messengers from Ava.[2] The Rajputs reconcile this to their conscience by considering the image as Budh Avatar.

I have already mentioned that west from the north end of the Sannyasis' convent, there are traces of a very large building called the Rajasthan or palace of Dharma Asoka. These extend about 1,300 feet from east to west and about 1,000 from north to south. On the east, north and west sides are traces of a ditch, and on the west and south sides there are traces of an outer wall with a ditch between it and the palace, but by far the greater part seems to have been a very large castle probably containing many small courts, as the ruin, except on the sides where there are traces of a double wall, is everywhere an uniform terrace consisting chiefly of bricks now covered with soil. Immediately south from the palace and separated only from it by a road was the temple of Buddh, which by the messengers from Ava was called Mahabuddh, [it] has been about 800 feet from east to west and about 480 from north to south, and it also seems to have been composed of various courts now mostly reduced to irregular heaps of bricks and stones, as immense quantities of materials have been taken away. The largest heap now remaining is at the north-east corner, where there is a very

Passages subsequently crossed out by Buchanan—

(1) "The place first became celebrated by [ ] King of Singhala having planted a pipal tree which he calls Buddh B rup or the tree of Buddh and which is now called Brahma Pipul, and continues to be an object of worship with the orthodox. This was about two thousand two hundred and fifty years ago. About one hundred and twenty-five years afterwards the present temple—."

(2) "Although they considered the whole place as holy and took water from every tank near it to form a bath for their King."

large terrace on which are two modern small temples. The one to the east is called Bageswori, and was erected by one of the Mahants of the convent. The image was dug up from the ruins and obtained an orthodox name. It had been employed before as an ornament, not as an object of worship. The temple of Tara Devi is towards the west, and its history is the same. In the east end of this terrace is now making a great excavation to procure materials for building. The workmen have laid open a chamber of brick, a cube of about 20 feet, without door, window, or stair. South from this terrace and separated from it by a road which is said to have been covered with an arch, and to have extended all the way to the river, but which now only remains at its west end, has been a vast range of buildings, but the greater part of the materials have been removed and there now only remain some heaps of broken bricks and images, one of which is very large.

South from thence has been a tank. West from these two masses of buildings has been a court surrounding the two principal objects of worship, that is, a Pipal tree placed on the west side of a terrace forming the lower part of a (Mondir) spire or pyramid, containing the image of Mahamuni. The arched way led from the east into this area in front of the great Mondir. On the right in entering is a small brick chamber, probably modern, and containing no image. On the left are two small chambers, both modern. That nearest the entrance contains several large images said to have been taken from the ruins and built into the wall. Five of them in the usual sitting posture adopted by the Buddhists to represent their Munis are said by both the orthodox and heterodox to represent the five sons of Pandu, who are claimed by all sects. The other small chamber is the tomb (Somadh) of the first Mahant of the convent of Sannyasis. This person in the course of his penitent wanderings came to the place, then overrun with wood and bushes, and finding the temple a convenient shelter, ook up his abode in it, until his extraordinary sanctity attracted the notice of numerous pilgrims and he became a principal object of veneration among the powerful chiefs and wealthy merchants who occasionally frequent Gya. From these he received the various endowments which his successors enjoy. Before the porch of the great Mondir is a stone containing impressions of the feet of a Buddh, and called Buddh Pada, and round it have been heaped many images. Among these, one representing a Muni has a short inscription under its legs; another has an inscription round the head. A male figure with two arms, having the figure of a Muni sitting on his head, has an inscription round his head and another below his feet. Adjacent to the Buddh Pada is lying a stone with a transverse inscription.

The great Mandir is a very slender quadrangular pyramid or spire placed upon a square terrace from 20 or 30 feet high. Except ornaments, the whole has been built of brick, but it has been covered with plaster and as usual in Hindu buildings has been minutely subdivided into numberless projecting corners, niches, and petty mouldings. The niches seem each to have contained an image of a Buddh in plaster, and on each projecting corner has been placed a stone somewhat in the shape of a beehive and representing a temple. On one of the sides of these small temples is a door much ornamented and a cavity containing the image of a Muni, and on the three other sides are niches containing similar images. The number of these small temples scattered all over the neighbourhood for miles is exceedingly great. The Mondir has had in front a porch containing two stairs leading up to two upper stories that the temple contained, but the roof has fallen in, and almost every part of the Mondir is rapidly hastening to decay, except the northern and western sides of the terrace, which have [been] very recently repaired by a Maratah chief. The reason of this repair is that on the east side of the terrace there grew a pipal tree, which the Buddhs call Buddh Brup, and some of them allege that it was planted by a King of Singala before the temple was built, while the Burma messengers alleged that it was planted by Asoka Dharma. The orthodox with equal probability allege that it was planted by Brahma, and it is an object of worship with all. It is a fine tree in full vigour, and in all probability cannot exceed 100 years in age, and has probably sprung from the ruins long after they had been deserted. A similar tree however may have existed there when the temple was entire. Around the roots has been raised a circular heap of brick and plaster in various concentric stages, and on one of these have been placed, in a confused heap, various images and carved fragments of stone taken from the ruins. On the pedestal of one of the images representing what the orthodox call Hargauri, the messengers of Ava engraved their names and the date of their arrival.

The original stairs leading up to the terrace were through the porch which has fallen, but the stairs are still entire and for Hindu workmen tolerably easy; but the access to a holy place through a heterodox temple appeared so improper to the Marattah who repaired the terrace that he has constructed a new stair on the outside. The chamber in the Mundir on the ground story is very small, and is covered by a gothic arch, the plaster work on which has been divided into small compartments, each containing the image of a Muni. The whole far end of the chamber has been occupied by a throne (Simhasana) of stone in a very bad taste, which has however been much disfigured by a row of images taken from the ruins and built upon the front of the throne on which the image of Mahamuni is seated. This image consists of clay, and is so vastly rude in comparison with all the other images as to favour very much the truth of a current tradition of the image having been gold and having been taken away by the Muhammadans. In fact the present image would appear to have been made after the sect had felt persecution and were no longer able to procure tolerable workmen. The two chambers above this temple are no longer accessible, but many people about the place remember the porch entire, and have been often in them. The second story has a throne at its far end, but no image

The uppermost was empty. These three chambers do not occupy one-half of the spire, even in its present reduced state. It perhaps may be 150 feet high, but is not to be compared with the great temples in Pegu. There is nothing about this work to induce one to believe that it has been originally constructed of ruins. All parts not evidently quite modern are built with the symmetry which shows their materials to have been originally intended for the parts they now occupy. The outer door of the porch is indeed composed of various fragments rudely placed together, but that is said to have been done after the roof fell in and broke down the door.

Some of the images are in the best style that I have seen in India, but in general they are much on a par with those at Gya. Indeed, it is alleged that a great part if not the whole of the images built into the walls there, as also all the doors, windows, pillars and inscriptions that accompany them, have been taken from these ruins. It is even alleged by the Rajput convert that all the images now worshipped at Gya were originally in this temple as ornaments, and have had new names given to them by the Brahmans and suited for their present belief. That by far the greater part of them belong to the sect of Buddh there can be no doubt, and it is admitted by all that most or much of the materials in question have come from Buddh Gya, but I cannot take upon myself to state whether or not he is accurate in comprehending the whole. He denies that Gya was ever a place of worship among the Buddhists, and asserts that it owes its celebrity to Vyas the son of Parasara, who long after the time of Gautoma made an attack on the Buddhs and introduced the worship of Vishnu. He it was who pointed out the various places of worship at Gya, but the Buddhists continued their own worship until the doctrine of Siva under Sankara gained a decisive victory. It must however be observed, as I am informed by Mr. Jameson, surgeon at Gya, that in the Dubustan Mozhayeb, a book by many attributed to Fyzi the brother of Abul Fazil, which gives an account of the various sects in religion, it is stated that the ancient Parsis[1] claim Gya as a temple of their foundation, where Gywa or the planet Saturn was worshipped. This Gya is by the Buddhists claimed as a Muni, and by the Orthodox it is alleged that he was an infidel. Certainly the worship of the Sun was once very prevalent, no image is still more prevalent in the vicinity, and one temple still continues an object of adoration. Between the temple and convent is a rectangular space containing the tombs of the Mahants. In its wall is built a large standing image with an inscription.

The followers of Buddh say the Gyasur was a Muni who performed religious ceremonies at Kolahal hill, ten coses south in Ramgar, the same place where Harischand Raja, King of the world in the Satyayug, performed his worship. Rotasgar was built by Kowar Ruedas his son. But Harischand lived long before Gyasur, who flourished at the end of the Laba or beginning of the Duaper. Gyasur is no object of worship among the Buddhs. They had no temple near the present Gya, but say that Gautoma lived six years under the Akshiya Bot, which they call Gautama Bot, and the tank called Rukminikund the Buddhs call Gautamakund. Vishnu Pad, Preth Sila, are not considered by them as holy. The messengers of Ava denied altogether Buddh Avatar, but consider themselves as of the sect of Brahma, on which account they allege that all men were Brahmans. That the distinction of caste was introduced by Vyas the son of Parasara, who lived long after the time of Gotoma, who was one of the ancient Brahmans. Vyas pointed out to the people the places now considered holy. Sankara afterwards destroyed the Bouddhs. The messengers from Ava considered the Buddh Brap as the centre of Jumbudwep, and reckon all distances of places in the world from thence. The Buddhists of Ava pray to the Sun but make offerings, nor do they ever burn offerings, and abhor the fire worship.

*10th December*.—I returned to Gya.

---

(1) Persians; in Report.

*12th December.*—I went to Singutha,[1] passing through Sahebgunj. About a quarter of a mile I crossed the Fulgo above the island, where it is fully half a mile wide, and beyond it is a barren sandy space. Having proceeded east along a wide but bad road for rather more than four miles, I turned south and went rather less than half a mile to a place where Soda is scraped by the washermen. It is an uncultivated plain of perhaps 300 yards diameter, intersected by a small winding stream. The soil is sandy and the grass thin and short. The soda effloresces on the surface, and after having been scraped, in 10 or 12 days is again covered, but the quantity procurable in a year would be trifling as the whole plain is by no means covered. The efflorescence takes place only in certain spots of very irregular shapes. From this field I went about 1¼ miles to the low ridge, the south end of which I passed on the 30th November. It consists of four distinct hills besides the one which that day I left on my right, and behind it are two peaks, one pretty high. I went first to the north end of the second hill, which consists of white quartz, rather mealy with a few black specks. From thence I saw nearly north a high hill named Tetuya,[2] which is one cose east from Patarkati. Near Tetuya is a quarry of Khori and a clay called Pilamati. South-west from Tetuya is another considerable lower hill called Narawut.[3] The space between the second hill of the ridge and the highest peak is cultivated, and may be 300 yards wide. From the peak proceeds a low rugged ridge, about ⅔ of a mile in length, which consists of quartz tinged red. Between this and the next ridge towards the north, is a rugged space through which the Kewar river flows. It is a narrow rocky channel with a fine little stream, by no means, however, clear or clean. On the western face of this fourth part of the ridge is an imperfect Khori[4] which has

(1) **Singhatiya.**
(2) **Tetua.**
(3) **Narawat.**
(4) Appendix, No. 18.

been dug up to a very trifling extent, so that being superficial no judgment can be formed of the position. The adjacent rocks on the left of the Pungwar[1] are quartz stained red.[2] The south end of this hill and the north end of the one on the opposite bank of the Kewar river are called by the same name, Kurheripahar,[3] while their two other ends are known by different names owing to the villages that are adjacent. The hill on which the Khori is found is almost a mile in length, and from its north end I passed about a quarter of a mile to rejoin the road, on the other side of which were two detached rocks and a long low ridge, all exceedingly rugged.

From thence I proceeded to my tents not quite four miles, having on my right the high hill of Moher with a row of hills passing east from its north end. Where we halted is some way north from the road, for what reason I know not, as where we struck off there was a fine village with a mud castle.

*13th December.*—I went to Bijabiga,[4] which was said to be only five coses distant, but I am persuaded we travelled at least eight. The road however, in order to avoid the rice fields, was exceedingly circuitous. In the first place I went about $\frac{2}{3}$ of a mile south to the road. I then went rather more than three miles east to the north-east corner [5] of the Moher range of hills, where the rock is an aggregate of fat and mealy quartz with some black and red specks[6]. From thence I went to the Dukari,[7] a small channel filled with dirty stagnant water perhaps owing to its being damned up. The channel may be about 20 feet wide. A little beyond it is a large village called Kenar,[8] beyond which I found no road. About $1\frac{1}{2}$ miles from the Dukari

---

(1) **Palmar.**
(2) Appendix, No. 79.
(3) **Kharhari.**
(4) **Biju Bigha.**
(5) Asrah, R. and B.A.; **Hanera or Sobhnath Hill.**
(6) Appendix, No. 73.
(7) **Dakhin Gaawan?**
(8) **Kenar Paharpur.**

I came to the banks of the Darhar,[1] at a village named Paharpur. The river here forms the boundary between Sahebgunj and Nowadeh,[2] and is a sandy channel 60 or 70 yards wide. Trenches drawn obliquely across it collect fine little streams that are conveyed by canals to water the vicinity. Beyond the Darhar the people become more stupid. Most of the people ran away, and none could be procured to show us the road. Not quite three miles from the Darhar I had to the north, at about two miles distance, a large hill named Majhuya,[3] and to the west of it two small hills[4] between which and it the Darhar passes. East from it are some low hills in a ridge, which towards the east approaches a pretty considerable peak.

From opposite to Majhuya I went about 3½ miles to Sita Mauri, where there is a low ridge of granite, in most parts so smooth and low that a cart codul pass with ease, but many blocks come to the surface and there are some low broken peaks. Sita Mauri is a small chamber dug into a great block of granite. The door is very small, and the chamber may be 15 feet by 10, and about 7 feet high in the middle. The polish has been attempted, but is inferior to that of the caves at Burabur. In the far end are placed two small images supposed to represent Ram and Sita. Both seem to me to have been taken from Buddh Gya, as one is a Muni and the other a female figure very common in these ruins. The cave is quite dry, and has probably been the residence of some well endowed hermit. A mela is held two days in the year, the merits of attending which are greatly enhanced by there being no water near. I had been told that there was an inscription at the place, but I found none. On the same ridge about a mile farther east is a small brick Dorga of Sheikh Muhammed.

From Sita Mauri to my tents beyond the village of Bija Biga is about three miles, mostly south.

(1) Dahder R.; R. and B.A.; **Dadar N.**
(2) Nowadah; R. and B.A.; **Nawadah.**
(3) **Majhwe Hill** near Jamuawan R.S.
(4) at **Tilera.**

Bija Biga is a small town belonging to the late Mr. Boddam's Munshi. When he purchased it, mostly waste. He is said to have laid out a good deal on canals, plantations, etc., and having brought in much land has had a very good bargain.

14*th December*.—I went to Rajauli,[1] six coses called four. I first went about ⅔ of a mile and came to a wide sandy channel on my left, called Teliya.[2] About ⅔ of a mile farther I crossed it where it seems to be formed by the junction of the Teliya and Harhari. The former is a large sandy channel with a small stream, like the united rivers which may be 100 yards wide. The Dunaiya [Tilaia] is the western branch. The eastern is a much smaller channel, but contains nearly as much water, which in some places is damned up so as to fill the channel. I went up its right bank for a little way, and without crossing it I went about 4⅔ miles to the Donaiya,[3] which I crossed immediately above its junction with the Danarji.[4] It is a wide sandy channel with water in small cuts which form streams. About half a mile beyond this I came to a village called Kanpura,[5] at which are some heaps of bricks said to have been the residence of Bandawuts. Rather more than a mile from thence I came to the left bank of the Dunarji, and proceeding up that bank for about a quarter of a mile I crossed it. There is no stream, but water for irrigation may be had at this season by digging a little way. About 2¼ miles [further] I came to this river again and crossing it obliquely passed to my tents, through the town of Rajauli situated among fine mango groves. These were all planted by a Fakir, a most venerable personage, by whom I was visited on my arrival. He is a Saiud born at Baragong near Mirzapur, and after some adventures in the west came and sat down here in the midst of wild beasts and the devils worshipped

---

(1) Rajouly, R.; Rajowly, B.A.; **Rajauli.**
(2) **Tilaia N.**
(3) **Donaia N.** (called Tilaia N. further south.)
(4) **Dhanarje N.**
(5) **Khanpura.**

by the Infidels. After a residence of 25 years he attracted the notice of Kamgar Khan, from whom he obtained a considerable grant of lands, which he has brought into cultivation and ornamented with fine plantations. His abode is large, but slovenly and mean. He has been a fine-looking man, very fair and of good address, but has too much of the ascetic, his face being bedaubed with ashes. One of his chelas wears a turban of hair like a Sannyasi. He has the character of having been very intelligent, but his faculties seem to have been greatly impaired.

15*th December*.—I went to Belem[1] in order to see some quarries of Mica that are beyond it. About two-thirds of the way I found my tents, which had been stopt on a pretence that no water was to be had at Belem. I ordered them however to proceed. In the first place I went about half a mile to the Dunarji which I crossed. The cultivation round Rajauli extends a little farther. Beyond this is a stunted wood in which, about one mile from the Danarji, I came opposite to the south end of a small hill consisting of immense blocks of granite, with small trees in the crevices. A low ridge of granite extends from thence across the Suknar,[2] a small mountain torrent now dry, and placed about half a mile beyond the hill which is called Loheri. East from the torrent this ridge rises into a small peak. About $\frac{2}{3}$ of a mile beyond this torrent I came to a miserable Rajiwar village, about a quarter of a mile beyond which I crossed the Kuri,[3] a sandy channel now quite dry and about 20 yards wide. From thence until I came opposite to the end of Kukdihi, a low hill, I had woods with swelling ground of a sandy poor soil for about $1\frac{1}{2}$ miles. From thence for about $1\frac{2}{3}$ miles was over swelling ground near the Kuri, but the soil good and clear. It is finely shaded with large Mohual trees, with a few others intermixed, and much of it among the trees is cultivated. The chief crops seem

(1) **Belam.**
(2) Sucknour R., R.; **Sukhnar N.**
(3) Coory R., R.; Cooree R., B.A.; **Khuri N.**

to be Maize, Orohor, Til and Cotton. The Orohor very good, as in Bhagalpur. The inhabitants of two villages, Bhunguyar or Ghatwals belonging to Abadut Singh. The huts made of clay but very wretched. Much Seem about them supported on Ricinus, as is the case in the Hindi villages intermixed with these rude tribes, such as Rajauli.

In the evening I was visited by Obadut Singh Tikayit of Domni,[1] to whom all the country on this side of the Suknar belongs. He calls himself a Surjabongsi Rajput, and such of his people as live pure are called Ghatwals. Those who adhere to their old impurity, and eat beef, pork, fowls and every other abomination, are called Bhungiyas. All towards Korokdea east and south is thinly inhabited by other Bhungiya chiefs belonging to Ramgar. The roads only penetrable for people on foot. The high-born chief is like an ordinary farmer, intelligent but without education. He has lost his nose, not in the wars of Mars. The people of his village exceedingly alarmed at my appearance, a very timid small ill-looking people.

16*th December*.—I went first to visit a mine or quarry of mica, and proceeded up the banks of the Belem, about three miles, which I crossed six times in a narrow valley, but in some places cultivated by the people of Belem. I then ascended a hill for perhaps 150 feet perpendicular height, when I came to the mine, which runs easterly and westerly along the northern face of the hill, which is there called Dorpayi. The vein may extend 200 yards, but is interrupted in the middle by a watercourse, to which there is a considerable descent from both the places that are wrought. The vein seems to wind very irregularly among the rocks that form the matrix, and nowhere comes to the surface, little shafts and trenches are made, and from the shafts, small galleries are dug into the vein as far as the workmen venture to go, which seems to be a very little way owing to the danger of the roof falling in,

(1) Dumnee, B.A.; Dhamni.

although the galleries are miserably narrow and low. This is not attributed to their want of skill but to the wrath of the Gods. A stone-cutter in my employ was going into one of the shafts to bring out a specimen, and although a Brahman was going on without fear, when a Moslem guide called out, Pull off your shoes, will you profane the abode of the Gods? The shafts are seldom above 6 feet deep, but some require a latter (ladder) of 10 or 12 feet, but are not above 2 or 3 feet in diameter. The galleries are so narrow that much of the mica, which would be in large masses, is broken in forcing it out with crows. The lead being easily procured the mine should be regularly sunk from the surface and the vein laid entirely bare, so that the pieces of mica might be taken out entire. All the workmen fled on our approach, although they reside the whole year on the spot. I understand that one of them takes the mine for a certain sum annually, works at it with the assistance of his companions as he pleases, and sells the mica to merchants. The quantity taken must be pretty considerable.

The rock in the channel of the Belem at the foot of the hill is a 'granitel consisting of a little white quartz and much black shining matter, in some places perhaps hornblende as it is light,[1] and in others probably micaceous iron ore as it is very heavy,[2] and some detached stones which I saw seemed to have lost almost all the quartz and to have become an iron ore,[3] but I saw no rock of this kind. The granitel in some places is a solid rock, in others it is granular owing to decay. It approaches very near to the mine, but I saw it nowhere adjacent, and seems to form the basis of the hill while quartz the matrix of the mica occupies the higher portions. Many masses of the quartz, however, and some of them containing mica are intermixed with those of the granitel, but probably they have fallen from the top. There is however

(1) Appendix, No. 22.
(2) „ Nos. 25, 112.
(3) „ No. 36.

adjacent to the mine in some places as well as lower down intermixed with the granitel, rocks of granite in a kind of intermediate state between the quartz containing mica and the granitel, for it is fine-grained and consists chiefly of white quartz intermixed with grains of the mica and black shining matter.[1] The rock of quartz commonly adjacent to the vein of mica consists usually of white masses, about the size of a filbert, conglutinated and partly glassy and diaphanous, partly white and opaque and more or less intersected in various directions by plates of mica. On breaking one piece which was almost uniformly white and opaque, I thought I could trace the transition from quartz to mica.[2] The surface of the fracture was smooth and glassy like a plate of mica, and for a little way in there was somewhat of a foliated structure. More or less of this foliated structure may in general be observed. The mica of Dorpayi (ধরপাই) although when split thin it is perfectly pellucid, in thick masses has always somewhat of a brownish[3] cast. Owing to the absence of the miners I could procure no large mass, but am told that such are to be had, although most of the pieces free from rents are very small.

Having examined the mine I returned to Rajauli. Up the same valley watered by the Belem are three other mines of mica, named Durhi, (ডারহি) Beluya (বেলহিরয়া) and Sophi, (সফিহি) all within a cose of each other and about three coses from Dorpayi; but the road is so difficult that I could not have visited them without walking the whole way. I have since learned that there is another vein named Durkora, (ধরখরো) but the whole were carefully concealed and it was by mere chance that I found them, by means of a trader who has been threatened for showing them. It was then pretended that they were all in Chatra, but this I found is false. They all belong to Buniar Singh.

---

(1) Appendix, No. 107.
(2) „ No. 69.
(3) „ No. 71.

The channel of the Belem in some places is quite dry, in others contains small stagnant pools, and in others a little clear stream. This is owing to various springs, which run a little way and are then absorbed by the sand.

In the evening I went about $3\frac{1}{4}$ miles north-west to Amaiya[1] to see an old fort said to have been built by a Maga Raja, but on coming to the place the people assured me that it had been the residence of a Runjit Rai, zemindar of Jorra, who was a Rajput chief destroyed by Kamgar Khan or his ancestors. There remains a long quadrangular space elevated by means of broken bricks, which is said to have been a fort, but it rather has been a castle perhaps 100 yards long by 50 wide, and near it have been several smaller edifices of brick all nearly levelled with the ground, so that the place may be of great antiquity. There is no hill near Amaiya as Mr. Rennell lays down.

*17th December.*—I went among the hills to visit other mines of mica or Abarak. My route lay along the Dunarjun which I crossed eight times. Having crossed it twice about $1\frac{1}{2}$ miles north[2] from Rajauli, I came to a small peak of large-grained granite west from my route with another beyond it in that direction. The river here, and where I crossed it next about half a mile beyond the little hills, is not quite dry and may be 100 yards wide. Where I crossed it next, half a mile farther, it contains a fine little clear stream which continues all the way up. A rock of large-grained granite here in the channel. A quarter of a mile farther up I crossed it again between the north ends of the great hills, and found a rock decaying into vertical masses running east and west, a fine-grained aggregate.[3] This I learned is a continuation of the rock on Durbasa, as I sent there and procured specimens of the entire rock, fine-grained red felspar, white quartz and black mica.[4]

(1) Amayah, R. and B.A.; **Amanwan.**
(2) Should be "South."
(3) Appendix, No. 26.
(4) Appendix, No. 108.

This is therefore probably the rock of the north end of Singra,[1] to which the mass in the river stretched. Another specimen from Durbasa contained most quartz, a little red felspar, and little or no mica, forming a granitel.

Having proceeded rather less than four miles south from Rajauli and crossed the river seven times, I had passed the hill towards the east called Durbasarikh. I then turned east and crossed a low ridge, round which the river takes a sweep to the south, beyond this ridge I crossed it again for the last time and proceeded east along its left bank to Dubaur,[2] a village of Bhunghiyas belonging to Brijomohun Saha, a Ghatwal. I here crossed two small torrents coming from the south, through a long narrow valley belonging to this chief, and extending to Pangch Bahini [3] ghat, the boundary with Ramgar. This pass is situated between two hills named Brahma Devata and Gunde. This valley is bounded in the west by a continuation of Sringarikh, and on the east by a very extensive mass of low hills, which is separated from Durbasa Rikh by a narrow valley watered by the Dunarjun, which there however is called by various names, and after coming from the east through this valley for about four coses, turns south through the valley of Dumchatch[4] in Chatra, bounded on the east by a great hill, Maramaku, and on the west by this cluster of Dubaur.

This village of Dubaur is about half a mile west from the hill, and I proceeded up the valley between the hill and the Dunarjun about a mile, when I came to the first mine named Chirkundi, which is about south-south-west from the highest peak of Durbasarikh called Anyari. Immediately adjoining to a fine rich level there rises a small peak of fine fat quartz [5] not above 40 feet perpendicular, and joining to the southern hills by

(1) Singur, R. and B.A.; **Singar** or **Sringirikh.**
(2) **Dubaur.**
(3) **Panch Bhurwa.** ?
(4) Doomchauns, B.A.; **Domchanch.**
(5) Appendix, No. 44.

a short ridge. On the summit of this is found the mica without any gangue except the quartz, nor has this intermixed with it any portions of mica. The vein runs north and south and has been wrought entirely by shaft, but has it is said been given up for two years, although I see appearances to indicate that it has been wrought very recently, although to a very small extent. From this quarry I went to another mine named Bandur Chuya, about one mile south-south-east from the former, with a considerable ascent the whole way among the little hills, on the summit of one of the most considerable among which it is situated. All the rock as I ascended,. until near the summit, was exceedingly rotten but is a schistose mica intermixed however with red grains, perhaps garnets [1]. The specimens are the most entire that could be procured. Towards the summit the hill becomes quartz, in some places pure white, in others glassy, sometimes without the least intermixture of mica, in others containing small plates of it. The gangue in some places is the pure quartz, in others beautiful, a white resplendent matter like felspar such as yesterday I took for quartz passing to mica; and sometimes both this spar and glassy quartz are intermixed. [2] In some parts the gangue has, intermixed with it, portions of mica, in others it is quite free. The mica itself is disposed in tables of various sizes, heaped together without order, as will appear from a specimen of small pieces taken from a mass that rises above the surface. [3] Deep in the veins, where the tables are large, they are heaped together in the same disorder and exactly resemble what I saw yesterday. This mine is wrought chiefly by trenches running north and south and now in some places 20 feet deep, but this seems merely to have been owing to the vein having been originally superficial, and to have been followed just where pieces could be most easily had. No pains have been taken to

---

(1) Appendix No. 62.
(2) ,, No. 110.
(3) ,, No. 58.

remove rubbish, so that the workmen descend into the trench by ladders made of single bamboos, the branches serving as steps, or by still worse contrivances. The whole fled on our approach, nor could I procure one fine piece as the tables are miserably broken in taking out by the workmen.

The only village I saw was that of Dubaur, inhabited by Bungiyas who shunned me. It is a poor place. The valley in which it stands is not very extensive, but were it all cultivated might produce a considerable revenue and would be exceedingly beautiful. The huts in proportion to the abundance of materials seem more and more wretched. From Rajauli to the hills might become a very valuable possession, as abundance of water from the hills might be secured in reservoirs. What I have called Rajauli is properly Salabatgunj,[1] on the side of the river opposite to Rajauli an insignificant place, so that Salabatgunj is usually called by the name Rajauli as being a new place in its vicinity. It is a tolerable village, with a good many petty traders and shops [and] besides the Fakir's residence has a Sangot of the followers of Nanak, a large neat-looking place with a tiled roof.

19*th December*.—I went about eight miles, called three coses, to Akbarpur.[2] I first crossed the Dunarjun at Rajauli, and proceeded mostly through stunted woods about three miles to Bahadurpur,[3] where there is a ruin consisting of a small mud fort that has surrounded some buildings of bricks. The walls of two of them are still in part standing, and they seem to have been small dwelling houses. Akbarpur is a village occupying the left bank of the Kuri for about half a mile. The streets are narrow, but some of the houses are pretty large and a few are tiled. It contains many traders and shops. The channel of the Kuri is small but contains a fine limpid stream.

(1) Salabatgong, R. (West of the Dhanarje).
(2) Akharpur.
(3) Bahadarpur.

*19th December.*—A Trader of Akbarpur who has long dealt with the hill people in bamboos, mica, etc., and with whom I met at Belem, having there offered to show me the place where the people of Behar procure rock crystal (Phatik), at a village named Buduya, [1] I went to see the mine, with which he said he was perfectly acquainted, and in the evening he had shown me two small hills about five or six miles from Akbarpur as the place [2]. On arriving at a small hill about four miles east from Akbarpur I ascended it to have a view of the country and to see a Dorgah, and was highly delighted with the view, the valley being rich and the hills and woods highly picturesque. The Dorgah is nothing. The hills consist of schistose mica, white quartz and silver mica, running south-west and north-east with an inclination to north-west. On desiring the trader to conduct me to the two little hills close by, I was a good deal surprised when he told me that there was no crystal [and] that the place he meant was about two coses farther east on a little hill that could not be seen from Akbarpur. I accordingly proceeded in that direction. A little less than three miles from the Dorgah I came to a number of fine little streams, branches from a fine spring named Kokolot,[3] which are distributed through the fields and lost. Here I met a Tikayet, owner of the neighbourhood, a good-looking young man. He ran after my palanquin all the way I went on his estate, and no persuasion would induce him to go home. On coming to his boundary I met his neighbour, the Thakur of Patra,[4] who acted in the same manner. On coming to his village, about a mile beyond the Kokolot, the trader halted and declared that he knew no farther, and had purchased the crystal there. Some of the Thakur's people said the place was eight coses, others two coses distant. On threatening the trader for having given me so much useless trouble and expense, he agreed with those who said that the place

(1) Buduwah, R.; **Budhuwa.**

(2) At **Ektara.**

(3) **Kakolat.**

(4) **Pathra.**

was two coses distant, and undertook to show it. On our way we were still followed by the Thakur, and having advanced through woods for about $1\frac{1}{4}$ miles we came to a small clear stream called the Dighar, which [he][1] asserted was his boundary with Salguma[2] of Ramgar, which I believe is not true. We then went rather more than two miles through a thick wood to the foot of Mahabhar hill, where a fine clear stream, the Mangura, comes from it through a narrow ravine. This rivulet is the finest torrent that I have seen in these parts, containing more water and that clearer than any yet observed. On its east side, just clear of the hills, I was shown some bare stiff soil on the surface of which were lying small bits of quartz, some of them pellucid and glassy, and some crystallized, and among them some opaque pebbles somewhat like those found in the Rajmahal hills.[3] The people endeavoured to persuade me that this is the only place from whence the workmen of Bihar are supplied, but this being absurd the trader confessed that he had been terrified by the threats of the owners and traders. He then said that the quarry was two coses farther, but sometimes alleged that it was on the south and sometimes on the north of Mahabar; so that it appeared evident to me that he would not show me the place, and I sent people to search the hills which he had first pointed out.

The rock in the channel of the Mungara, just within the hills, is decaying in vertical layers running east and west of an aggregate of quartz, red, white and glassy, and consisting of fine grains with somewhat of a schistose structure.[4] The fragments that have rolled from the summit are similar in their materials, but the grains are larger and their structure solid.[5]

Having returned to Akbarpur by the same way I went to Nawadeh.[6] About $1\frac{1}{4}$ miles north from Akbarpur I came to the east end of a low narrow ridge of fat

---

(1) "I" in M.S.
(2) **Satgawan**?
(3) Appendix, No. 32.
(4) Appendix, No. 106.
(5) Appendix, No. 98.
(6) Nowadah, R. and B.A.; **Nawadah.**

quartz, consisting of large grains aggregated and mixed with black dots.[1] This ridge is called the hill of Serpur.[2] On the opposite side of the Khuri I had on my right a long ridge called Kulana[3] and south from its west end a rocky heap called Dhakni.[4] From this hill to the Kuri opposite to Nawadeh is about 3¼ miles. By the way I passed an old mud fort now ruinous,[5] which belonged to Kamdar Khan. Near it a small neat mosque. By the way also, under a tree at a village named Karha,[6] I saw some broken images. One is that of a Buddh in the usual posture, which has been new-named and is worshipped by the vicinity. Such I am told are very common all through the division, and the images are supposed to have been brought from Rajagrihi. For above a mile, by the side of a canal for watering the district, was a narrow space on which soda effloresces, and it is the most extensive of any that I have yet seen. It is carefully scraped, so soon as it effloresces, by those who make glass and by the washermen.

The people that I sent to look for the crystal on the two hills near Buduya, although they had seen that the zemindar would not show the place, immediately on my leaving them applied to these very men, who took them about two coses farther among the hills, from whence they brought some small fragments such as I had seen.

A man whom I sent to the hills on the right of my route gave me the following account :—The smaller hill of Dakni towards the south-east consists of a schistose mica, of white mealy quartz in plates with silver mica intermixed.[7] The larger hill towards the north-west consists of earth containing many masses from two or three feet in diameter of very fine hornblende in mass with small crystallizations and very heavy.[8] The west

(1) Appendix, No. 57.
(2) **Sherpur.**
(3) **Kulna.**
(4) **Dhakni.**
(5) At **Barew.** (Burdhoo, B.A.).
(6) **Karhar.**
(7) Appendix, No. 30.
(8) „ No. 87.

end of Kulna hill consists of fine-grained granular quartz or hornstone, red towards the bottom of the hill,[1] and white towards the summit.[2]

21*st December*.—I went about a mile and a half northerly to see Nukaur[3] tank and the Jain temple which it contains. The tank extends east and west in its longest direction, and is much choked with weeds, especially the Nelumbium. The temple occupies the centre, a small square terrace, and is a neat but inconsiderable building covered with one dome. A road in very bad repair with a very rude bridge of brick lead into it. The temple is in very good repair, so that if built 100 years ago as said, it must have been several times repaired. It contains two stones, much carved and perhaps old, as one is defaced. On the top of each are resemblances of the human feet surrounded by short inscriptions. There is not the smallest trace of any ruin in the vicinity of the tank to induce one to suppose that it had been formerly a place sacred to the worship of the Jain; to which they were allowed to return when the Muhammadan conquerors looked on all Hindus with equal contempt and favour. Neither is there a single Jain near the place. Why it has therefore been selected I cannot say. Perhaps the tank is old, and the Jain knew from their books that the stones, the old object of their worship, were contained in the island. Its vicinity is waste and covered with bushes. Nawadeh is a small market village, very poor.

24*th December*.—Although the Duroga pretended that a predecessor in office had actually measured the whole roads, in the district, I found that no two persons agreed concerning the distance of the places that were proposed for this day's stage. Tetari[4] was fixed upon as an easy march of five coses, but it is somewhat more than 15 miles. About 1½ miles from Nawadeh I crossed the Sakri[5] obliquely. It is a sandy channel like the Fulgo,

(1) Appendix, No. 74.
(2) „ No. 30.
(3) Near **Gonawatola**, (*see* page 102).
(4) **Tetari.**
(5) Sackry N., R.; Sacry N., B.A.; **Sakri R.**

about six or seven hundred yards wide. At this season its stream is very inconsiderable and is chiefly confined to small cuts made to convey the water into the canals for irrigation, which are numerous. About five miles farther on, I saw at Morera[1] a considerable brick building, the residence of some Sannyasis, it is called a Math. Besides the brick building they possess several large ones of mud. Near this was gibbeted a murderer, whose body was little decayed although it had hung almost a month. The crows and vultures, for what reason I do not know, do not appear to have touched it. Titari is a small village on the bank of an old tank.

25*th December*.—I went eight miles to Pally.[2] About $1\frac{1}{2}$ miles from Tetari I came to Rukaur,[3] where are the ruins of a mud fort on a very fine rising ground which commands a noble view. The fort has contained a large mud castle, and is said to have belonged to the Mayis. About a quarter of a mile beyond it is a small heap of bricks with two Lingas, and about half a mile farther, beyond a tank, is a more considerable heap of brick. The place has therefore been probably of some note among the Hindus before the Moslems came. About three miles beyond this, I came to a small dry torrent with woody banks. The villages contain many large mud houses; but are miserably huddled together, with such narrow streets that an elephant can only pass in some places, and that always with difficulty. The houses, however, as all between this and Gya, are surrounded by small gardens of Ricinus and Seem, and are not contiguous.

26*th December*.—Polly is a very sorry village, and seems to have decayed. I see no trace of the fort laid down by Major Rennell.[4] I went between ten and eleven miles, called four coses, by a most villainous and circuitous route to Islamnagar.[5] The only object of the guide

(1) Mariah, R.; **Marra.**
(2) Pollay, R. and B.A.; **Pali.**
(3) Rupaw, R.; **Rupau.**
(4) Not in R., but only in B.A.
(5) Islamnagur, R. and B.A.; **Islamnagar.**

seemed to be to keep us at a distance from the villages. About 5½ miles from Polly, I crossed a small sandy torrent called the Lala, and a little beyond it a larger channel which is said originally to have been a canal from the torrent, but now it is much the larger. The villages as yesterday. The people very poor and dirty.

Islamabad was the residence of Sundar Khan, the elder brother of Kamgar, who being a quiet man allowed his brother to manage as he pleased. He resided in a mud fort about 300 by 200 yards in extent, with a ditch and a wall strengthened with circular bastions. His house within, built of brick, has been pretty considerable, with a zenana mahul surrounding a small square court in which there were baths like the plots of a garden for the use of his women. There are a good many Moslems about the town, which is a pretty large village. The fort had a small neat mosque in the gateway, and is finely situated on a rising ground which commands a very fine prospect.

*27th December.*—I went between seven and eight miles, called four coses, to Lechuyar.[1] For about one half of the way the soil was poor, and appeared in several places to contain soda. In one place about a quarter of a mile from Islamnagar I saw the saline effervescence, and I observed that the people had scraped it off and thrown it together in a shallow pit with water, so as to allow a crust to form on the surface. At a large village beyond this, a Muhammedan landlord has a neat small thatched bungalow in a large flower garden, but this is far from neat and has no walks through it. Between three and four miles from Islamnagar is a large village with two or three tolerable huts, called Mirzagunj.[2] Lechuyar is such another place on the west side of a small torrent named Kawarmata,[3] which has a sandy channel and contains a small stream. The people not so dirty nor the huts quite so bad as near the hills of Nawadeh.

---

(1) Lichwar, R. and B.A.; **Lachhuar**.
(2) Morjagunge, R.; **Mirzaganj**.
(3) **Bahuar N.**

People that I sent to various hills between Nawadeh and this, gave me the following stones :—

Dilawa, the western extremity of Sujur, consists of quartz. The top is composed of fine white grains with black dots and some mica in crevices.[1] In the middle of the hill the rock is an imperfect glassy quartz with some reddish matter intermixed.[2] At the bottom of the hill the quartz is more perfectly glassy.[3] At Hurkarghat in the middle of the same ridge is a granitel of hornblende and white quartz.[4] The small hill Sumba, north from Hurkarghat, consists of a schistose mica,[5] and all the small hills in front of that great ridge are vastly more rugged than the great ridge itself. The next of these small hills, Bonsaha, consists of a rude jasper, reddish and white. Some portions covered on the surface with some imperfect crystallizations of white quartz. [6]

Lechuyar is a pretty considerable village, with an old ruinous house and mud fort which belonged to the Gidhaur family, the original proprietors of Bishazari. The principal residence of the family would seem to have been at Sekundera[7] in sight of Lechuyar towards the east, where there is a brick fort still in repair and occupied by the agent of the Moslem who holds Bishazari in Altumga. The Gidhaur family still receive the commission of ten per cent. on the revenue, which was all that the zemindars in the Mogol Government could claim, as on the Moslem obtaining this Perganah as Altumga he took possession even of the family residence.

28*th December*.—I went to Sejorighat[8], between twelve and thirteen miles by an exceeding bad road or path. About a mile from Lechuyar there is much soda in the

---

(1) Appendix, No. 46.
(2) ,, No. 2.
(3) ,, No. 85.
(4) ,, No. 59.
(5) ,, No. 88.
(6) ,, No. 7.
(7) Secundra, R.; **Sikandra.**
(8) **Sijhori.**

soil. Indeed it seems to continue from that village about 1½ miles in a northerly direction, but about a mile from the town I saw more than anywhere else, and some of it was collecting. I recrossed the river at Lechuyar, and met with no other channel until I came to Sejorighat, where there is a small channel with pools of dirty stagnant water. The villages generally occupy fine eminences and look tolerably well at a distance, but are miserable enough on approach, being miserably dirty with very narrow lanes. Some chief tenant or petty zemindar has however in general a kind of small mud castle, which produces a good effect.

29*th December*.—I went between nine and ten miles to Sheikhpura.[1] For about a quarter of a mile I continued along the bank of the channel, which is called Dundu.[2] I then went rather more than a mile to a village named Kewara,[3] where there is an old mud fort said to have been built by the Rajewars. From thence, rather more than two miles, I came to a narrow channel in clay containing a good deal of stagnant water and called Korhari.[4] About half a mile farther I had three small hills on my left, in one bearing, about south-west. The one nearest me, Chakonggra,[5] consists of rude jasper[6] disposed in white and red blotches. About two miles farther on, crossed a narrow clay channel containing a little water. About two miles farther on I came to the Sheikhpura hills which, like the others, look smooth at a distance and contain no trees, but on a near approach they seem to consist mostly of rock without the least appearance of stratification, but cut into cuboidal masses by fissures vertical and horizontal. The stone is a quartzose approaching to rude jasper or to silicious hornstone,[7] in most places stained reddish or intermixed with black matter somewhat of the appearance of

(1) Sheikpour, R. and B.A.; **Sheikhpura.**
(2) **Nata N.**
(3) **Chewara.**
(4) **Kaurihari N.**
(5) **Chakandara.**
(6) Appendix, No. 33.
(7) „ No. 70.

Amiantus, but in many white and often aggregated of various grains, mealy and fat. I passed through an opening immediately west from the town. The two hills almost unite at the north end of the pass and leave an exceeding bad passage. The pass is not quite half a mile in width. I then turned west for more than half a mile, and halted east from the town situated at the west end of the largest hill in the range, which is a mere rock of quartz rising into many tops with very little soil, but not near so rugged as granitic peaks. The northern face of these hills is much barer than the southern.

Persons whom I sent to the small hills east from Lechuyar brought me the following specimens :—Tek at the bottom consists of a strange kind of glassy and brownish quartz. At the top it contains two kinds of irregular small-grained granite, one white with dark greenish spots,[1] the other brownish.[2] These are probably the rocks of which the hill consists. The quartz is probably sporadic. In the adjacent hummock called Nabinagar, the granite or rather gneiss has a very anomalous appearance.[3] On the hill of Satsunda, west from Tek, are two granites, one grey tolerably perfect,[4] the other yellowish.[5] On Majuya, between Tek and Satsundh, is a kind of blotched anomalous granite of a very strange appearance.[6] On Donayi, south from Satsunda and Tek the rock is a silicious hornstone, whitish, livid or red.[7] In many places, especially where red, it seems to me to be a slag.

31*st December*.—I went to Jainagar to examine some remains attributed to Indrayavan Rajah. I proceeded, first, east along the ridge of hills to its end, which is about four miles road distance from my tents, or 4½ from the Thanah. The first hill of the 4½ may

(1) Appendix, No. 64.
(2) „ No. 97.
(3) „ No. 14.
(4) „ No. 20.
(5) „ No. 45.
(6) „ No. 39.
(7) „ No. 114.

occupy $1\frac{1}{4}$ miles, the second as much. I did not perceive the opening between the third and fourth which I suspect join by a low and stony ridge, and the second and first do [so]. The whole is evidently one rock, with fissures dipping from the north to the south at perhaps 25° from the horizontal, and with others vertical. East and west and north and south, although all evidently was originally one, now split by the action of decay, its various parts assume exceeding different appearances. The greater part is an imperfect quartz or silicious hornstone,[1] in some parts white, in others red, in others blackish, with all manner of intermediate shades, sometimes the colours of pretty considerable masses are uniform, at others they are intermixed in veins, dots, and blotches. The red I presume is from iron. The black seems to be owing to an intermixture of amianthus. In one specimen the silky fibres are very discernible. In some specimens the grain is very fine and uniform. In others again, the stone is evidently an aggregate, composed of glassy particles intermixed with others that are powdery. If it is necessary to suppose that this rock has ever existed under a different form from [that] which it now has, for which however at present I see no strong evidence, I would certainly suppose it has been in fusion and slight agitation, and that different parts assumed different appearances from circumstances attending their cooling. The distinctly granular parts seem to me very strongly to resemble rocks which I consider as granite having undergone a partial fusion.

About four miles farther on, I came to the part of the country which is liable to inundation from the lower part of the Fulgo river, and reached this about two miles farther on. It was here called Hurwar,[2] and is a deep dirty stagnant watercourse, but not near so wide as at Gya. The water although deep seems to stagnate entirely back from the Ganges. The banks at present are about 14 feet high, very little commerce seems to be carried on by this channel. I saw only five or six

---

(1) Appendix, No. 70.
(2) Harohar N.

boats, and these were not employed. I proceeded along its bank for rather less than two miles, when after passing a dry channel I came to the Sumar,[1] here a wide channel containing stagnant water from the Hurwar. I then proceeded east along the Hurwar to Balguzar, rather more than six miles.

From Balguzar, which I had already seen, I went southerly for about two miles to a wretched Invalid Thanah, near which there is a small dorga of brick in which some ornamented stones taken from ruins have been built. About two miles farther I halted near the hills of Joynagar,[2] in the lands of a village whose owner, a zemindar Brahman, very civilly undertook to be my guide after several rustics had given me a denial. For the last mile, the ground contains many scattered heaps of bricks, but none larger than what may be supposed to have arisen from the ruin [ of ] a small temple, or of a dwelling house of very ordinary dimensions. These heaps are intermixed with many small tanks, which extend all round the hill to about a mile's distance, except where the Keyol river diminished the space. If the town extended wherever these tanks do, it has been very large, with a diameter of perhaps three miles, but the hills of course occupy some of the space. I am told that there are no heaps of bricks in any quarter but that by which I came, but this may have been the fashionable part of the city and the remainder may have been huts; the numerous small tanks being a strong presumption that the city occupied nearly the ground which I mention.

There are two hills, one about a mile long and 400 yards wide, another, much smaller, towards the north, and consisting almost entirely of a rugged broken rock. The larger is also rocky, but admits of trees, and has an ascent of tolerably easy access. I went to this in order to see Raja Indrayavan's house, as it is called, which occupies the summit of the hill and consists of two parts or courts. The one which occupies the very summit of

(1) Some N.
(2) Immediately south of Kiul.

the hill has been a small court, perhaps 15 yards square on the inside, and has been surrounded on all sides by a very thick rampart of brick, or perhaps rather by narrow rows of building, the ruins of which have left the appearance of a rampart. At the north-east angle of this square, and projecting beyond it, has been a small chamber of large squared stones. The chamber within may be ten feet square, and the walls eight feet thick. The stones very large. This is called the Rajah's chamber. The outer court, which is lower down the hill towards the east, is nearly of the same size with the inner, but seems to have been merely a terrace with a small building in its middle. The small chamber has evidently been made of great strength as a place of security, but it is too confined for the den of any Raja, in whatever terror he may have lived. Nor can it be supposed that Indrayavan, who possessed such a large abode near Gidhaur, could have breathed in such a place. As it contains no water, it could not be intended as a stronghold against an enemy, and the use of the building was probably to secure the revenue against thieves, who in India surpass far in dexterity those of all other countries. The town was probably the residence of the officer who managed the revenue of a large district on the banks of the Ganges, for which it is well situated, being on the boundary of the inundated tract but having at all seasons a communication with the capital near Gidhaur.

The building on the other hill I saw was still more trifling, and the difficulty of ascent and distance I had had to return at night induced me to decline visiting it. At the east end of the hill has been a small temple, which the people say contained a Linga. They complain that Mr. Cleveland took it away to Bhagalpur.[1] If this be true it was a most wanton

The following notes have been made in pencil on the R. A. S. copy of the Report, on this subject (page 330), a portion of the Report which has been omitted by Martin :—

(1) "Mr. Davis carried away from this place the Image of Sureya (Soorooge) at present in the Museum of the India House. This is probably the transaction alluded to. The most remarkable things here are the fine tanks which Dr. B. has not noticed."

outrage, and his conciliatory measures to the natives must have consisted in lavishing on the hill tribes and zemindars the public money and resources.[1] On the opposite bank of the Kiyol, in Bhagalpur but probably attached to Joynagar, I could see a lofty narrow building raising its broken summit above the highest trees. It has probably been a temple, but the people with me could give me no account of its date or use.

The rock [2] on the hill, where entire and undecayed, resembles entirely the hard stone from the millstone quarry at Loheta,[3] consisting of small masses of fat quartz united by a greyish powdery substance, in some places tinged red. Various detached masses[4] lying scattered on the surface, more or less tinged red, and some of them slaggy while others retain portions of the felspar entire, induce me to think that the whole has been a granite in an imperfect state of fusion, so that the quartz remained entire while the other ingredients were changed. This opinion is confirmed by the red slag found south from Jainagar at no very great distance, at Donayi mentioned [on the] 29th inst., and near Mallipur [5] mentioned in my account of Bhagalpur. Donayi is about eight miles south from Jainagar, and Mallipur may be ten miles south-easterly from thence. The anomalous appearance of the granites near Donayi seems to show that they have undergone great changes. Among the detached fragments on Jaynagar are many of whitish silicious hornstone, and the rock is intersected by narrow veins of quartz running in various directions

(1) "Mr. Davis did not consider that he carried the images away from the *Villagers*, but from a bear that had made the ruined temple which contained it his den. The place was buried in unfrequented woods, and no villages within the distance of several miles. He purchased the consent for what he did of a bramin who was the only person claiming anything to do with the image."

(2) Appendix, No. 83.

(3) **Laheta,** five miles north-west of **Maira Hill, Monghyr.** *See* East India, Vol. II, page 180.

(4) Appendix, No. 48.

(5) At **Katauna Hill.** *See* East India, Vol. II, page 182.

to a considerable distance. Can it be that all rocks of quartz, hornstone, jasper, potstone, trap, etc., are granite that has undergone various degree of fusion, and has been cooled in different manners ?

*3rd January.*—Sheikpura is a very large village or small town, closely built and extending more than a mile from east to west. It is however very narrow, consisting of one very narrow street with many short lanes on each side. It was with great difficulty that I could squeeze an elephant through the street, and at the west end is a place between two houses not above three feet wide, where of course I was stopt and with great difficulty scrambled over a mud wall. The Daroga had informed me that the road to Behar was very good. This sample under his nose was a proof of what his ideas of roads were, and accordingly I found no road except a foot-path and that not much frequented, although it is the line of communication between two of the chief towns of the district. Sheikpura contains some tolerable houses of brick cemented with mud. One entirely of mud, belonging to a Bengalese merchant, is a very comfortable place, being kept smooth and clean and in some places painted, three points very generally neglected. From the west end of the town to a small round hill is about three-quarters of a mile, and about the same distance farther, leaving two other small hills to the left, I came to the north end of the southern of the two chief hills of a small range lying west from Sheikpura. This hill consists of a rude jasper, blotched red and white[1], exactly resembling that of Chakoongga. I passed between these two chief hills, and then had two detached rocks on my right and one on my left, as in the plan. A very little beyond this hill the country becomes liable to inundation from the Tati,[2] a small channel in a deep clay soil. At present it is stagnant, and is about $\frac{2}{3}$ of a mile from the hills. The country liable to inundation extends almost two miles west from the Tati and is very dismal, being much neglected.

(1) Appendix, No. 13.
(2) Tati N.

Beyond that is a finely wooded country all the way to Sawos,[1] where I halted. The mango plantations are quite overdone. Sawos is about ten miles from Sheikpura, about three miles before I reached it I came to Maldeh[2],—which notwithstanding its name (the abode of wealth) is a miserable village, situated on the ruins of a mud fort which has contained some brick buildings, part of their walls is standing. The people said that they had belonged to an old zemindar, which seems very probable. He had probably been destroyed by Kamgar Khan. Sawus belongs to a Pewar Rajput, who says that his ancestors have had the zemindary for many ages. During the rule of the Mahi they were deprived of the management, but were allowed the usual commission, a favour that was shown to very few. The village stands on the north side of a large heap, evidently containing many bricks and said to consist almost entirely of that material. It extends east and west about 60 yards, and half as much from north to south. It contains no cavity on the summit, nor are there any traces of a ditch, so that it has been rather a house or castle than a fort, but is called Banwatgori or the fort of the Banwats, who are said to have been Goyalas who very long ago possessed the country. At its east end there is a large projection towards the north. At its west end is a conical heap of bricks with some stones on the summit. This is said to have been the place where the Rajah sat to enjoy the cool of the evening. It seems to me more like the ruin of a solid temple of the Buddhists. This is confirmed by a number of broken images placed under a tree on the great heap, several of which are those of Munis, while the others are exactly such as are usual about Gya and Kewa Dol, especially the female and buffalo. These are said to have been taken from a small temple some way east, beyond the ruin of a square building. The temple was of brick supported by stone pillars, some of which have been dug out to build into a wall. South from the great heap is a tank choked

(1) Sanwas.

(2) Maldah.

with weeds and earth, among which are standing two large images which have probably been thrown in by those who destroyed the place. The others were lately dug out from the ruins of the temple and have again become objects of worship; the people, not knowing what they represent, have given new names. They are all broken. The two in the tank represent Munis, but are called Bairab and Lakshmi Narayon, although there is only a male represented. The one called Bhairab has round his head the images of several Buddhs.

*4th January.*—I went about thirteen miles to the fort of Behar.[1] About four miles from Sawos I came to the Sakri, which is here a small channel about 100 yards wide. It contains some stagnant pools of water. There is a small branch of it between Sawos and the main channel, but so inconsiderable that it escaped my notice, although it properly is called the Sakri, and the main channel is called the Kumuriya.[2] About a mile and a half west from the Sakri I came to a large tank or reservoir, about 400 yards by 600.[3] It has been made partly by digging and partly by a bank to confine the water of a canal from the Sakri, and is a very pretty piece of water, being quite free of weeds and covered with teal. About 4½ miles farther on, I came to a small nallah containing a little water, the name of which I could not learn.[4] About 1¼ miles from the fort of Behar I crossed the Adya, a sandy channel 400 yards wide. It has no water on the surface, but supplies many wells for irrigation. The road all the way was a path. In some places very bad. There were many large villages. The houses so huddled together that no passage is left for a carriage of any kind, or even for an elephant.

*6th January.*—Two Moslems of rank in the place, Meer Nasser Ali and Mulovi Mahummud Bassawan, decent men, know nothing of the history of the Maga

---

(1) Bahar, R. and B.A.; **Bihar.**

(2) **Kumhara N.**

(3) At **Jiar.**

(4) **Golthawa N.**

Rajahs, except that they were sovereigns of a considerable country and resided here. The name Behar they say is Hindi, and therefore must be Vihar, meaning pleasant. They say that the Rajah on building the fort found that it was commanded by the hill, guns placed on which could lodge a ball in any part of it. He therefore pulled it down, but guns probably were little used when the fort was built, and if they had we cannot conceive any Rajah so stupid as not to have taken the hill into consideration before he began so great a work, for the ramparts have been very strong and built of very large rough stones. It is very irregular, with all the angles strengthened by large round bastions. It is probable that the Moslems, when they found it no longer tenable against guns, neglected the work : but for some time at least they must have continued it as a place of strength, as one of the gates is built of ruins taken from a Hindu work, as a stone built into it contains a Buddh and Ganesa. The original gate probably contained too many emblems of idolatry and was destroyed by the saint who took the place.

These gentlemen whom I consulted denied that the town was destroyed or deserted. An Amil always resided at the place, but it was never the station of a Subah or person of very high rank. Patna had always this preference. The Amils within the old fort had fortified their Kacheri, and this was pretty entire within the memory of some of the gentlemen, but it has gone to ruin The work was small, intended merely to resist sudden outrages from the zemindars. It would appear (for there are few traces of it remaining) to have been a square mud fort, perhaps 150 yards each side with a small bastion at each corner. The buildings were probably huts, as the office of the Amil, the walls of which are standing, has been built of mud with a few bricks intermixed, but has been neatly ornamented and plastered with lime. These officers held their appointments by too precarious a tenure to think of paying out money on buildings.

I visited several places in the vicinity. I first went north a little way to Mosatpur[1] to look after the Rajah's house, but my guide did not know it. This part of the town is the neatest that I have seen. The houses though small are built of brick or of mud plastered, and are covered with sheets of paper stuck on to dry. This gives them a clean look. This part of the town is inhabited by paper-makers. Between it and the fort is a pretty large mosque, quite ruinous.

From thence I went to see a house that had been built by a rich individual, not an officer of government, and it has been very considerable, but the family has subdivided into many branches so that, though they still occupy the dwelling houses, these are very ruinous, the places of worship have been allowed to fall, and the places intended for pleasure and ornament are lying waste. There is a semi-subterranean building called a Bauli, which was intended as a retreat during the hot winds. An octagon space was dug down until water was found. This was lined with brick and a building erected all round. This was square on the outside, without any windows, but within formed an octagon court adjacent to the pond. A suite of rooms opened into this court by eight doors, and without them were various galleries, stairs, closets, and bye corners. The floor was sunk so low that in the rainy season there is no access, and even now there is a foot of water on the floor, but in the heats of spring they become dry and the water is confined to the octagon court. The hot winds are then entirely excluded, and it is said that the chambers are then very cool and pleasant during the day. Buildings on somewhat of a similar plan, with a supply of water brought in pipes so as not to affect the floors, would probably be a great luxury. Adjoining to this building has been a garden, with many small canals and reservoirs built of brick and covered with plaster, in which there were *jetd'eaus*. Beyond this was a solid square building of one storey, called

(1) Musadpur.

Novoroton from its containing nine rooms, one in the centre, one at each corner, and one at each side. They are arched with brick, and had the roofs been high and the doors sufficiently large the building might have had a good effect and been very cool. The execution is exceedingly clumsy.

From thence I went to the hill, which extends north and south with a very abrupt face towards the west and a gentle slope towards the east, but is the barest rock of such a shape that I have ever seen. It consists of granular quartz or silicious hornstone, in most places white or grey, but in others stained red.[1] It is disposed in parallel layers rising from the east towards the west at an angle of about 26° from the horizon. The layers are from one-half to two feet thick, so that the rock might be considered as composed of horizontal strata. To me it appears that they are occasioned by mere fissures produced by cooling, desiccation or decay, I will not take upon myself to say which. The rock is also intersected by vertical fissures, running east and west and north and south. The fissures running east and west have become very wide, often several feet, owing apparently to the action of the rain running down the declivity of the hill, while those running north and south are mere fissures. On the summit of the hill are several Dorgas of different saints with inscriptions in the Togara character. They are all ruinous except that of [ Malik Ibrahim Bayu[2]] a very rude building, although the bricks have been smoothed with the chisel although noways ornamented. In this manner they are as smooth as the bricks used in England and make of course as neat a wall, so that the joinings do not admit of fig trees. This wall, although not plastered and built without lime in the mortar, is perfectly fresh although said to be above 400 years old. It is a massy square, the walls sloping considerably towards the top, which is covered with a very clumsy dome. The

(1) Appendix, No. 42.
(2) Left blank in M.S.

door is the only aperture in the building. The others are much in the same style. One of them is said to contain part of the body of the saint of Pir Paingti, and the keeper pretends that along with the saint is included a Siva linga. On the grave, indeed, is made a projection of plaster as if formed by the point of that emblem of the deity, which has probably been done lately to extract money from the infidels. I do not suppose that 400 years ago any such idolatrous practice would have been tolerated.

From the hill I went towards the south part of the town, where I passed the largest mosque of the place, now quite ruinous and of no repute. It is covered by five domes in one row. Near it are some decent houses surrounded by high brick walls. Some way beyond there is a pretty large tank; and a heap of earth and bricks, called Pajaia, which has probably been a Hindu temple. Beyond this I went to the principal place of worship, the tomb of Ibrahim. The buildings are of no great size and uncommonly rude, but although slovenly are in tolerable repair. From thence I returned through a very long narrow bazar, the dirtiest and poorest I have ever seen. Near the Thanah within the fort is the monument of Kadir Kumbaz, a poor place but in tolerable repair.

In none of these buildings are there many ornamented stones, nor are many such scattered about the place. A few rude pillars have been built into the different Muhammedan places of worship, and I have already mentioned those in the gate. There is therefore no evidence that this Hindu abode has been a place of much splendour. The fort must have been strong, as the stone rampart has been very massy, as it has many salient angles strengthened by round bastions, and as the ditch would appear to have been enormous. It is now entirely cultivated, and small canals wind through it, but where most entire, on the east face of the fort, it would seem to have been about 600 feet wide. On the west side where narrowest it would seem to have been about 400 feet.[1] The extent of the heaps of brick within the fort shows that it has contained many large buildings of that material, but no traces of their particular form remain. It is however probable that they all belonged to the palace of the Rajah,[1] while the town surrounding the ditch on the outside was open. It now indeed surrounds the old ditch, but in its present state of decay has divided into separate villages ; before the famine, however, and before it had been twice sacked by the Marattahs, it went entirely round in a form as compact as is usual in Indian cities, and probably in the time of the Hindu Government may have been very considerable. The Rajah was probably of the sect of Buddh, as several broken images collected round a tree and also round a small modern temple, both in the fort, are evident representations of Munis.

I find that scarcely two persons agree concerning its history, and the chief Moslems of the place have no copy of Ferishta nor other historical work, although one of them is called a Moulavi, and all they say as well as what is said by others seems to rest on tradition, in general rendered very suspicious by its being intermixed with the miracles performed by the numerous saints of the place.

Some people pretend that the place continued to be governed by the Magas until the time of Ibrahim, but they do not know the Rajah's name. Others again pretend that the Magas lived very long ago, 15 or 16 centuries, and that their fort had long been destroyed before the arrival of any Moslems. Among these is the owner of the Dorga of Bara Sistani. He says that on

---

1 Crossed out—" The earth has I imagine been thrown on the inner part of the fort which is very high, nor can the height be attributed to the ruins of brick buildings, for although the surface and the interior everywhere consists of broken bricks I see many parts where the people have dug and where the bricks extend only a few feet into the soil. I do not suppose therefore that the fort has contained many great buildings, there is nothing remaining to show that any one was of great dimensions, but it was probably occupied by various small courts surrounded by small brick buildings in which the Rajah, his family and immediate dependants resided, *while the town surrounding.*"

the arrival of his ancestor 700 years ago, this part of the country belonged to Sohel Deo, a Rajah who lived at Tungi [1] near Behar, but no traces remain of his abode, which was probably therefore petty. The country was then infested by Daityos or cannibals, the chief of whom the saint destroyed by miraculous power, on which the Rajah was converted to the faith, and gave his daughter in marriage to the saint. The heathen temple was then pulled down, and the tomb of the saint has since been erected in its stead. One door of the temple has been allowed to remain, and forms the entrance through a wall which surrounds the tomb. It has contained many images in relievo, the spaces for which remain, but Moslem piety has carefully eradicated the idols, by which the door has been so much defaced that it would not be worth while to take a drawing. When the saint arrived, the fort of the Mag Rajahs was covered with trees and entirely waste. Many people say that this is a mere idle fable, but it appears the most probable.

The colony of Rajputs say that they came as soldiers with a Mogul Amil who was sent to manage this part of the country, that on their arrival the town was large, but the fort was entirely unoccupied except by the Fakirs belonging to the tomb of Kadur Kumbaz. It was then that the small mud fort was built, and the Rajput soldiers were cantoned in and near it. About 15 years ago they planted a tree in the old fort and placed under it a Siva Linga. About the same time they built a small temple for another Siva. Having found several old images lying about the ruins, they collected them near these two places of worship, and these are the images of Munis that I have before mentioned.

Many allege that Behar is not the original name of the place, and was given to it by the Moslems after the conquest. Behar however, so far as I can learn, is neither a Sangskrit nor a Persian word, and is probably original. The Hindu town had probably gone to ruin with the Maga dynasty, and the Moslem city arose into

(1) Tungi (about two miles south-east of Bihar).

consequence from the numerous saints belonging to the place.

A little west from the old fort is a very considerable heap of bricks, called Pajaiya which means a brick kiln, and people allege that it was the old brick mill of the Magas, but its elevation and size renders this opinion untenable. It has probably been a large solid temple, and its ruins indeed may have supplied bricks for the modern town to a very considerable extent, to which the name may be attributed.

The only detail concerning the Magas that I can learn is that one of their Queens, Rani Malti, had a house about 2½ cose east from the town. It is said that there remain no traces except a considerable heap of bricks.

*8th January.*—I went about seven miles westerly to Baragang,[1] where there was said to be many ruins. I first went about a mile south to the end of the bazar, which extends in a direct line from the edge of the ditch. Behind the wretched sheds which form the shops are many houses of brick, some of them pretty large but in general very slovenly, and neither plastered or in good order. The bricks seem to have been all taken from ruins. Near the far end [is] a large building of stones similar to those of the fort and probably taken from thence. It is said to have been the Kachery of the Phaujdar, and is a kind of rude castle. About one-third of a mile west from the end of the bazar is a long ridge of stones on the east side of a pretty considerable tank, in the centre of which is a stone pillar. The Dorga of Gungam Dewan has been erected on the ruin, which probably has belonged to Maga Raja. About 1¼ miles beyond this I crossed the principal channel of the Punchanun,[2] which may be 200 yards wide and contains a small clear stream. About four miles from thence I came to a tank called merely Dighi, which is the

(1) **Bargaon.**

(2) Panchany R., R.; **Panchane N.**

commencement of the ruin. It extends east and west about 1,000 yards, but is not above 200 yards wide. No weeds, and covered with Pintails. Immediately west from this tank is a very considerable space elevated with the fragments of brick. Its north end is occupied by part of the village of Begumpur,[2] and a small ruinous mud fort erected by Kamgar Khan. This occupied the highest part of the heap, which sinks towards the south, but on that end are four smaller heaps which have probably been separate buildings, and their ruins have formed the heap by which they are united. On the one next the fort is a large image which the people call Bairubh, but this name they strangely mis-apply. It seems to me to represent Narayan riding on Garuda, but is exceedingly rude. On the most easterly of the four heaps are two images, both male, one sitting with its legs crossed like a Buddh, the other with its legs down as Europeans sitting on a chair, and like this I have seen some images of Jain in the south.

South from this mass of building has been another much more considerable, on the north end of which is situated the village of Baragung. The two however seem to be connected on the east side by an elevated space filled with bricks. Between these two masses is a conical peak of bricks, which has evidently been a temple. West from it is a small tank called Surjapukhor, where a great Mela is annually held. On the north side of the tank has been a considerable mosque, totally fallen to ruin. At the north-west corner are three images. One a Linga with a man's head and shoulders on one side. There are several others such among the ruins. Another is a male standing, with a short inscription round his head. The third is a Buddh. The image of Surja is said by a Fakir to have been thrown in the tank, but this seems doubtful. On the south side of the tank, near a small heap of brick, have been collected several images. Among others a Buddh sitting in the usual posture, with several others as

(1) Begampur.

well as other human figures carved on his throne and round him, also a row of Buddhs. Also one very usual near Gya, namely, a male standing, with four arms and leaning with two of them on two small figures, one of which is a female. On the east side of the tank temple a large fig tree has destroyed a small temple, and under it have been collected many images. The largest, of very considerable dimensions, is turned upside down so that the figure cannot be seen. (On my return I had it placed erect and found that it was a Varaha.) It is probably that which was worshipped in the adjacent conical heap, which is called Tarhari. The most remarkable image under this tree is one of a male with a boar's head (Varaha), on each side a Nagini or female ending in two serpents in place of legs. The serpents are twisting their tails round the feet of the God. Many Buddhs or Jains here also, for I do not know how to distinguish them, but on the whole most of the figures have a strong resemblance to those of Buddh Gya. Among others at this heap, I saw one of Surja such as he is represented at Gya. The real image however, to which the tank is dedicated, has been probably conveyed to a small modern temple built in the middle of the village of Baragung.. In its walls have been built several images, and a good many are lying about in the area before the temple. One of the Buddhs in the wall of the left hand of the temple has a short inscription. Here as well as elsewhere, several Lingas with human faces on four sides, an idol very common near Gya also.

In the street of the town, near this temple of Surja, is a large image which the people worship as Kala Bairobh.. It is seated in the usual posture, one hand over the knee, with two small Buddhs above and two below in the same posture, and one reclining on a couch. Also a figure standing on each side. On this image there is a short inscription.

Nearly west from the town of Baragang, a wretched place, is a conical heap of bricks called Dorbar, with three others of the same name running in a southerly direction towards a large tank choked with weeds; at the foot of this hill are three large images of Buddhs sitting in the usual posture. Two are erect, one supine. This has a short inscription, but it is much defaced. Its hand is over its knee, as is the case of that farthest north. The southernmost of those that are erect, which is the largest, and seems to have had its hands joined before the breast but they are broken, has two short inscriptions. Between this conical heap and the next towards the south is a small temple, where a Dasnami Sannyasi is Pujari. The third image, which is an object of worship, he calls Baituk Bairobh, but it is evidently a Buddh or Jain sitting in the usual posture and clothed, with one hand on the knee. It is of great size, seated on a throne ornamented with lions, and the execution better than usual. It is not a relief but a full figure. A vast number of images and fragments of all sorts are lying near it.

The next heap has been opened for materials, and seems to have contained only a very small square cavity. The door has been of stones, among the fragments an image of an elephant.

Parallel to these conical heaps, evidently temples, has been a very long range of buildings between them and the great elevation extending south from Baragung. Traces remain to show that at its north end there has been a row of five small courts surrounded by buildings. The south end seems to have been one mass, as there are no cavities on the top but such as may be supposed to have originated from the falling in of the roof of large rooms. On the east side of this and parallel to it, but much larger in all dimensions, is an elevated space containing many bricks, and extending south from Baragung. It would rather seem to have been formed by the ruin of a congeries of buildings than to have been one mass of buildings, or palace. On its north end, adjacent to the town, has been erected a small temple of the Serawaks, which probably however isnot above 100 years old. It is in charge of a Mali, and in tolerable repair but very slovenly, the court round it being cultivated with mustard or filled with rubbish. The terrors of the Jain seem to prevent them from living near their temples, and they study concealment as much as possible. The doors into this temple are made so small that I was under the necessity of creeping in on all fours.

A considerable way south from thence, on this range of ruins, is a considerable conical heap, evidently a temple. Near it but at some distance are two large images, one a Buddh or Jain, the other a female supported by two lions. At the south end of this mass is a very considerable long heap with two smaller risings on its west side, probably a large house or palace. Beyond this I saw no more heaps. There appear to have been many small tanks round. At the south-west corner of this large building is the ruin of a small temple called Kapteswori, in and near which have been collected many images of all kinds, some of them though Buddhs smeared with the blood of offerings made by the neighbouring peasantry. One of them, evidently a fat-bellied male, without a proboscis and sitting with one leg hanging over the throne, they call Devi or the goddess. Three female figures at this place have short inscriptions. One of them is standing under two Buddhs. Another is very curious. It represents a small female sitting on a throne, supported by swine, tolerably well done but called elephants by the neighbours. Above her is striding an enraged Sakti with three faces, two human and one porcine. A Buddh on the ornaments of each head, and an inscription.

Such are the ruins of the place which the people all agree in calling Kundilpuri and the residence of Maga Raja, but that merely is to say that it was the residence of the King of the country. The nature of the heaps and the number of images induce me to suspect that it has been merely a place of worship, although it is possible that the long range with the five small courts in its north end may have been a palace. I further suspect, from the few traces of religious buildings about Behar, that the King usually dwelt there in the fort, and that this was his place of worship, where indeed he might also have a palace. There is no trace of any fortification near it. Vast heaps of the materials, I am told, have for ages been removed to Behar and other neighbouring places for building. Great quantities still remain.

The Jain priest at Behar (Jeti) says that the proper name of Behar is Bisalapur, which first belonged to Raja Padamuda who had a country extending 48 coses round. He was succeeded by his son Sujodun, and his son Duryodhon, his son Ugrieva. These Rajahs were Khatriyas of the Jain religion. Padamuda lived about 2,800 years ago, and there are no remains of his work. After this dynasty came Rajah Srinik, a Jain, who dwelt at Baragong, the proper name of which is Kundilpur. He only raised one temple of the Jain, where he placed the mark of Gautom's feet.

The Jain here acknowledge Gautom as the chief of eleven disciples of Mahavira one of their Avatars, and pay him divine honours. The priest says that at that time the bulk of the people were Buddhs, and that all the other temples and images belonged to that sect. Raja Srinik lived about 2,400 years ago, contemporary with Mahavira and Gautoma, and his country extended 48 coses. He left no heirs, as he betook himself to a religious life.

The temple of the Jain at Baragang is called Buddh Mundol, and is the place where Gautoma died. The present temple was built by Sungram Saha, a merchant, who lived about 250 years ago and placed in it an image of Santonath, one of the Avatars. Kundilpur is also called Pompapuri. The Buddh temples had been there before. There were no other Jain Rajahs here. Raja Maga (a proper name) afterwards built the fort of Behar, but the Jain have no account of him, as he was not of their religion. They have no account of Jarasindha as being an infidel, but they say he lived before Padamuda. Four of the Avatars, Molonath, Subodnath, Kuntonath and Arinath, performed hermitage (Topisya) at Rajagrihi, on which account it has become a holy place and was published as such about 2,200 years ago. Four maths have been built by the house of Jogotseit within these 100 years. It belonged to Raja Srinik.

At Pokorpur near Pauyapuri is a temple of Mahavira, when he died he was carried as usual to heaven but some of his remains were left at that place. The temple built lately. At Gunauya[1] near Nawadeh, Gautama Swami performed Topissia. He says that Vaspujiar died at Champanagar. Kurna Raja was not a Jain, but Raja Dodibahun was Raja of Champanagar an exceeding long time ago, at the time of Vaspuja. He was after Karna Raja.

Twenty of the Avatars died at Sometsikur hill, called Parswanath, in Palgunj. Neamnath died at Grinar near Gujerat, Adinath at Setrurija near Palitana city. The places where the 24 Avatars were born and where they prayed are also holy, some were born at Kasi, some at Ayudiya. All the Avatars were sons of Rajahs except Nemnath, who was son of Samududra Vijayi by Siva Devi. Samudra was a Jodobongsi, or of the same family with Krishna.

The whole Jain are called Srawakas, but they are divided into 84 castes (Jat), Osuyal, Srimal, Agarwal, Porwar, etc. The Osuyal and Srimal can intermarry, but none of the other castes can intermarry nor eat together. Besides these are a class called Bojok or Pushkarna, who are Brahmans. These were admitted about 350 years ago, when a King threatening the Srawakas with destruction, a number of armed Brahmans undertook their defence and have been received as Purohits for the whole. Formerly they had no Purohits

(1) **Gunawatola**, (east of the tank described on 21st December, and of the main road between Giriak and Rajauli).

The Bojoks although outwardly Jains are generally supposed to be privately of the sect of Vishnu. At first he said that there were no Brahmans among the Jain, but he afterwards said that he had heard of Gujerati Brahmans belonging to the 84 castes, and called Gujewal. The Agarwal, Osuyal, Paliwal, Srimal, and others perhaps, are Chitris. Bazirwal are Jat or Goyalas, Golavaris and Poriwar are Vaisiyas. Any one of the castes or a Brahman of any kind may become a Joti, or the Gurus of the Sarawaks. My informant in fact says that he was born a Gaur Brahman, and that his father was of the seet of Vishnu. My people think that privately he still continues of that faith. None of them are married, and they give upades to the Sarawaks, who are all married. The abode of the Jotis is called Pausal. One Joti usually lives with his Chelas and such guests as he chooses to entertain. They also are divided into 84 sects or Gueh, each of which has a chief Sripuj. If a Joti leaves no chela the Sripuj is his heir. They are also divided into two maths, Digumba and Swetumba. The Digumbas should go naked, but they now content themselves with using tanned clothes. They follow the same gods, but have some different books. None of them here worship the Astik gods, but they have a Chetrapal god of cities, as other Hindus have Grama Devatas. Their temples here they call Deohara. They perform Hom, that is, burnt offerings of honey and ghi. They make no sacrifices. They admit the sun and heavenly bodies to be deities, but do not worship them.

The Rajahs of Jaynagar were Jains until the time of Protapsingh, the son of Sewai Jaisingh, who became a worshipper of Vishnu. The Astiks here deny this, but I heard the same from a Gaur Brahman who had come from Jainagar as an artificer. Many of the Rajputs of Bundeli, Mewar, Marwar, Kundeir, Lahor, Bikaner, Jodpur, etc., are Jain, but many also are Vaishnavs. They admit the Buddhs to have preceded them, but know nothing of their history. The Buddhs were succeeded, partly by the Vaishnavas, partly by the

Jains. He says that Mahapal, Devapal, etc., were Jain merchants, not kings.

In the Bhagawati Suth in 45,000 slokes is contained an account of the Avatars and Jain Rajahs. The Tara Tambul gives an account of the places of pilgrimage, with their distances. He has a good many books in Sanskrit, but not the Bhagawati Suth. The Jains' images that are sitting have both their hands supine and across. Those standing have both hands down, with the palms turned forwards. They have 48 female deities, Padmawati, Chukreswori, Chundrakangta, Sri Maloni, etc. They make offerings of flowers and fruits to them. Some have many arms.

He says that Vihar is the proper name of the place, and has always been its name in the vulgar dialect. It obtained the Sangskrit appellation Bisalapur in the time of Mahavira.

The old images in the fort at Behar, the Joti says, are all of the Buddhists. One, a small stone with a muni on each of four faces, contains a short inscription, but so much defaced that no meaning can be extracted from the parts that are legible. Without the south gate, under a young tree, some broken images have been collected, but I had no opportunity of consulting the Joti concerning them. One is a female sitting, with two elephants above her head.

*9th January.*—I visited the old Kacheri of the Moguls. The mosque alone remains, and has been by far the largest of the place, but exceedingly rude. The walls, pillars, and arches have been built of rude stone taken from the fort, and have been covered by domes of brick. The domes have been 21 in three rows. The spaces between the pillars have been about 15 feet wide. The pillars are masses about six feet square and seven feet high. This may give an idea of the taste. The walls have been rudely plastered. The size in the inside has been about 57 feet by 141. It was built by a Mir Mahmud, and a descendant, venerable by age and appearance but of a very querulous disposition, retains the property of the ground, which may be three or four acres. No traces of the other buildings remain except a few walls, partly stone, partly brick. About 100 years ago the Kucheri was removed into the fort by orders from the King. It seems to me as if the south gate alone had been rebuilt and formed into a small kind of castle, by blocking up some openings with bricks. This has probably been done by the owner of a Dorga, who occupies most of the space within.

10*th January.*—I went to Puri. Having passed through the bazar and the Dorga of Mukhdum, I found encamped a party of Jain pilgrims, and proceeding south, by a road not however practicable for carts, about six miles, I came to the Panchanan. It is here not above 200 yards wide, but contains a good deal of water, notwithstanding numerous canals that are taken from it for irrigation. I followed its bank for above half a mile, and then turning easterly went to the Tirth, about a mile farther on. Here I found another camp of pilgrims. The whole of the pilgrims assembled are Poriwars. There are fully as many women as men. Most of the women are elderly, but some are young and a few have children. They are in general dressed in a red gown with a petticoat, and a cloth round their head and shoulders, not as a veil, for like the women of the south of India they show their faces. Many of them wear shoes and are well made girls but very great hoydens, their clothes being thrown on without the smallest neatness. They have many horses, some oxen, and small tents. They went first to Kasi, then to Ayudiya, then have come here, they go on to Rajagiri, Palgunj and Champanagar, and then return home. They say that the whole of their tribe are traders, and at first said they were Sudras, but then recollecting themselves said they were Vaisiyas. They never heard of any Brahmans among the Serawaks, but said that west from Bandlekund there are many Rajputs among the Jain. The doctrine of caste, at least of Brahman, Kshatri, Vaisya and

Sudra, seems to me a mere innovation. Finding the three first titles become honourable among their neighbours, the men of learning take the title of Brahmans, the powerful call themselves Kshatris, and the traders call themselves Vaisiyas. The Poriwar admit of no Gurus except those of their own tribe, and pay no sort of attention to a chela of the Behar Joti who is here looking for employment. He is so like the Joti that I suspect that he is his son. The Guru of the Poriwar resides at Gualior. They have no Purohit, each man offers for himself. They seem to abhor the Brahmans, yet they say that they give them sometimes a couple of Paisahs for some yellow powder, with which they mark their faces.

Pauya Puri, I am informed by the convert, is considered by the Burmas as the place where Gautama changed this life for immortality. For some time previous to that event he resided at Gya, but coming to Pauya Puri he died, and his funeral was performed with great pomp and splendour by Raja Mol, then sovereign of the country.

I expected to have found Pauya Puri an old city, but on coming there I found that Pauya[1] and Puri were two distinct places distant from each other above a mile, and that at Puri there was not the slightest trace of the Buddhists. On the contrary, everything there seems to be comparatively modern and to belong to the Jain. Some of the people of Pauya having come to have a peep into my tent, I by chance asked them if they had any old temple. They said that they had a temple of the Sun, and that there were many broken images lying near it. I accordingly went to the spot and found the village situated on a considerable elevation, about 600 feet in length and perhaps 150 in width, consisting of a mixture of earth and bricks, in general broken to small fragments. The greatest length extends east and west, and at each end is a tank nearly filled up. On the west end of this elevation is the temple of Surja, a small quadrangular

(1) Paowah, R. and B.A.; Pawa.

building with a flat roof, divided into two apartments, and perhaps 100 years old. It contains two images, one called Surja and the other Lakshmi, both males standing with two arms, and exactly resembling many that are to be seen at Gya. The one called Lakshmi has a short inscription which my people cannot read, and on her head a male figure sitting cross-legged with both his hands on his lap, as the Jains are usually represented. On the outside of the temple are several broken images, mostly females standing, but two small ones are of Munis of the Buddhists, having their right hands on their knee.

This place, I have no doubt, is the proper Pauya Puri, and seems to have been a large temple. The Jains afterwards, having dedicated a place near, it, called it merely Puri or the Abode, while the other is now called simply Pauya. The people of the village have not the smallest tradition concerning the bricks found in their village, but that is not surprising, as they do not know who built their small temple, and are astonished how any person should conceive them to know such a circumstance, as they say it was done three or four generations at least ago, and that is beyond the extent of their chronology.

The Jains at Puri have erected three places of worship. That farthest south is the place where Mahivera was burnt. It is a small temple placed in the middle of a fine tank, and surrounded by a wall with very narrow doors. The temple was erected and is kept in good repair by the family of Jogotseit. A Brahman of Telingana, of the sect of Vishnu, and a Mali have charge of it. The former takes the offerings, and the latter sells flowers, but neither is employed in the worship. Immediately north from the tank is an eminence formed by the earth thrown out. On this has lately been erected a place of worship in honour of the feet of Mahavira. It is round, and rises by several stages gradually narrower, but as each stage is only a reasonable step high and very wide the whole elevation is trifling. In the centre is a place like a large beehive, in which is placed the emblem of the deities' feet.

North from this some way, at Puri village, is the most considerable temple. It consists of two courts surrounded by a brick wall, with very small doors as usual. In the centre of one is a temple in excellent repair and of no great antiquity. The ascent to it is by a wretched stair, on each side of which are two small places like beehives, each containing a lump of earth covered with red lead, which is called Bairubh. The temple consists of a centre and four small mondirs at the corners. In the centre are three representations of the feet of Mahavira, who died at this place, and one of each of those of his eleven disciples. In the corner buildings are also representations of the feet of various persons. Each has an inscription, which has been copied, only the inscriptions on four have become obliterated by rubbing and are no longer legible. These inscriptions are in Devanagri, which my people read. One is said to be very old. The Joti reads the date of the year of Sombot five 5, but the Karji thinks that what the Joti calls Panso, or five, are the cyphers 160 which would give the date 1605. The oldest. All the eleven disciples were made in the [year] 1698 by one man. One of the new ones of Mahavir, made in 1702. The other, when the feet of the disciples were made. There is an inscription giving an account of the persons by whom the eleven Padukas were made. At each side of the court of this temple is a building. One serves as a gate, two for accommodating strangers of rank, and the fourth for a Joti, disciple of the person of Behar. He is said to have been a Brahman and is I suspect a mere pretended Jain. The Poriwars will have nothing do with him. The Oshuyals alone seem to have admitted these Brahmans as Gurus, on their professing their faith and studying their law. The court is tolerably clean and planted with flowers. The other court contains a building intended entirely for the accommodation of pilgrims of rank.

11*th January.*—I went to Giriak,[1] about two coses. The village is situated on an elevation containing ma. bricks, at a little distance from the Punchanon, towarc.. the east. Immediately south from the village is a tank, much filled up, called Dobra, south from thence some way is another called Dunsar, and south-west from that is another [called] Puraniya, from its being covered with the leaves of the Nelumbium, called Puran as the flowers are called Kamal. North from Puraniya, and running along the banks of the Punchanan between it and the two other tanks, is a very large elevation composed of broken bricks, rude masses of stone taken from the hill on the opposite side of the Punchanan, and earth. That this is not a natural heap or hill I conclude from there not being the smallest appearance of rock, for all the hills of this country are mere rocks with a little soil in the more level parts. Its shape also showing traces of symmetry supports the same opinion. It may be traced to consist of two parts. That to the south considerably the lowest, both have a projection towards the east and west, like porticos or perhaps gates.[2] The elevation of the northern part cannot be less than 80 feet perpendicular. Nor is there any trace of a cavity within. If it has been a mass of building, as I doubt not has been the case, it must have been a great castle or palace, without any courts or empty areas which could have left any traces in decay. The whole however, probably by the removal of the materials, has been reduced to a mere irregular mass in which no traces of building remain. On its top has been erected a small square fort with a ditch. The rampart and bastions have been faced with bricks, taken probably from the ruin. This fort is attributed to a Bandawot Rajah who governed the country before the Batana Bamans. This fort is called the Boragara, while some irregular traces on the east side of the large heap are called Chotagar, and are also attributed to the same Bandawats, who were Rajputs.

(1) Gireek, B.A.; **Giriak Babhoipur.**

(2) The river is cutting away this mound on its western side, exposing wells and the brick foundations of buildings, and the projections on the western side have now disappeared.

The most sensible natives of the place have no tradition concerning the elevation on which the Baragara is situated, but think that it was made at the same time with the fort, which is an opinion quite untenable, the fort-ditch having evidently been dug into the heap of ruins. A Dosnami indeed pretends that the old name of the place is Hangsa Nagar and that it was built by a Hangsa Rajah ; but he is a stupid fellow, and no other person has heard of such a tradition. At Patna, however, I heard the Hangsa Rajah lived at Phulwari.

The greater part of the stones, as I have said, are rude blocks of quartz or hornstone taken from the opposite hill, but a few images and fragments of potstone are scattered about. Two of the images are pretty entire, although much defaced. One represents a female killing a buffalo, exactly like the Jagadombas of Kewadol. This is lying on the surface of the hill under the fort towards the east. Near it is a very neat pedestal on which five images have stood, but only their feet remain. The other image that is entire is placed leaning against the wall of a small modern temple of Siva, built on the northernmost of two small heaps that are north from the great ruin. It is exactly like one of the most common figures at Gaya. A male with four arms, leaning on two small personages, one male and one female. Two small images below in form of adoration, two angels hovering above with chaplets in their hands. His head has a high cap with an old regal coronet. By the people it is called Lakshmi Narayan, and is the same with that so called at Pauya, only that it wants the Jain on the head, being too small. Under a tree, between the great heap and the river, have been collected some fragments of images. The male part of a Linga, part of a Ganesa, two fragments of the male last described, with some others so much defaced that it is impossible to say what they were. On the north end of the great heap I found a fragment of the same male image, being one of the angels that has hovered above his head. Under a tree on the east side of the large heap is a fragment of the human form, which the Musahors have put upon a heap of bricks and worship as one of their saints or devils. This large heap is evidently what the people of Nawada called Jarasandha's house, but the people on the spot have no such tradition. The buildings attributed to Jarasandha are on the hill called Giriak, just opposite to the village of that name. He is considered here as having been an Asur or Daityo of immense size, so as to stand with one foot on Giriak and another on Rajgiri, three coses distant, and from thence throw bricks into the sea at Dwarka on the other side of India. On account of this vile trick by which he disturbed the 1,600 wives of the God who lived at Dwarka, that God came here to war with Jarasandha, and killed him by the hand of Bhim the son of Pandu. At that time Krishna gave orders that people should bathe in the Panchanan, and 50,000 are said to assemble for the purpose in Kartik.

*12th January.*—I ascended the hill to see the antiquities. Crossing the Panchanan at the upper end of the great heap, I ascended a very steep precipice to the small temple called Gauri Sankor, which is situated at the bottom of an immense rock, on the summit of which is the monument called the Baitaki of Jarasandha. In this temple, which is very small and probably not 100 years old, are two small images, one of Ganesa, the other of a male sitting with a female on his knee, such as is usually called Hargauri or Krishna and Radha, but very common at Gaya. Near this is the tomb of a late sanyasi, predecessor of the present pujari.

I went from thence east along the face of the hill, to another larger temple of the same shape, and perhaps six feet square, which is built over what is called the impression of Krishna's feet, which at Nawada was called the impression of the feet of Rama. The marks are small and like real impressions, being excavated, and not elevated like the feet of the Jain. In this temple are the fragments of an idol that has been broken into so many pieces that no judgment can be formed of what is represented.

Ascending from thence a steep precipice between two immense rocks, I came to a comparatively level place, where I found the proper road, paved with rough blocks of stone cut from the hill. It seems to have been about twelve feet wide and winds in various directions to procure an ascent of moderate declivity, and when entire a palanquin might perhaps have been taken up and down, but it has always been a very rude work, and in many places is almost entirely destroyed.[1] I followed its windings along the north[2] side of the hill until at length I reached the ridge opposite to a small tank, excavated on two sides from the rock and built on the two others with the stones cut out. The ridge is very narrow, extends east and west, and rises gently from the tank towards both hands, but most towards the west. I went first in that direction along the causeway, which is there at least 18 feet wide, and rises gradually above the ridge. This causeway led me to a mass of bricks which is very steep, and I thought in ascending it that I could perceive the remains of a stair, somewhat like the trace of two or three of the steps being discernible. At the top of this steep ascent is a hollow space with a thick ledge round it. This has probably been a court, open above but surrounded by a wall, and formed a terrace surrounding the building on all sides. West farther has been a square mass of building, of which the foundation at the north-east corner is still entire and built of bricks about 18 inches long, 9 wide and 2 thick. They are laid on clay, but have been chiselled smooth so that the masonry is very neat, and have never been covered with plaster. In this corner the ends of five pillars of granite project from among the ruins, and in other parts three other pillars are still standing. They are of no considerable height, about ten feet and quadrangular, while only one of their faces has been ornamented with carving and that very rudely. They

(1) Dr. Buchanan did not notice the fortification walls, which can be easily traced, going round the hill on the west, everywhere below its crest, and crossing the narrow valley between this hill and the southern range.

(2) Should be " south," *see* page 113.

probably therefore formed a corridor round this court, and the carved face has been turned towards the direction intended to be most conspicuous. They consist of a very fine grey granite, white felspar and quartz, and black mica, and have been brought from a distance, there being no such stone on the hill. Immediately west from this building, which has probably been a Nath Mondir, is a conical mass of brick placed on a square basis. There is no cavity in its summit, so that it has probably been a solid temple like that of the Buddhists. On its north[1] side would appear to have been a small chamber, built in part at least with granite. The terrace beyond this cone has terminated very steep towards the west, and the rock appears to have been cut away to render its west end more abrupt and to procure materials. A small plain has been thus formed on the descent at its west end, and in this is an excavation probably made to procure materials. West from thence is a very picturesque view of a narrow parched valley between two ridges of rocks. In all other directions the country is exceedingly rich.

I then returned to the tank, which is now dry, and in its bottom I found a small female image with traces of her having had a child on her knee, but it has a Chokor or disk in one hand and Goda (Mau) in the other. On this account the Brahmans deny that it can represent Ganesa Jononi, the mother of Ganesa, but I have no doubt that it represents the same circumstance, that is, the warlike Semiramis with the infant Niniyas on her knee.

Going east from the tank a little way is another small conical heap of bricks, quite a ruin, behind which on a square pedestal is the circular base, 68 feet in circumference, of a fine column, the most entire part of the ruin, and which is called the Baitaki or seat of Jarasandha. It is a solid building without any cavity, as may be known by a deep excavation made in its western face, probably in search of treasure, and has been built

---

(1) Should be "south," as shown in Buchanan's own sketch plan.

throughout of large bricks laid in clay. The external ones within reach have been removed, but higher up some part remains entire and surrounded by the original mouldings. The whole outer face has been cut smooth with the chisel, and the mouldings have been neatly carved, but they contain no traces of animal figures. The square pedestal has been built in the same manner and much ornamented. In what the column terminated it is impossible to say, as what now remains is merely the basis, and the whole northern face of the precipice under it to the bottom is covered with scattered bricks which have fallen from it. The terrace on which it stands extends a little way towards the east, forming a little plain from whence there is a most extensive prospect of rich plain.

The building towards the west is called by a Sanyasi (Pujari of the two modern temples) Hangsapur, but all other persons are ignorant of this name. Both parties admit that it was the house of Jarasandha, but this is evidently a mistake. No prince could have lived in such a place, and the building has evidently been a temple. The use of the column is not so obvious. It may have been merely an ornamental appendage to the temple, or it may have been the funeral monument of a prince. The last is the most probable opinion, and it may be the tomb of Jarasandha, who is said to have been killed at Ronbumi about four coses west. If Jarasandha had a house here, I have no doubt that the heap on which Baragara has been built is its ruins. None of the images here are of a size fitted for worship in such temples, and have been mere ornaments. The proper images, if there were any, are either buried in the ruins or have been destroyed.

I returned all the way by the stair or road which descends by the north side of the hill, whereas I ascended by the south side. The hill consists entirely of quartz or silicious hornstone.[1] In most parts it is white, in some ash coloured, and in a few red. It

(1) Appendix, No. 111.

is nowhere that I saw an aggregate, but is composed of an uniform substance, in some parts glassy, in others powdery. In a state of decay, as at the small temple of Gaurisankar, it looks as if passing into Khorimati.

Some invalid native officers have been within a year or two settled at Geriak. They complain that their lands produce nothing except Kurti, being too sandy. I am however told by the farmers that the soil is good, and when fully cultivated will produce all kinds of rubbi, or Janera, Meruya, etc. It was lately covered with stunted woods of which a good deal still remains in the vicinity, but of late years much has been reclaimed. Near Giriak are many Musahars and a few Bhuiyas. These here have no chiefs, and eat everything.

13*th January.*—I went six coses to Hariya,[1] but the road or path is very circuitous. About $5\frac{2}{3}$ miles from Geriak I crossed the Teluriya,[2] a sandy channel about 200 yards wide, with a little stream of water, full however as large now as the stream of the Fulgo was at Gya when I was there. About five miles farther on I crossed the Dadur,[3] much such another channel as the Puri. The villages closely built. Many of the inhabitants Musahars. They speak a Hindi very obsolete and difficult to understand. Their noses very small and rather flat, faces oval, lips not thick, eyebrows prominent. Hair long like all original Hindu tribes.

14*th January.*—In the first place I went about a mile northerly to see the rock from whence Silajit proceeds. I ascended the hill[5] to about its middle by an exceeding steep rugged path through a stunted wood, of bamboos and Boswellia chiefly. I then came to an abrupt rock, of white quartz in some parts, and grey

(1) **Hanriya.**

(2) **Tilaia N.**? Puri crossed out. Probably **Khuri N.**

(3) Dahder R., R. and B.A.; **Dadar N.**

(4) By taking this route, Buchanan missed the hot springs called Agnidhara, at Madhuban near Giriak, which also are not referred to in his Report. Maximum temperature observed since 1909, 129° on December 25, 1920.

(5) **Handia** or **Hanriya.**

hornstone in others, the same as I had found all the way up the hill. Scrambling along the foot of this perpendicular rock some way I reached the mouth of a considerable cave, which has a wide mouth, and may be 50 or 60 feet in diameter and 10 or 12 feet high where highest. The floor rises inwards with a very steep ascent and is very rugged, and the roof looks very threatening, and its crevices shelter wild pigeons. The cave itself is quite dry, and near the mouth is cool and airy. It is said to be an usual haunt of bears and tigers. At the far end of the cave is another, with a mouth about 12 feet wide and 4 or 5 high. On approaching this I was struck by a hot vapour and stench that constantly proceed from it, and I heard the chattering of bats from whom the stench proceeds. The heat is very considerable, so as instantly to produce a violent perspiration, but unfortunately I had not with me a thermometer.[1] I looked into the mouth of this inner cave, and could see all round it without perceiving any ulterior opening, but I saw none of the bats who were probably hid in crevices. And the heat and stench being exceedingly disagreeable, I did not go in. The cave consists entirely of white quartz, stained red on the surface of some parts.[2] What has caused the rock to slide out from it, I cannot say. All before and under it for a little way is a rock composed of small fragments of quartz imbedded in a tufaceous substance. This I saw nowhere else on the hill. There is no appearance of stratification. The rock, as usual, divided into rhomboidal masses by fissures horizontal and vertical. In many parts it is quite naked and abrupt, and everywhere (it has) the hills composed of it have the most arid sterile appearance. The hills of quartz are in general very inferior in grandeur to those of granite. The latter rise into peaks of the most magnificent boldness, and the crevices are much more favourable to vegetation. The hills of quartz, however, produce more springs and little

(1) "Not due to any physical cause, such as high temperature, but merely to physiological causes, owing to the fact that the air is stagnant and extremely foul." *See* J. B. O. R. S., 1917, Vol. III, Part III, pages 309—310.

(2) Appendix, No. 40.

rivulets, and in the recesses formed by these there are often abrupt precipices and scenery of astonishing grandeur.

Standing before the cave and looking up, I saw the Silajit besmearing the face of the rock about 30 feet above my head, and procceding from a small ledge, in which I am told it issues from a crevice in the quartz. It was impossible for me to proceed farther. One old Musahar alone ventured on this, and before he set out he fortified himself with some spirituous liquor, having made a libation to the ghosts of the saints (Vir). A young active Harkarah attempted to accompany him. They went round the rock until they found a ledge, and proceeded by this, holding on by roots of trees, until they came over the mouth of the cave, 40 or 50 feet above the Silajit, and the old man descended from one crevice or projecting point to another, until he reached the little ledge from whence it issued. The young man's heart failed him and he did not venture on so dangerous an exploit. The old man brought back about an ounce measure of the Silajit, which he collected in a leaf. It is about the consistence of new honey but rather thinner, and mixed with dust and other impurities that crumble down from the arid precipice above. It is of a dirty earth colour, and has a strong rather disagreeable smell, somewhat like that of cows' urine but stronger, although it cannot be called very offensive. The whole appearance is however disgusting.[1]

The place belongs to Rai Kosal Singh of Patna, and all the Silajit that is collected is sent to him. The people say that the old man goes once about three days during the months Paush and Mag, and does not collect above one or two sicca weight in the day, and that the whole

---

(1) Writing in 1819, Buchanan says in his Account of the Kingdom of Nepal, page 80 :—"In many parts of these mountains, the substance called *silajit* exudes from rocks. I have not yet satisfied myself concerning its nature; but intend hereafter to treat the subject fully, when I describe the natural productions of Behar, where I had an opportunity of collecting it, as it came from the rock." For an explanation of its nature, *see* J. B. O. R. S., loc. cit., pages 315—318.

procured in a season is not a seer. This seems to be doubtful. The man with any pains might to-day have collected a couple of ounces, and it exudes in a similar manner from another place about a quarter of a mile farther east. It is very likely, however, that the owner does not get more than a seer, and that I should suppose is quite enough. I heard the Hanumans, but doubt much of their eating the Silajit, as is pretended.

Having descended, I went along the bottom of the hill towards the west. About five miles from Hariya, the hill on which the Silajit is ends in a low point,[1] and another from behind it comes in view, but sinks into a deep gap in less than half a mile farther.[2] Beyond the gap it rises again, and continues beyond Topobon, which is about six miles from Hariya. These hills consist also of quartz, and are similar in their appearance. Their lower parts covered with bamboos and stunted Boswellias, their upper, sterile dismal rocks with tufts of withered grass. A canal about 24 feet wide has been dug all the way along the hill, and the earth has been thrown towards the plain. The bottom is now cultivated and it seems intended to collect the water into reservoirs, that extend across the plain at right angles. The plan is judicious, but might have been more carefully executed. About three miles east[3] from where the Silajit exudes is a deep recess in the hill like a broken crater, as it is funnel-shaped and the hill is not lower at that part on any side, except towards the south where the edge has given way and shows the hollow.

Tapaban is a place where a Mela had been held two days ago, and it is supposed was attended by eight or ten thousand people. It forms part of the holy places of Rajagriho, and some Brahmans had come from thence to receive contributions. They are most importunate beggars, and call themselves Magaiya Srotriyas, but say that they are Maharasta Brahmans, brought here by

---

(1) Aral or Saphi ghat.
(2) Jethian ghat.
(3) Should be "west."
(4) Sarsu ghat.

a certain Raja whose name is the same with that of Krishna's father.

The holy places are five ponds or pools containing small springs of water, but very inferior to even Sitakund. The water however serves to cover some rice fields even at this season, but here the cold at this season is too great for that grain. The water however is turned on the fields in order to enrich them. The pools are situated in a row at the foot of the hill, which like those farther east consists of quartz and hornstone. A great deal of the latter especially above the Kunds is red,[1] but there is no rock immediately adjacent to them. It is there covered by fragments that have fallen from the precipices above. The easternmost Kund is named Chundakosi, and is the finest. It may be about 20 feet square, and at this season three feet deep. The water however, as in the others admitting of the people bathing in it, is very dirty. It has been surrounded by a wall of brick plastered, descending to the water's edge with a narrow walk round the water. In the side opposite to the stair is a small door leading into a petty temple, in which is an image exactly like that at the temple of Siva at Geriak, and is here called Vasudeva. The thermometer, being 70° in the air, rose in the water of this Kund to 116°.[2]

At the west side of this tank have been gathered together several small images, mostly defaced. I observed fragments of five or six of such as is called Vasudeva, but from the enormous distension of ears these are admitted to belong to the sect of Buddhists. I observed two of the goddess sitting on a lion couchant, which my people had never before seen ; also two of Gauri Sangkar, and three lingas. A little south-west from thence is a terrace of brick and stone, said to have been erected by Dototraia, who was killed in Nepal by Bhimsen. On this are three modern and petty temples of Siva.

---

(1) Appendix, No. 24.

(2) Now called Sanatkumar Kund or Surajkund. Maximum temperature observed since 1908, 113·4° on December 28th, 1908.

Immediately south-west from thence is a small pool of cool water, called Hangsatirtha. It has been surrounded by brickwork, but this has gone to total ruin, and the water is exceedingly dirty. Immediately south-west from it is a small brick temple, the roof of which is fallen,[1] in the centre of which is a linga, and in the back wall are built three images of Gauri Sankar, on one of which is carved a person's name by whom probably it was dedicated. Near this temple is lying one of the images called here Vasudeva and at Gya Narayon.

Some way south-west from thence is the pool called Puran Hangs, lined with brick in good repair. The water in it raised the thermometer to 100°.[2]

Near this is Sanantanakundo, also lined with brick, which raised the thermometer to 102°.[3] At some distance farther south-west is Sonok Tirtha, also lined with brick, and like the others in tolerable repair. It raised the thermometer to 112°.[4] In none of these ponds was there any issue of air bubbles as in those of the Bhagalpur district, except in the last, and there they issued in very small quantities. I observed that in the two middle Kunds, where the heat was at 100° and 102°, there were some small fishes and a great many frogs; but in the two extreme ponds, where the heat was 112° and 116°, none of these animals could live. This points out the heat in which these animals can live with comfort.

*15th January.*—I went to Amaiti,[5] which was said to be five coses distant, but I found it less than 3½. The

(1) No longer traceable. A large modern temple probably occupies its position.

(2) Now called Sanaksanandan or Sitakund. Maximum temperature observed since 1908, 104·4° on December 12th, 1909.

(3) Now called Sankaraditya or Brahmakund. Maximum temperature observed since 1908, 101·8° on December 12th, 1909.

(4) Now called Sanakkua or Chamarkund. Maximum temperature observed since 1908, in hottest part of the Kund, 123·4° on December 27th, 1915; but on December 28th, 1917, a small spring issued direct from the ground, the temperature of which was 128·7°. *See* also note on page 115.

(5) Amethi.

country a fine level between two ridges of rocky hills, much of it under stunted woods, but the soil good. Less than a mile from Amaiti I crossed a narrow rivulet in a clay channel, but filled with stagnant water. It is called Mungora.[1] Amaiti is a small place belonging to Mitrjit. The people, as usual on his estates, very attentive.

16*th January*.—I went to Norahu,[2] about 5½ coses A little south from Amaiti I saw the soda efflorescing on the surface of a small barren space. I continued skirting the two small hills west from Amaiti for about 1½ miles. I then skirted the ridge behind them, which consists of an exceeding bare rock of a granular rude jasper, in. sometimes prettily variegated white, grey, and red, which if it takes a polish will have a fine effect. The specimen taken at Kharghat.[3] No appearance of strata; as usual broken into rhomboidal fragments. Rather more than a mile farther, I had on my left a small conical peak which, with the two hills of Amaiti, five small hills farther south, and two considerable ones farther on, are a continuation of the ridge of Tapaban.

Rather more than 2½ miles farther, I came to a wide gap in the ridge towards my right, opposite to the third of five small hills above mentioned, and between the two ridges there is a beautiful plain, a great part of which is covered in the rainy season with water, a reservoir having been formed by a bank about half a mile in length drawn across the gap. The bank made only of earth. The ridge continues only a little way farther south, in two short hills. I turned round the south end of the reservoir and went north-east to Nowadah,[4] and from thence north through a very fine plain for about three miles to a little conical hill named Korwa, from whence to

---

(1) **Mangura N.**
(2) **Narawat.**
(3) Appendix, No. 4.
(4) **Nawada.**

Norahur at the west end of the hill so named is rather less than three miles. Korwa hill consists of a red rude jasper,[1] with veins of white quartz. Adhering to it are masses,[2] half crystallized, of a fine white substance, either quartz or felspar, I cannot say which. The country in the recess between the two chains of hills to my right seems to be overrun with low woods, and to be very stony. To the left it is very rich.

Narawat is a small village belonging to Pitumber Singh, cousin german of Mitrjit. His agents say that until lately the country round had been waste for some hundred years, and that Narawat was the residence of a Nol Rajah, who lived in the Tritayog and is celebrated in legend. There are several heaps of brick near the place, but of very little elevation. Whether this is to be attributed to extreme antiquity, or to the buildings having been originally inconsiderable, I cannot say. Many images, in general much defaced, are scattered about these heaps, and several pillars of granite, very rude and resembling those on Giriyak Pahar, are projecting from the ruins or lying above them. The most considerable heap may contain 10 bigahs and is nearly square. On it about 50 or 60 years ago a barber was killed by a tiger, and his ghost became the terror of the neighbourhood, until a small temple was built to his memory. In it has been placed the lower half of a Buddh. The door is supported by an old lintel very much worn, which has a row of angels like those at Mongeer on each side of a sitting figure, much defaced but probably the same as found there. Near the temple of this ghost a pillar projects, and there are four Sivas lately erected but said to have been found on the spot. Two pillars project at no great distance.

Near the present village are standing two granite pillars, and several long stones are lying near them as also several images. A large Linga, three Gauri

(1) Kobwa.
(2) Appendix, No. 55.

Sangkors, with very high diadems. Two fragments of the image called Vasudeva, a Naugraha, a Dosavatar, one stone—the fragment probably of one of the Gauri Sankars, as it has evidently gone round the upper part of a stone containing images below—contains two Jains and a Buddh, that is taking the Joti of Behar's diagnostic to be true, that is two of them have their hands crossed on their lap, and one has its hands joined in adoration. Ramajai[1] however says that no dependence can be placed on this, as several Buddhs in Nepal had both hands crossed on their lap.

A little east from thence, just at the west end of the hill, is a large Gauri Sankar broken in two. About a quarter of a mile east from thence is an old dry tank, called Pukhori by way of eminence, and attributed to Nol Rajah. About half a mile farther east, under a tree, is a fragment of a small Gauri Sangkar quite neglected, while the Goyalas that form the chief population worship under the name of Goraiya four Jains with their hands crossed on their laps that are carved on one stone. The stone seems to have been a lintel and to have contained probably as many more images of the same kind. At the end is represented a solid temple such as is used by the Buddhs but not by the Jain, which confirms Ramajai's opinion. The name of the person by whom it was made is written under it in no very ancient character. This part of the country is said to have belonged to the Bundawuts who are here called Rajputs, but most of the inhabitants in their old territories seem to have been Goyalas. The Kol, it is said, possessed all the country west from this to the Son, beyond which was the country of the Cherin. Nol Raja, I presume, was a Bundawut and a Buddh. The character on the stone is modern, and the images are all probably of the same era. Inder Dovon is said to have been a Bundawat, and his country probably extended so far west at least. It must

(1) Ramajai Bhattacharyya, Pandit attached to the Survey; see Preface to the Account of Nepal, page 1, and Dr. Buchanan's letter to Wallich, of 12th March, 1819, in Sir D. Prain's Memoir, page xxx.

however be observed that Keyadol was said to have belonged to the Bundawats after the Cheru, and that the Cheru and Kol are considered as the same.

*17th January.*—I went to Saren[1] Nateswor,[2] reckoned five coses but my route was about six, partly owing to the winding of the road, and partly owing to my having visited several places by the way. In the first place, I proceeded about half a mile to the south-west corner of Narawut hill, and leaving it on my left proceeded north-east to its other extremity. It may be near two coses long. The country between it and the Tapaban ridge about half-occupied, the Goyalas endeavouring to keep as much waste as possible. My people killed here an antelope, and a wolf descended from the hills at night and alarmed my sheep.

Having passed between Narawut and Tetuya,[3] I passed north-east with the Tetuya ridge on my right, and opposite to Majholighat,[4] the passage between the second and third hill of this ridge, I came to a small hummock called Kariari, which is situated about a mile from the ridge and perhaps 3½ miles from the south end of Narawut ridge. About a mile and a half from Kariyari I crossed a small winding canal called the Liyani, which contains a good deal of stagnant water.

Khori is at present wrought in Khariyari, from whence its name is derived. It is a small round hummock. The rock is a kind of intermixture of imperfect reddle [5] and hornstone or quartz, in some places containing imbedded in it fragments of Khori, and in some places stained yellow. The Khori has been wrought in two places, but to no great extent. One near the bottom of the hill [6] is in a very irregular nest, surrounded by the imperfect reddle more or less

---

(1) **Saren.**
(2) **Natesar.**
(3) **Tetua.**
(4) **Majhauli ghat.**
(5) Appendix, No. 93.
(6) No. 17.

approaching in nature to the Khori. The derivation of the latter from the former is so evident that the natives say that the Khori is the reddle corrupted or putrified (Sor). The mine has been conducted with very little skill. The workmen first dug a narrow gallery into the Khori until stopt by water. They have gradually since been beating pieces from the sides and roof, so that now they must have recourse to ladders to reach it and every piece tumbles to the bottom, from which it is brought up with much trouble. This Khori is harsh, and consists of various layers of different shades of pale red. In the other vein the Khori[1] is white and very harsh and contains bits of quartz unchanged. The vein is very superficial and has as yet been only just opened. Farther in it will probably improve.

From this hummock I went rather less than a mile to another at the village of Majholi. This consists of somewhat similar materials, but in a great state of decay[2] and becoming schistose. It may be considered as an intermediate state between rude Jasper and Khori. None of this substance in a perfect state has been yet discovered here. About a quarter of a mile farther on, is still another small hummock on which Khori[3] was formerly dug, but the vein has been exhausted. The rock in decay is splitting into vertical thin strata running east-north-east and west-south-west or thereby, and the vein has run the whole length of the hill in that direction, and has been wrought about four feet wide and deep. The rock on its southern side shows in my opinion the transition from hornstone to reddle or Khori.[4] On one part are curious minute crystallizations like those near Malipur.[5] That on its northern side is very curious.[6] It seems to be a kind of porphyry, consisting of an argillaceous cement strongly impregnated with iron, containing concretions

(1) Appendix, No. 5.
(2) ,, No. 53.
(3) ,, No. 54.
(4) ,, No. 21.
(5) At Katauna Hill, *see* Bhagalpur Journal, 19th March, 1811.
(6) Appendix, No. 3.

partly silicious and partly changed, and has a strong resemblance to the gangue of the Khori which I saw near Neduyanalah.

From thence I went obliquely to Jornaghat, the passage between the third and fourth hill of the great range. There is no plain between the two hills, which are united by a very steep rugged chain of grey hornstone,[1] in some places stained red. The whole of this range from Narawut seems exactly of the same nature with the southern range of the Rajgriho hills, only the northern face is not quite so parched, and the bamboos and stunted trees extend farther up the rocks. At the foot of the hill is found an unctuous yellow clay, called Pila mati from its colour. Potters use it, but the quantity seems to be inconsiderable. It is quite superficial, and mixed with many fragments of rock, which are separated by throwing the whole into water and collecting the [lighter sediment].[2] Near it is a pit from whence the people have dug some indurated schistose clay, red white and yellow. From thence I went obliquely for about a mile to Saren Nateswor, a village situated at the east end of a more considerable hummock than the three above mentioned.

The second and fourth hill of the great ridge are the most considerable for elevation.

The country at Saren [is] said to have formerly belonged to the Bandawats, who called themselves Rajputs, but many of them still live in Perganah Chay in Ramgarh. They speak Hindi, and eat pure, but perform Sagai. It is said that before the Bandawats the country belonged to the Kol. These are different from the Cheru. The Rajah of Palamo is a Cheru. The Bandawats and Kol entirely banished from this country. There remain many Bhungiyas.

The hummock or hill of Saren, the most considerable of this low range, consists of a variety of rocks, all

(1) Appendix, No. 57.
(2) Left blank in Journal. *See* East India, Vol. I, p. 262.

decaying in vertical masses running east and west. In some parts is a Khori more or less perfect,[1] some of which is dug for teaching children to write. Indurated reddle[2] is still more common, but is very inferior in quality to that brought from Gwalior, which is used by the Sannyasis for dyeing their clothes. The great mass of rock on the north side of the hill, and especially towards a peak at its west end, appears to me evidently a slag[3] containing much iron, partly reddish, partly blackish, and in many parts containing nodules of quartz and khori. On the south side of the hill is what I consider as hornstone impregnated with iron[4] disposed in waved layers of various shades of colour, exactly like some Khoris but very hard. It has nothing of a slaggy appearance.

Saren is a pretty considerable village belonging to Mitrijit, with fine lands towards the north, and in a very picturesque situation.

18*th January*.—I went to Rajagriho,[5] said to be distant six coses, but my guide attempted to take me by a passage between the transverse range and the great hills, which being impracticable after having advanced two miles, I was obliged to return, and then to proceed by Dukrighat almost two miles from where I turned. Dukrighat passes over a corner of a large mass of hills, which may be considered as a continuation or as the principal part of the range of hummocks containing Khori, and it fills up the space between the great quartsoze range of Rajagriho and the granite range of detached peaks that extends east from Patalkati, or rather from Burabur. The granite[6] on the easternmost of these peaks[7] is very perfect and small-grained, white felspar and quartz and black mica. Dakrighat itself consists of an exceeding tough hornstone, of different thin layers

---

(1) Appendix, No. 94.
(2) ,, No. 99.
(3) ,, No. 102.
(4) ,, No. 47.
(5) Radgejir, R.; Rajegur, B.A.; Rajgir.
(6) Appendix, No. 66.
(7) Bathani Hill.

of various shades of grey and of very fine grain.[1] It resembles the stone of the hill of Saren except in not being iron-shot.

From Dakrighat I went rather more than four miles to Singhaul,[2] a village in Nawada. Before entering it I found some broken images on the ground. One differed from that called Vasudeva or Narayon by having two small figures on each side, in place of one. The other seemed to have been the throne of some idol, and containing a Buddh sitting above the head of a male figure, with two arms and standing.

From Singhaul I followed a very grand old road attributed to the infidel Jarasandha, and on that account called the Asuren. It has run in a perfect straight line, and is about 150 feet wide, rising from the sides with a very gentle ascent to the middle, which may have been about 12 feet perpendicular above the level of the plain, which is very low land. The people imagine that it was a reservoir intended to collect the rain water and convey it to Rajagriho, and then this water was to be raised to the flower garden, which the prince chose to have on the top of the hill. That it served for a reservoir I have no doubt, as it does so to this day, and during the whole rainy season the space between it and the hills forms a lake, but in the dry season the water disappears, and the bottom of the lake is cultivated. The object of the work, I have no doubt, was for a road, as it extends over this low plain only for about four miles, and ends about a mile before it reaches Rajagrihi where the land rises, so that it never could have conveyed water to that place. The road was a noble approach to the residence of the prince, and may have extended to (Patana) the royal city, although it can now only be traced where it formed a very elevated bank. Originally perhaps it was not so wide and much higher, as the natural operation of so many rainy seasons would be tc reduce the height and spread the breadth. The wate

(1) Appendix, No. 9.
(2) Singhaul.

collected in the lake has broken down the bank in several places, so that as a road it has become perfectly useless, for the small banks with which the gaps have been filled up to preserve the work as a reservoir will with difficulty admit loaded oxen to pass.

19*th January*.—At Rajagriho are two ancient forts, one occupying the south-west corner of the other is attributed to Sheer Shah, the external one I presume is the Rajahgriho or abode of Jarasandha. I went round this on an elephant in 48 minutes, keeping on the outside of the rampart and inside of the ditch, which may in most places be traced, being lower than the adjacent fields, quite level, and cultivated entirely with winter crops, which are watered. It is however most entire on the south side where, the land sloping down with some declivity from the bottom of the hills, it has been probably deeper. It would appear to have been above 100 feet wide and, so far as I can judge, the original rampart has consisted entirely of the earth thrown out from the ditch, and has contained neither bricks nor stones. Several gaps are formed in the rampart, but whether or not they were originally gates would be difficult to say, the position being quite irregular and some being evidently too large. I can observe no traces of outworks nor flanking defences in this original rampart, which is indeed reduced to a mere mound of earth with some small fragments of stone from the adjacent hills, perhaps originally intermixed with the soil. The present town of Rajahgriho occupying the north-west corner of the fort and the adjacent plain has occasioned considerable deficiencies there, which owing to the narrowness of the lanes I could not trace, but I suspect [that] at that corner which is the lowest, there have been two or three lines of defence, and some irregularities in the contour. The general form is very irregular, extending about 1,200 yards each way.

The fort attributed by tradition to Sheer Shah occupies the south-west corner of the above for about 600 yards square. The west and south faces are evidently continuations of the original rampart, but have been much strengthened. Their surface is everywhere covered with bricks, which perhaps have proceeded from a parapet of that material, but no traces of it remain except these fragments. These however are quite superficial, and the mass of the rampart, above 60 feet wide and 30 high, consists of earth. Where gaps have been formed in the rampart, a new one has been built up entirely of large rude blocks of stone from the adjacent hills. This rampart is about 16 feet wide, and exceedingly broken down. All along the old earthen rampart it would appear that there has been laid a platform of these stones some feet high, which probably served for the foundation of the brick parapet, and this has been strengthened at short distances by semi-circular projections constructed of stone. The eastern and northern faces have had no ditch, and the eastern one has consisted entirely of rude masses of stone, with many semi-circular projections and about 18 feet thick. The eastern half of the northern face has been built in the same manner, but the western end has been constructed of brick.

Both these ramparts, especially that of stone are much more decayed than one would expect from so short a period of time as has elapsed since the reign of Sheer Shah, and although in these ramparts, as well as in the external ones, there are several gaps which may have been gates, there is not the slightest trace of the buildings of a gate to be observed. This I confess staggers me with respect to any part of the building having been erected by Sheer Shah. It may be supposed that the two works are coeval, but besides the gaps filled up with stone I observe that at the north-west and south-east corners of the small fort a wide breach has been made in the earthen rampart to serve as a ditch ; but had the smaller fort been a citadel more strongly fortified than the town, we should have expected that the ditch would have been continued round it. Both areas contain many irregular heaps having very much the appearance of the debris of building, but rising to very little height, either from the lapse of many ages or from removal of the materials. In some parts it would appear that there have been tanks surrounded by these eminences, and these are the only thing resembling ruins that retain any trace of symmetry. The heaps consist chiefly of earth, but contain many small stones and a few broken bricks. I have some doubts whether or not they may not be natural, or formed of earth thrown out from the tanks. By far the largest is in the outer fort, and if it has been a building, as on the whole I think probable, it has been very large. Two conical mounds on its west side can scarce be natural eminences.

The Seruyak here assembled say that the fort was built by Rajah Senok or Srinik, and as being his residence was called Rajahgriho. The same person built Baragong, and was contemporary with Mahavira. He lived long after Jarasandha, who they think lived at Ayudiya. He lived 2,563 years ago. Senok's father and grandfather, Upasenok and Mahasenok, possessed the country. He was Nathbongs. The first family of kings was Akwakbongs, of whom was Rikub Deo of Ayudiya, Sombongs of Hustinapuri. Sriangs was one of these. An account of these families is contained in the Hori Bongs, Padma Puran, Adapura; books belonging to the sect. Jara Sandhu was of the Judobongs and a Jain, as were also Ramà and Krishna and Siva. They know nothing of the Buddhs. They claim the whole images, Siva, Ganese, Surjo, etc., and all the hot springs, which they call by the same names with the Brahmans. They say that their images are known by both hands being joined on their lap, but on the same stone here I find images with their hands in all positions. They know nothing of Hangsapuri. They say that some Seruyaks are Brahmans, some Kshatris, some Vaisiyas, no Sudras admitted, but any man may become a Seruyak. No one can be made a Jetti or Guru except of the three pure castes, and any man of pure birth, whether his ancestors were Jain or not, may become a Jetti. All the 84 castes are Vaisiyas. But in the south there are Brahmans, and in the west many Kshatris. They pray to all the gods of the Brahmans.

The Brahmans of Rajagriho say that the road attributed to Jarasandha was made by some infidel, they know not whom. Rajahgriho belonged first to a Rajah called Chatorboj, and then Raja Bosu, who brought 14 gotras of Brahmans from Maharastra to worship the gods of the hills. He gave them the whole Parganah, which was taken from them by the Muhi. They say that Jarasandha lived at Geriyak. They say that Raja Senik was Raja of Hansupurnagar, in the plain between the five hills. The only remains are a math called Moninag, and another called Nimulpuri, where the Serawak worship, but there are no tanks nor appearance of a fort or city. Bosu lived after Srinik, and Srinik after Jarasandha. The last was a Kshatri of the Asurimath, and derived his power from the worship of Jora Devi. The Ron Bhumi, where he was killed, is in the plain between the five hills, a little west from Sonbondar. He was burned on the field, which has made the earth red. The Brahmans give the same names to the five hills that the Jain do, but do not consider them as holy. Many images on all the hills, but most on the two northern. On that to the west of the gap above Brihmakund is shown a stone building, said to have been the place where Jarasandha was wont to sit after bathing. The old road very generally attributed to Jarasandha leading directly to the fort gives great room to suppose that the fort was the real abode of that prince, or rather perhaps the garrison to secure his various abodes in the vicinity. The whole space between the fort and hill is very irregular, and many eminences may be traced resembling the foundations of buildings. In one or two, indeed, fragments of the foundation of large stones may be traced, but there are very few bricks. I suspect that a great part of all the buildings have been of stone, and that those of the more modern fort have been taken from the ruins. From the north face of the fort to the gap in the hills are traces of a double rampart with a road between.

Having visited the fort, I went to visit the curiosities towards the roots of the hills. Immediately west of the fort is a circular mound, containing a small cavity surrounded by a rampart of earth, on which are some broken bricks. The Brahmans say that this was a math or abode built by a Dosnami named Gytanand; but this is quite absurd. A house could never have left such a ruin. He may have indeed dwelt upon it, and some small temples of Siva in the vicinity support this opinion. The rampart entirely resembles that of the fort, and this may have been some outwork, there being only the ditch between the two ramparts. A small river which comes from the gap between the hills passes through the old ditch.

A little up its bank from this circular work, on the west side, is a small ghat of brick recently made at a place called Baiturni, which is holy. Here are lying a Ganesa, three fragments of the image usually called Vasudeva, and a stone—apparently the throne of an image—which contains rows of sitting images, some with their hands lifted up, some with both in their lap holding an offering, and some with one of their hands over their knee. This shows that nothing from the position of the hands can be determined concerning the sect to which the images belonged. The Serewak indeed said that those images with both hands in the lap represented Gods and the other men, but the position of the various figures does not favour this opinion.

Some way up this torrent, at a place called Soriswati in the passage between the two northern hills of the great range, is a new ghat on each side of the torrent. Here is a very dirty pool in the torrent, which is considered holy both by Jain and Astik. Immediately above this ghat, on the lower part of the hill to the west of the river, is a collection of various springs and buildings, none of them old and some of them quite recent. The most celebrated is Brahmakund, a square cistern very deep and built partly of stone, partly of bricks. The water is collected in a pool at the bottom, and the thermometer in this stood at 109°, being at 62° in the air when shaded[1]. An image of Ganesa is built into the wall. Below Brahmakund towards the east is a terrace for the accommodation of religious mendicants at the Mela, on its south end is a small temple of Varaha with two Naginis somewhat different from those at Baragang. Below the terrace is a square reservoir of brick, containing five sacred springs [2] which issue from an equal number of spouts made of stone, and the water as it falls is allowed to run off so that it is perfectly clean, limpid, and tasteless. Where collected in kunds in which the people bathe, it is abominable. The first spring named Panchanon has stopped. In the second, named Kasi, the thermometer stood at 107°. In the third, called by some Panchanod but by others Langai because the Jain women wash there naked, the thermometer is 104°, in the fourth, called Panchanod, the thermometer [is] 94°. The fifth, called Gaumukhi, has stopped. In the reservoir is lying an image of Surjo.

Immediately south from Brahmakund and west from the temple of Varaha is a small temple of Siva, and extending the whole length of this temple and of Brahmakund, on their west side, is a long narrow reservoir built of brick, containing seven holy springs which issue from stone spouts, and the water is allowed to run off as it issues, except that as usual part is allowed to collect in puddles filled with frogs and other vermin and overwhelmed with weeds and rubbish. The first spring in this reservoir is named Gautam, and its heat is 104°. The second named Baraduyar is of the same heat. Viswamitra, the third, raised the thermometer to 110°. Jumdagani, the fourth, raised it to

(1) Mean temperature of the hottest place in Brahmakund, as measured on twenty-eight occasions since 1909, 107·3°. Maximum 108·3° in September, 1914.

(2) There is no independent spring in this Kund, which is used exclusively by women. The outflow which Buchanan called Panchanon has disappeared, the others are merely overflows from tanks higher up.

102°. Durbasa, Vasishta and Parasari, the fifth, sixth and seventh of these springs, have become dry.[1] In the wall of this place has been built an image of a Buddh or Jain, with both hands in the lap. It has lotus flowers on the soles of the feet, and lions on the throne. It has a short inscription. In the cistern is lying a male figure somewhat like that usually called Vasudeva, but somewhat different. Notwithstanding its sex the Brahmans call it Devi or the Goddess.

Immediately west or above this reservoir and two small temples (Maths) of Siva, and south from them, [is] a reservoir containing a spout of stone which emits the the finest stream in the place[2]. It is 110° hot, and perfectly limpid and tasteless, but not near so copious as the fine springs of the Mongger hills. In the reservoir are lying two carved stones, one a Ganes. The other, such an octagonal ornament as is so common at Buddh Gya, and containing four images of Buddhs.

Immediately south from thence is another spring, nearly as fine, and named Markunda[3]. In the reservoir are lying some images. A Gauri Sankar. A male and female standing, both called Devi. Two such as are usually called Vasudeva, with large ears as usual. In one side of the reservoir is a dark hovel called a temple of Kamaksha, but it contains no image. All these images except such as are objects of worship are said to have been brought from the hill above, and the same has probably been the case with those which are worshipped,

(1) In the Saptrishi tank, the third to seventh outflows, as well as that in the Anantrishi Kund to the north-west, which Buchanan did not notice, are all connected with a common underground source, above the Veda Vyasa tank, which in turn is connected with the same source. The third outflow is closest to the source, and is therefore the hottest, though usually more than a degree cooler than the source itself. Its mean temperature since 1909, 104·6°. Maximum 107·4° in October 1914; minimum 96·3° in April, 1909, when, with the exception of Brahmakund, the whole of the springs were practically dry.

(2) The Veda Vyasa Kund, called Vyas by Buchanan in his drawing and in the Report. Mean temperature since 1909, 105·3°; maximum 107·0° in April, 1912.

(3) Fed from the same source as the Veda Vyasa, but the subterranean channel from the real source is longer, and the outflow is slightly cooler on this account.

as they are in the same style and all resemble those at Buddh Gya and Baragang. The whole water from all these springs unites at the bottom of the hill, and forms a stream rather larger than that of Sitakund[1].

Advancing a little farther up the river on the same side with Brahmakund is a fine little spring of clear water issuing from a small square cistern cut in the rock. It is called Vanur Vanuri, from a monkey and his wife having been immediately translated to heaven from bathing in it. A little farther up, the rivulet divides into two branches, and in the fork is a small conical mound of earth and stones. On it is a small modern temple, but the traces of one more ancient and somewhat larger are observable. The size of the mound could never have admitted a large one. The image is broken and is carved on a small stone. It represents one of the most hideous forms of the destructive power that I have seen, with three heads and eight hands, dressed in armour and holding in its hands two serpents, various implements of destruction, and a human head. It seems to me clearly a male, and is probably the same deity with the chief figure in the caves of Elephanta, although that represents only the head and shoulders and this represents the whole body. By the attendant Brahmans it is considered as a female, and called Jaradevi, and to its worship it is supposed that Jarasandha owed all his power.

Beyond this is a considerable plain surrounded by five hills held sacred by the Jain, but neglected by the Brahmans. This plain with the adjacent hills is called

(1) Buchanan did not notice the Ganga-Jamuna tank west of the Anantrishi, which is the third independent outflow. Mean temperature since 1909, 106·6°; maximum 107·8° in March, 1911. Being at the highest level, it is often dry. In the Report, he says :—"I suspect that those near Brahmakunda have, in a state of nature, been one spring; which has been subdivided and conveyed by various channels, so as to supply the various pools and spouts from which it now issues; and in this manner I account for the different degrees of heat observable, and for several of the spouts that formerly flowed being now dry." This observation is correct. The whole of the area occupied by the springs and temples has been built up artificially against the side of the hill. No substantial changes have been made during the last century, and the general agreement with Hiuen Tsang's account suggests that the subdivision of the springs dates from a very early period.

Hangsapurnagar, and is supposed to have been the situation of a city, but of this I see no traces; some zigzag structures of stone both here and at Giriyak were pointed out to me as walls of the old city, but I have not the smallest doubt that they have been roads, and it is probable that there has been a route communicating by the hills with Giriyak, as the zigzags of Rajagriho ascend the west end of the same hill on the east end of which those of Giriak are. It consists of five bends, in all 1,200 cubits long, with a roundish resting place at each turn, and is four cubits wide. The people I sent to measure it could trace it no farther, but they might lose it by a very short interruption, as the hill is covered in many places with thick reeds.[1] They saw no images nor traces of buildings.

A road leads through the hills, towards the south as well as to the north, and there is a narrow passage towards the valley between the two ridges. On all other sides are rugged hills. The situation is exceedingly strong and in that respect well fitted for a city, and the extent is considerable, three coses by one, but would no doubt be exceedingly unhealthy. The situation however is very grand, and well adapted for occasional visits or for inspiring religious awe, and accordingly the three great Hindu sects have all chosen it as a favourite residence and claim it as their own. The Buddhists of Ava came to it, directed by their books, and considered Rajagriho as the residence of Jarasandha, one of the most religious princes of their sect.

In the south side of the hill by which the central plain is bounded on the north and west, has been dug a cave called Sonbundar. The door is small, but there is also a window, which occasions a circulation of air and gives a light unknown in the dismal caves of Burabur. The materials here however are vastly inferior, as the rock is everywhere intersected by fissures, so that some parts have fallen down, and it admits

(1) This zigzag road leads to a flat-topped stone *garh* on the top of Ratnagiri, not far west of the Jain temple.

water which has stained the walls with a red ferruginous crust. The stone is an imperfect Khori[1], variegated, red and grey in veins, layers, and blotches, and is evidently the rude jasper of the hills, similarly marked, passing into an indurated clay. This cave is called Sonbundar, and is an object of worship with the Jain. In its middle is left a small kind of quadrangular pyramidical figure, on each side of which is carved an erect man with two arms. The chief figure is the same on all the four sides, but on each he is accompanied by different emblems. On the wall is a short inscription in a strange character. It probably merely contains the name of some pilgrim.

On the east side of the rivulet also there are sundry places of worship common to all sects. At the west end of the northern hill is a cluster of springs and small temples, similar to those opposite, and surrounding Surjokundo.[2] This is a small reservoir in which the water is collected in a pool, and does not fall from a spout, so that it is beastly dirty and swarms with frogs. Its heat is 103°. An image of Surja somewhat different from that at Kasi Tirtha is built into the wall, and near it a fat male figure with two arms, and one leg hanging over the throne. It is surrounded by an inscription. This figure is in several other places intermixed with Buddhs, and seems to me to represent the cook of Gautama that I have seen in Ava. Before the feet of Surja has been placed [a] small figure of Buddh. In a small math of Siva southwest from this kund is an image of Buddh, and on the outside [are] two throne-like stones such as I saw at the west end of the great Asuren road. Each has a sitting figure of a Buddh over a standing figure, but in the two the position of the hands is reversed. Here a wretched Sannyasi has taken up his abode. He sits all day besmeared with ashes in the position of a Buddh

(1) Appendix, No. 56.

(2) Surajkund. Usually in the cold weather the level of the water in these tanks is kept above that of the spouts which lead the water into them. Mean temperature of the inflow since 1909, 104·8°, maximum 107·0° in April, 1910.

He neither moves nor speaks, and those who choose bestow alms on him. If he gets none he fasts It was alleged that some thieves had stolen his blanket, but I suspect that this was a mere allegation to endeavour to extract a rupee from me; no thief in all probability would steal from so wretched an animal, especially as viewed as being of the utmost purity and enjoying divine favour.

West from that is a small ruined math, with a stone containing two feet, and a short inscription in relief, which is not common. The Brahmans call it the feet of Dototreya, one of the 24 Avatars of Vishnu, but from the inscription it evidently belongs to the Jain, as it commences with the charactor called Balaminda, which the Jain prefix as the Astik do the name of Ganesa.

South from Surjakund are two temples of Siva with one of Tulasi between them. One of them is called Halokeswar. Here are several old images. A pedestal like those already mentioned, containing a Buddh sitting above a man standing. A Gauri Sangkor. A Vasudeva. Two Sahusera Lingas, which implies 1,000 Lingas. A Lion rampant, which is an ornament of Gautama. South from thence is Santonkund,[1] a pool similar to Surjakundo. Its heat [is] 106°. North from Surjakundo is that of Som or the moon[2]. Its heat [is] 102°. Near it is lying an ornament similar to those of Buddh Gya, with four Buddhs on the four sides. Ganesakundo north from thence[3]. The heat also is 102°

(1) The position of Santonkund in this account corresponds to that of the present Sitakund, but in Buchanan's rough plan it is shown as east and slightly north of Surajkund, thus occupying a site where in 1917 I found that the earth had fallen in, exposing channels leading from the hillside further east, and diverging to the present Sitakund, Surajkund and Chandramakund. Mean temperature of Sitakund inflow, 104·7°. Maximum 106·0° in May, 1912.

(2) Chandrama or Somkund. Mean temperature of inflow 104·7°. Maximum 106·0° in May, 1912.

(3) Ganeshkund. Mean temperature of inflow, 104·0°. Maximum, 106·0° in May, 1911. At the steps leading into this tank, as well as those of Sitakund and Chandramakund, the temperature since 1909 is between 97° and 99°, and has never reached 100°.

Proceeding[1] from Surjokundo some way east, along the northern face of the hill, I came to the Dorga of Surufuddin Behari, built where that great saint passed much time in prayer. The buildings although destitute of architectural merit are neat and clean, and the area includes a hot spring formed into a pool, called Singriki kundo.[2] The Hindus are still permitted to bath in the place, and have a small temple of Siva in the side of the pool. The heat of the pool is only 97.°[3] During the Ramazan from eight to twelve hundred of the faithful assemble, and are entertained by the successor of the saint.

*20th January.*—I visited the Baitaki, or seat of Jarasandha, which is a considerable way up the hill above Brahmakundo. No road has been made to the place, which is a platform built against the sloping side of the hill, of large rude blocks of jasper from the adjacent rock. Its upper surface is 79½ feet by 72¾, and its perpendicular height at the highest corner is 27¾ feet. There is nothing about it to indicate its real era, except that the stones having been altered by the action of the air for about an inch have probably been quarried at a very remote period. It is very possible that when Jarasandha from policy or awe bathed in these sacred pools he may have sat on such a place, and may there have received presents from his courtiers as is usual on such occasions. A few stones have fallen from one corner, but if not disturbed it may remain to the day of judgment. Even now, near the kunds and a considerable way above them, various religious mendicants have erected small Baitoks or platforms of brick, on which they sit during the months that pilgrims frequent the place, and raise

(1) The Ram-Lakshman tank was not in existence in Buchanan's time, but was made about fifty years ago. The tepid water in the spout called Lakshman comes in a long channel from a point on the hillside about half-way to the Makhdum Kund.

(2) The Makhdum or Sringgi Rikhi Kund flows into a cistern from a long channel leading from the hillside. It is distinctly cooler than the other springs, mean temperature since 1909, being 95·1° and maximum 96·4° in March, 1911; and unlike the others it appears to be coolest during the rainy season, probably from admixture of water from cold springs during this season.

voluntary contributions. If Jarasandha ever sat on the place the contributions were probably somewhat more than voluntary. A Moslem saint has been buried on the platform, and his tomb has gone to decay. He seems to have been too petty to have procured such a platform to have been built on purpose for him. One would have supposed that Jarasandha might have had a road cut for him to ascend this seat, but perhaps the difficulty of access was a necessary part of the ceremony. The rock consists of rude reddish jasper with white vein.[1]

I also ascended the opposite hill to visit a mine of rock crystal, Futik, situated a considerable way up. The lower part of the hill consists of a grey very small-grained hornstone [2] or petrosilex with veins of white quartz. [3] Further up it becomes more granular, is in some places stained red, and in others contains rounded concretions of quartz, and the surfaces of fissures and little cavities are covered with minute crystals. The rock among which the crystal is found [4] has been reduced to a kind of sandstone, but is surrounded on all sides by the petrosilex, and is disposed in trapezoidal masses in a similar manner. Some of these blocks are white, some ferruginous inclining to red. It must be observed that all the upper part of the next hill, situated south from this and named Rutenachul, consists of a similar sandstone [5] while the lower part is a red and white rude jasper. [6] Among these blocks the workmen have found interstices from two to four feet in diameter, and winding in various directions. These are filled with small angular fragments of quartz, generally semidiaphanous, but stained red externally and intermixed with a red ferruginous harsh earth. Among this are found small masses of the Futik or rock, crystal generally in imperfect hexagonal prisms terminating

(1) Appendix, No. 12.
(2) ,, No. 35.
(3) ,, No. 72.
(4) ,, Nos. 15, 29.
(5) ,, No. 49.
(6) ,, No. 12.

in hexagonal pyramids.[1] All that I could find were very small, irregular, and of a bad quality, nor do the workmen procure any larger than can be made into beads, and these seldom clear. The beads have generally a good deal of a smokiness in their colour. I saw none of the crystals adhering to the matrix. They were all detached and in distinct crystals. There was another mine of crystal lower down the hill, near a small temple of Ganesa, but for some years since the one I visited has been discovered the workmen have deserted this old one. In the new one ten or twelve excavations have been made, but to no great extent. None of them seem to have contained above five or six cartloads of gravel. The workmen say that they follow the veins sometimes 20 or 30 feet, and that they wind very much among the stones. They bring out the gravel for day's hire, and the Hukak or bead-makers pick out the pieces. Two crystals are never found cohering, nor do they ever adhere to the rock. At Chukra, [2] north from Sophi ghat, is also found rock crystal, but my informants do not know the particulars.

It is remarkable that the Jain know nothing of Hangsapur Nagar, while the Astik here pretend that it was the residence of Srinik Raja, chief of the Jain. The Ghatwal (who) is a Rajewar and holds his office hereditary. He was a custom master and levied a tax on all passengers going by that passage. *He now collects some duties on bamboos, etc. for the zemindar and receives a share of the profits of the Brahmans. He is quite impure and eats everything but says that his ancestors.* [3] Now the descendants of his ancestors and of a certain Bojok Brahman divide in equal shares all the offerings that the Jain make, and take care of the temples. He conducted one of my people to what he calls Hangsapur Nagar and the former residence of Srinik Raja. It is situated in the middle of the plain at the west end of Rutinagiri. Here is like the ruin

(1) Appendix, No. 84.
(2) Chakra ghat.
(3) Portions in italics subsequently crossed cut.

of a house about 80 feet by 60, part of the walls, built of rough stone and clay, standing four or five feet high. This is called the fort of Senek Raja. Near it is a small temple of the Jain with an inscription. It is built above a well lined with brick (Indera), which has been filled up. It is supposed that Srinik had 32 wives, to each of whom he daily gave new jewels and threw the old ones into the well. These were afterwards carried away by a lucky rogue of a Moslem. There is nothing like the remains of a town round, *but the people*—On the west end of Rutinagiri is a zigzag ascent built of stone, which the Ghatwal attributes to the Daityos, and does not lead to any of the places considered holy by the Jain.

*The Jain call the 5—The Rajagiri Mahaton mentions the 5 hills on which the Jain have most of their temples.*—The Astik have no places of worship on the five hills, nor do the pilgrims visit the hills. The Jain on the contrary put little or no value on the Tirthas of the Astik, and bathe in them merely for cleanliness or comfort. This seems to me doubtful. It was asserted by the Rajagriho Brahmans, but they are miserably ignorant and mere importunate beggars. Not one of them, I am told, understands Sanskrit, although they have the ceremonies by rote. Although many of them could repeat the verses of the Rajagriho Mahato containing the names of the hills, I found that no two of them agreed about the application of these names even to the two hills between which their holy springs are situated, and between which most of them pass their time. There are about 100 families, one half of which have become Bojoks and take the profits of the hills. The others take the profit of the wells, a great part of which arises from the offerings of the Jain. Both continue to intermarry and to take upadesa from the Ramanandis.

Vaykunt, who went up to copy the inscriptions on the two nearer hills, says that on the western one he saw no broken images nor any but those in the new temples of the Jain, which are five. Four contain Padukas, at three of which is writing. At two some images have been built into the wall. One is the Dos Avatars with an inscription. At another, eight females sitting on different animals, oxen, elephants, swine, peacocks and geese. This figure at Gaya was called Naugraha, and has an inscription. The other temple which I saw contains a Jain standing with the palms of his hands turned forward. It has an inscription.

On the western hill are about twenty temples still standing. Two are large. In the largest is a Paduka and inscription. The other is not quite finished. In the small ones, which are very old, broken, and covered with grass, some have images with hands in various positions, some are empty. They are not frequented by the Jain. They contain no inscriptions. Besides these he found many heaps of brick, formerly small temples but quite destroyed, with many pillars of granite such as at Giriak but larger, and parts of doors, partly standing partly scattered about. Many images such as those below were also scattered about. On only one did he find an inscription. It was a sitting Buddh.

*21st January*—I went rather more than five[1] miles called three coses to Baragang, passing through a very large close-built village named Silau[2] rather more than half a mile north[3] from the village of Rajagriho. It contains a few houses of brick and many that are tiled. Rajagriho is still a pretty considerable village, but has decayed much of late, having been deserted by a colony of Muhammadans of rank who have left behind them the ruins of good brick houses. The Jain have erected in it a temple and place of accommodation for pilgrims of rank. No resident Jain at the place.

On my arrival at Baragang I took another view of the ruins. The part of the ruins north of Surjo tank

(1) Rather more than eight miles.
(2) Silao.
(3) Rather more than three and a half miles, the only considerable mistake noticed in Buchanan's record of distances.

would appear to be of a more ancient date than that to the south. The heaps have been reduced to mere masses of rubbish, in which no symmetry of parts can be observed, and the number of bricks except at the four small heaps is inconsiderable. The swelling ground may indeed have merely arisen from its having long been the situation of a mud-walled village, as all such soon rise into eminences, the clay of old walls constantly raising the ground, while fresh clay is always brought to build new walls or repair old ones. The four small heaps, evidently temples, may have been the only buildings of brick.

Near the Baitok Bhairab as it is called is a stone containing an assembly of Buddhs such as I found at Rajagriho. A little south-west from the Jain temple is standing a very large figure of the three-headed Sakti. The Pandit calls it a female Varahun. I think it more probable that it represents the Jara Devi.

In the evening I went about two miles south by the way I had come, to see a large image said to be in that direction. I found it on the summit of a small mound of bricks called Yogespur,[1] which is situated on the west side of a small choked tank, on the east side of which also there is a small mound of brick, but that contains no images. On Yogespur are several, but the eye is immediately attracted by that of a great Buddh seated with one hand over his knee, under a Nim tree. On the stone round him he has many figures like that near the temple of Surjo in the streets of Baragang, but more numerous. It has a short inscription. This image is the object of worship, and two Brahmāns act as its Pujaris. They called it Jagadamba, that is the Goddess, for they totally disregard sex. Near it is half-immersed into the bricks a similar and less ornamented Buddh. Here are also two small Buddhs with uplifted hands, one has an inscription. Also a male standing with two arms, one leaning on a horizontal projection of the stone. I have seen the same at Rajagriho. Also two

---

(1) Jagdispur.

males sitting with one leg over the throne, one having a short inscription. Three Sesanags, very curious figures. They represent two many-headed Naga in copulation, each having a human figure under the hoods, and these figures terminate in the tails of serpents. The female embracing the male with her arms.

*22nd January.*—I went about 9½ miles to Sewan. The villages as usual close-built, and placed on considerable elevations evidently formed from the decayed mud walls of former buildings. The ridges here straight. Little or no garden. Some old mud castles, very rude but still occupied. Just before coming to Sewan I crossed the Mohane, here a channel of about 20 yards wide, with only a little stagnant water and deep clay banks. This was immediately below a dam by which the stream is turned out on the fields. The dam is of mud, and of course is renewed each season.

*23rd January.*—I went about nine miles to Hilsa,[2] by an exceeding bad path from one bank to another. About four miles from Sewan crossed the Nuni[3] (Nanaiwanj), a small sandy channel now quite dry. About 1½ miles farther on, at a village called Akbarpur,[4] I found a conical mound of bricks, on its top had been a small temple about six feet square within, but the walls had fallen, the threshold of stone and foundation entire. The image in its place occupied the whole side opposite to the door, and is such as I have seen nowhere else. It is a male standing with two arms, but has lost the head and both arms. It has long robes and boots. Above it are two Hangsas, beneath, six horses rearing. On each side are two small figures

(1) Suan, R. and B.A. Not shown in the new standard maps, though it was a stage on the old road between Calcutta and Patna through Gidhaur and Deogarh, and the site of the decisive battle on January 15th, 1761, when Law and his French force, who were assisting the Shahzada, surrendered to the British. Probably at **Bichloganj**, on the west bank of the Mohane, and about a mile west of **Paindapur** (Pondipour, R.).

(2) Hilsah, R. and B.A.; **Hilsa.**

(3) **Nanai N.**

(4) Acbarpour, R.; **Akbarpur.**

standing. On the right hand a male spirit with a bow, on the left a female. Against the side walls are resting several images which have been intended as ornaments. Two are Gauri Sangkor, as usual. One, a male sitting with one leg hanging over the throne, but with a slender waist. The others are so much defaced that they could not be defined, but I have not seen them anywhere else. Two Siva Lingas. The people say that it is a temple of the sun, and was built by a Bungiya Brahman whose descendants still have land in Perganah Pilich, from whence a tribe of that caste has its name.

*28th January.*—I went between eight and nine miles to Ongari.[1] The whole path pretty tolerable, and so far as I continued on the route from Hilsa to Sahebgunj there was a road practicable for a cart. About seven miles from Hilsa I came to Ekangur Dihi,[2] a pretty considerable village, near which is a heap extending about 400 yards north and south and 150 east and west. It has lost all symmetry and is [of] no great height, but contains many small fragments of brick. All entire ones seem to have been long ago removed. On it have been in late times erected two small mud castles, both entirely ruinous, and a Moslem saint has been buried on the place with some care, as the tomb is surrounded by a wall of brick. Under a tree are placed five or six images, two of which are objects of worship and pretty entire, the others are so much defaced that it would be difficult to say what they are meant to represent. Both the entire ones have inscriptions. The largest represents a female standing with two arms, supported on each side by a dwarf, and having a Buddh over each shoulder. She resembles exactly, except two small figures of worshippers under the throne, one of the figures at Kopteswori in Baragung. The other is a Buddh, sitting in the usual posture with a hand over the right knee. The people of the village attribute the whole to a Kuhi Chaudhuri of the Kurmi caste who was

---

(1) Aungari.

(2) Cangarh, R.; Ekangar Dih.

proprietor of all the neighbouring country, but the best informed persons both at Hilsa and Ongari say that Ruhi Chaudhuri was a mere zemindar of a very late period, and that the ruin was once the abode of Karna, a great King.

At Ongari is a good tank, (of) about 150 yards square and free from weeds. For a long period it seems to have been a place of worship, and is said to derive its name from one of the appellations of the sun. There are however no traces of any large building, but many images are found in the place ; and the temple of the sun seems to be old, although still in good repair. The door now faces the west, but formerly was in the contrary direction : for once on a time when the heretics were powerful they came determined to destroy it, but as they were about to enter, the door turned round, by which they were alarmed and desisted. There are in this temple two images that are worshipped. One called Surjo is of the form usual at Buddh Gya, etc. The other is called Vishnu, and entirely resembles those called Vasudeva at Giriak, etc. Before the door are lying many fragments, very much mutilated. Most of them would appear to have been portions of Vasudeva. One has been a Gauri Sankar. On the west side of the tank opposite to Surja (the temple ) is a clay hut called the abode of the serpent (Nagasthan). Here are several images, three pretty entire, namely, Gauri Sankar, Ganesa, and a Buddh sitting in the usual posture. A little farther west is another temple of clay, dedicated to Jagadamba. In the wall have been built several images. That of Jagadamba entirely resembles those of Keyadol, etc. Two Vasudevas. One of a slender man with two arms, sitting-with one leg over the throne, and called Saraswati. A small three-headed female standing, with eight arms as at Buragang. A man sitting, with a female on each knee. A bull, but no lion, beneath. It is called Gauri Sankar, but in there being two females, and in wanting the bull, it is entirely different nor have I seen it anywhere else.

Under a tree near the temple of Surja have been placed several images. Devi with four hands, sitting as usual on a lion. A Vasudeva. An eight-armed three-headed figure in armour exactly like the Jaradevi of Rajagriho. It seems to me a male, but the Pandit alleges that it is an old woman. It is called Kalli by the people of the village. A Surja. A female standing with four arms, with a small Ganesa sitting at her feet. All these images are attributed to Karna.

*29th January.*—I went almost eleven miles to Hulasgunj.[1] About five miles from Ongari I crossed the Mohane, a sandy channel about 100 yards wide only. It has at present no stream, but gives a supply for irrigation by digging a little way. Its banks, like those of the Fulgo, rise in many parts into barren sandy downs. Before reaching the river I passed some land on which soda effloresced, part was waste, but where the soda had effloresced in greatest quantity had this year produced rice. On crossing the Mohane I passed through Islampur,[2] a large village with a few brick houses, one of them pretty large. I here joined the great road from Patna to Gaya, which at this season is practicable for a cart with much difficulty, and that is as much as can be said in its favour.

*30th January.*—I went rather more than two miles to a village named Daphtu,[3] in order to see an old temple of Surja. About two-thirds of the way I came to the Jilawar,[4] a dry channel about 100 yards wide, but containing water under the sand. I went down its channel some way, but did not cross. The place is a little to the north of its left bank. There is a considerable elevation, consisting of clay with fragments of bricks intermixed, but the fragments would appear to have proceeded from the ruins of five small temples that have stood on the place. At the north end of the elevation is an old mud fort, built by the Rani of

---

(1) Olassgunge, R. and B.A.; **Hunathganj.**

(2) Islampour, R. and B.A.; **Islampur.**

(3) **Dabthu.**

(4) **Jalwar N.**

a Donawar Brahman who possessed the country before the present Dumkotars. The people have no tradition concerning the persons by whom the religious buildings were erected. The Pujari, a Sakaldwipi Brahman, says they belonging to the Tritaiya Yug. I shall follow his nomenclature, although it is liable to much doubt. Immediately south from the mud fort is a tree with several large stones of granite, said to have been a Pir's Dorga, but it has gone entirely to ruin. A little north-east from thence has been the largest temple of the place, but it has been entirely ruined. It is called Parswanath, but it seems rather to have belonged to the Jain, for on a very fine lintel there is at each end a lion rampant. On its middle is a female figure sitting in the usual posture of the Buddhs. A large stone is said to contain an image reversed.[1] One of the sides of the door also remains. The other seems to have been taken to form the lintel for the temple of Kanaiya when that was repaired. An image, said to have been taken from this temple, has been erected in a garden south from all the temples. It is called Jagadamba or the Goddess, but is quite different from those so called at Keya Dol, etc. It represents a female standing, with four arms. The two foremost leaning on two projecting cylinders. On each side is a lion rampant and a small human figure. An image exactly similar, but male, has been placed under a tree between this garden and Parswanath, but it has lost the head. I have seen similar at Buddhgya. It is called Kanaiya, but is different from the others so called. Near it is a male figure, also without a head. It has many arms, is in a dancing posture, and is called Puspotinath. One foot on a bull. An armed male without entrails on one side. A female standing on a lion on the other. Two musicians, one on cymbals (Kurtal). Under the same tree is a Siva Linga with four human faces, two male, two female, on its sides, and the Joni terminating

(1) "I sent people to raise and draw it, and it entirely resembles that usually called Vasudeva or Lakshminarayan, except that on each side it has the lion rampant, an emblem of the Buddhas. The people, on seeing it, called it Kanaiya." (M.S. Report).

in a crocodile's mouth. Immediately north from the garden containing the female figure has been a temple, but it is entirely destroyed. The image however seems to remain, but has been removed from its throne. It is called Kanaiya, that is, Krishna, but seems to be exactly the same with what in other places is called Vasudeva or Lakshmi Narayon. Immediately north from thence is the most entire temple, that of Surjo. It consists of a flat-roofed Nat mundir or propyleum, and of a pyramidical shrine or Mundir. The roof consists of long stones supported by stone beams, and these by pillars. The interstices between the outer rows are built of brick, and the shrine is constructed entirely of that material, except the door which is stone and much ornamented. Both this door and the stonework of the outer temple seem to be of much greater antiquity than the brickwork, which has probably been renewed several times, but there is no appearance of the image or the plan of the building having undergone any alteration. The image represents Surjo in the manner common at Buddh Gya, etc. On one side of it is placed the usual figure of Vasudeva, which the Pujari calls Lakshmi Narayon. In the outer temple are placed many images, pretty entire, and leaning against the wall without order. They seem to have been taken from the other temples that have fallen. They stood as follows— A small Surjo. The usual Jagadamba with buffalo, etc. Gauri Sangkar, as usual. Ganesa, dancing. Gauri Sangkar, again as usual. Lakshmi Narayon, that is, a male figure standing with four arms, and differing from the common Vasudeva by having two small figures on each side in place of one. A Surjo, with boots. Vishnu, a male figure like Vasudeva but in armour, especially his legs. Gauri Sangkar, but it is a male, sitting with a female on each side. No bull nor lion, but the male has his foot on a crocodile. Another Gauri Sangkar like the last. Narasingha. A male called Trivikram Avatar. A female sitting on a bull, with two arms and a porcine face, called Varahani. The outer door, very mean, of brick. On one side is an image representing a prince hunting. It is called Bairub, and the animal on which the prince rides is called a sheep, but it was probably intended for a horse. A little north from this temple has been another totally ruined. It has contained a very large linga, before which is what the Pujari calls Gauri Sangkar, but it is the male with two females. Immediately north from this is the temple of Kanaia, which consists only one chamber, supported by pillars of the same structure as that of Surja. The brickwork had fallen, but was repaired by the grandfather of Mittrjit, and has again gone much to decay. The door is of stone and much ornamented. The sides remain, but the lintel having been broken the side of a door from Parswanath has been put in its place. The broken lintel lying by the door. The image seems to me exactly similar to Vasudeva, and is of very considerable size.

*31st January.*—I went to a low ridge of hills in order to see the place from whence Mr. Law took his porcelain earth. About a mile from Holasgunj I came to the banks of the Jilawar, and proceeded about a mile along its west side. I then crossed, and proceeded up its bank about two miles farther. From thence to the north-east corner of the ridge of hills is about $1\frac{2}{3}$ miles. The ridge consists of three hills, Dhermpur,[1] Nuzera,[2] and Sophneri,[3] so called after three villages, and extends about three-fourths of a cose north-east and south-west, so as to hide Keni and Lodi. The mine is on the north face of Dhermpur, a little way up the hill. The stone on the ascent has a hornstone fracture, and seems to consist of grey hornstone containing disseminated in it grey felspar or shorl, with little clusters of black points.[4] The upper part of the hill consists of a stone similar, but the proportions reversed. The little black points form the greatest proportion, and the grey hornstone the least.[5] What is called the clay from which

---

(1) **Dharampur.**
(2) **Nadira.**
(3) **Supneri.**
(4) Appendix, No. 91.
(5) ,, No. 104.

Mr. Law made the porcelain is marl, and forms a very large bed or nest, but its extent has by no means [been] ascertained. The excavation however is considerable. This [1] exactly resembles the other marl which he is said to have used, and which I have described on the 23rd November. The nodules which it contains [2] are exactly similar, and are the same with the rock below the marl. In some parts, however, the marl is bounded by a rotten rock of a greenish colour, which seems to be the aggregate in an intermediate state of change into marl, and is a kind of steatite. [3]

These hills, although they consist almost entirely of stones and rocks, with a little mould in the crevices, are not near so rugged as those of granite, the masses being small and the interstices filled with earth. Nor do they form the abrupt precipices of quartzose hills. They have not the smallest appearance of stratification. Lumps of iron ore [4] are scattered about the bottom of the hill.

A little north-east from the corner of Dhermpur is a small rugged hummock of very perfect granite, consisting of middle-sized grains of white felspar and quartz with a good deal of black micaceous matter.[5]

*2nd February.*—I went about two miles north-east to a village named Lath [6] (pillar) to see a pillar which has communicated its name to the place. It is a very fine piece of granite, the pedestal, shaft, and capital constituting one piece, 53¼ feet long. The capital is 86 inches long and 36 in diameter, and the base 70 inches in length and 40 in diameter, [both] are quadrangular. The shaft has sixteen plain sides, and 38½ inches below the base contracts suddenly its diameter by about three inches, so that the shaft consist of two parts, the upper very short, and both taper in a very trifling degree.

(1) Appendix, No. 103.
(2) „ No. 68.
(3) „ No. 115.
(4) „ No. 86.
(5) „ No. 50.
(6) Lat.

The sides are quite straight and well-cut, but not polished. It is lying horizontally, about one-half sunk in the earth, and is situated in the midst of a cultivated plain without the smallest trace of buildings or of a tank near it. The tradition is that it was brought by two Gods, names unknown, from Nepal ; and cavities like that used for beating rice in a mortar and probably originally formed for that purpose, one in the capital and the other in the pedestal, are shown as the marks made by the heads of the Gods as they carried it along. It has become an object of worship, and a Brahman, its Pujari, has an endowment. It has probably been cut in the Burabur hills, and has been carrying to Baragang, but has overcome the patience of the people.

*3rd February.*—I went not quite six cose to Maniknagar.[1] I first ascended the bank of the Mohane for about two miles. I then crossed it, turned west, and about two miles farther crossed the Sungr, which is not so wide as the Mohane but contains a small stream, whereas the Mohane is quite dry. I then passed two granitic peaks, one on each side of Bisunganj,[2] at a little distance. I then went to the east end of the northern division of Burabur, and passed the whole way between the two. Maniknagar is a little west from their termination.

*4th February.*—I went first to Kesba[3], about six coses called four. About five miles from Maniknagar I crossed the Jamuna river, which is much farther from the hills than Major Rennell places it. The channel is not a hundred yards wide, but contains water from side to side, but nowhere above two feet deep, and though clear almost stagnant. The soil

(1) **Manikpur** (one mile north-west of Kawa Dol).
(2) **Bishunganj**.
(3) **Kespa.**
(4) In Rennell's maps, the Barabar Hills are shown as extending at least three miles to the west and two miles to the south of their true position. Opposite these hills, the Jamuna river swerves away from its northerly course, about two miles farther west, so that instead of running past the western border of these hills, as shown in the maps, it was at least five miles from them where Buchanan crossed.

seems peculiarly retentive of water, for some old channels beyond the river are even now quite full. Both banks of the Jamuna are very uneven, like the sandhills on the sides of the Fulgo, but they are not at all sandy. About three miles farther on, I crossed the Morhar, a sandy channel about 200 yards wide and containing a very small stream. Kesba is about three miles farther. Soda seems very prevalent in this part of the country. I saw it on this route in three places efflorescing on the surface, and saw some people gathering it. The whole quantity, however, appears to be trifling.

At Kesba is a celebrated image called Tara Devi, which I had gone to see. It is in a small square temple, evidently quite recent and built of bricks and clay without plaster, but it is situated on a heap of bricks and stones, evidently the ruins of a former building. Three Brahmans of the Panda's family were repeating prayers, and seemed offended when asked by whom or when the temple had been built. They first replied in a surly manner—in the Satiya Yug. They afterwards judiciously observed that it was needless to ask when temples were built, that the Gods were not the work of men. On such a subject indeed I find it needless to consult the officiating priest, who is always interested to veil the truth. The image is of the full human size, and is standing with a small figure on each side, but the body is entirely covered with a piece of cloth, so that it entirely resembles a Hindustani waiting-maid, but I suspect is a Vasudeva decked out in women's clothes. I could not unveil it without giving offence.[1] Many images are built into the wall, and others much broken are lying by the door, and all occasionally receive a smear of red lead. Some of the images, such as the Vasudeva with his hands on the cylindrical projections, Lingas, Gauri Sangkars, etc., are similar to those of Buddh Gya, etc. Some I have seen nowhere else, especially a female with many arms standing on a lion.

(1) *See* Beglar, Arch. Survey Reports, Vol. VIII, 1872-73, page 53.

I was going to return when I was desired to look at Rajah But, and the Burkandaz who served me as a guide told me that this had been a lustful tyrant to whom the country belonged, and who seized on all the beautiful women that he found. Tara Devi was an oilman's wife of great sanctity, who meeting the Rajah and being afraid of her virtue prayed to her protecting Goddess, and both were turned into stone. The image is erect, surrounded by a heap of bricks with many broken columns of granite, flags, and doors, which may have formed a pretty large temple. It is a male with two arms, in a standing posture. One of the hands hangs down with the palm turned forward, as usual with the Munis of the Buddhists when represented standing. A small male is seated at his feet. A short inscription over [his] head. Near are several broken images, with a Ganesa and a two-handed Goddess sitting on a lion, both pretty entire. I was now joined by two decent young men, who told me that all over the immediate vicinity there were heaps of bricks, and that when people were digging them out for building they had laid bare the stones and images, and said that in all ten or twelve temples had thus been laid bare.

As I had far to go, it was not in my power to visit the whole. I saw only one more, called Kober. The image represented a man with two arms sitting cross-legged, and supporting on his shoulders another male with four arms, fully as large as himself. The women pelt this image with bricks. The men had no tradition concerning any Rajah having lived at this place, but had heard that it had been the residence of Kasiop Muni. It certainly has been either a city or place of worship of very considerable note.

I then went three coses to Tikari, [1] in a southerly direction. Raja Mitrjit, and his son my acquaintance, were absent. I had therefore no opportunity of visiting the house. It is of abundant size for the residence of a man of rank, and has at a distance a picturesque

(1) Tickarry, R. and B.A.; Tekari.

castle like appearance, being built very irregularly with many projections and elevated towers. It is surrounded by a double rampart of earth and a wet ditch, which contain a considerable space besides the castle, but are now ruinous. Every village near has been fortified with a mud castle or fort, but all have been allowed to go to ruin. At a little distance is a garden surrounded by a brick wall with turrets at the corners, and containing some small buildings of brick. Also a tank where a Sannyasi resides in a good brick house, and entertains mendicants at the Rajah's expense. The castle is not all whitewashed, which gives it a mean appearance, especially conjoined to the decayed state of the defences and many wretched buildings in the outer fort. In the absence of the Rajah and his illegitimate son, I was visited by the Dewan, who gave evasive answers to almost every question. He would not even speak of the Kol, and pretended to think that the Rajah's ancestors had possessed the country from time immemorial. No person was more communicative, as without a special order from the Rajah no one dares speak. On each side of the fort is a large bazar, and in some places the streets have been made wide and straight like those of Sahebgunj. The houses are mostly of mud, tiled, but in general poor and slovenly.

*5th February.*—I went about ten miles[1] to Baraiya[2] by the way of Koch.[3] About four miles from Tikari I crossed the Sinane,[4] a small channel in a stiff clay soil, but it contains a good deal of water. About 2½ miles farther I crossed another similar rivulet named the

---

(1) In the Report (Eastern India, Vol. I, pages 25 and 67-68) Buchanan describes, evidently from personal observation, extensive fortifications at Kabar, considered as the principal remains left by the Cherus or Kols; but there is no record of this visit in the Journal. Kabar is three miles south-west of Koch, and he probably visited it on this day rather than on the 3rd December; though the last part of the Journal for 3rd December is irrelevant. In the Report, Buchanan says that Kabar is in the immediate vicinity of Bodh Gaya (page 25) and some way north of Barwan (page 67). It is about twenty-five miles north-west of Bodh Gaya, and six miles south and slightly east of Barwan.

(2) Berhah, R.; **Barwan.**

(3) Cowch, R., Couch, B. A.; **Koch.**

(4) Sidang, N., R. and B.A.; **Sinane N.**

Mera, [1] which sends off by a canal a fine little stream for irrigation. The soil here is such a stiff clay that the rivers make little impression in the rainy season, and in the dry are not swallowed up. Baraiya is a small village belonging to an invalid sepoy. It is on the banks of an old tank, which is merely called the tank, nor is there any tradition concerning the person by whom it was dug. Under a tree on its banks are some broken images. A Ganesa. Two Vasudevas, of the usual form. A Narasingha, and one similar to that of Kongh, where a male standing with four arms holds the hand of a female with two arms.

*6th February.*—I went about eight miles to Deohara, [2] through Go. [3] The whole road filled with pilgrims passing to and from Baidyanath and the west of India, each carrying a Kaungr. Few persons of rank among them. Many women in red petticoats. A little from Deohara I crossed the Ponpon, which is about 100 yards wide, but contains more water than any of the torrents in the district. It has now a fine clear stream, perhaps thirty yards wide and from twelve to eighteen inches deep.

In the afternoon, I went about a cose south to see a temple of Chinna musta, a goddess so eager after blood that she cut off her own head in order to drink the blood. I was curious to see how this practical bull was expressed, having been told that pictures of this goddess represent her dancing on a man and woman in the act of copulation, while three streams of blood issue from her neck. One falls into her mouth, she holding her head in her hand. Another stream is swallowed by a jackal, and a third by a serpent. On my arrival at the place I found the image was that of Gauri Sankar. A small Bouddh, with one hand over his knee, and several fragments of other images, were placed beside, and all come in for a share of the oil and red lead. Two

---

(1) Nehrah N., R.; **Nira N.**

(2) Dowra, R. and B.A.; **Deohara.**

(3) Gow, R. and B.A.; **Goh.**

Pujaris were at prayers by the booth. The temple is very small and rude; built of clay and bricks taken from the ruin of the old temple on the top of which it is placed. This has been a mut similar to Kongch, but more considerable. Round it are several Lingas and Somads of Sannyasis, but no traces of other buildings, nor have the people any sort of tradition concerning the old temple. From the number of mud stalls used by the Haluayis, a great many must attend the Mela.

*7th February.*—I went about ten miles to Daudnagar[1] through a poor swelling sandy country. The road pretty tolerable, and practicable for a cart with little difficulty. The road still swarming with pilgrims.

*8th February.*—I went about four coses to see some antiquities at a village called Manora.[2] It is a large village, and stands very high from the accumulation of mud from fallen houses for many generations, but has no bricks, so that it has always been a mere village. A little way east from it is the foundation of an old temple, which has probably been of the spire form. The chamber square, not above ten feet in diameter, but the walls are very thick, nor is there any appearance of there having been a Natmundir or of any other building. The image is a Buddh, sitting with his right hand over his knee and the podda flower on his soles. It is called Buddhrup, and not only continues to be an object of worship, but the Pujari is a Brahman and has the title of Patak. He however seemed to be ashamed, and kept out of the way.

A zemindar Brahman who showed me the place said that there was absolutely no tradition concerning the place, but he seemed afraid that I had come to make advantage of some old claim and to dispute his property, for a Dusad told me that he would show me the ruins of the house of the Kol Rajah, by whom the place had been built. He accordingly took me

---

(1) Daoudnagur, R. and B.A.; **Daudnagar**.
(2) Marownah, R.

about 200 yards north, where there was a heap of bricks about 20 yards square and of very little elevation. On the surface had been placed two lingas, and in the temple adjacent to Buddhrup are two of these images, and a small Vasudeva, which the people here all call Mahama, besides some other fragments. The ornaments on Buddhrup being very entire, and there being an inscription, I have directed a drawing to be made.

From Manora, I went northerly about a cose to Boutara, where I was told I should find the ruin of a small house belonging to the Kol. I accordingly found a small heap of bricks about twenty yards square and perhaps twenty feet high, although many bricks have been removed. It seems to me to have been rather a temple than a house, and the image which has been the object of worship is probably buried in the ruins. On the top are lying two small broken Gauri Sankars, which the people call Soka Bokta. The people of the village attribute the building to the Cherus, another proof of the Kol and Cheru being the same. I then returned to Daudnagar.

11*th February.*—I went about three coses east, by the road I had formerly come, to a village named Tal in order to see where a substance called Mus is dug. The village stands on a very long eminence, having low rice-ground on the south and a marsh towards the north, and this is said to have been an abode of the Kol, and it may have been a large village and the eminence may have been formed by the gradual accumulation of mud from the decaying walls, as usual in the country. The soil as usual contains many fragments of pots and a few bricks, but there is nothing about it like the ruin of a fort, large house, or temple.

The Mus is found in a small field of perhaps thirty yards square, on the slope towards the tank, and consists of small modules like the dross on some ores of iron. Two men that I procured to dig it said that it was found about a foot deep mixed with the soil, and that they never dug farther, the small quantity required for medicine being thus easily procurable. Accordingly, in digging a hole about three feet square to this depth, they found three or four pounds weight in small detached masses mixed with the soil, which is sandy. I then caused them to dig about three feet deep, the soil becoming stiffer as they descended, but after the second foot the quantity diminished, and at three feet I found no more; but to be certain that none is found at that depth would require a more extensive opening than I could make. It may be dross from an old iron work, although there is no hill near from whence ore could be brought, nor is there the smallest trace of furnaces, ashes, or cinders. No masses are found on the surface, but such may have been removed.

Daudnagar and Hamidgunj form one considerable town; the space between, where the thana is situated, being small. Some of the streets, in Hamidnagar especially, are straight and wide, but there are many miserable gullies and the streets are very irregular, a wide one often terminating in a lane, or being interrupted by a hovel in the middle. Daud Khan, in the town named after him, erected a handsome fortified serai. It is a square, enclosed with a brick wall with handsome battlements and loopholes. It is strengthened by round bastions, and has two large gates. His descendants occupy it as houses, in many poor buildings erected within. In fact it was probably intended as a stronghold, but called a Serai to avoid giving offence to the jealousy of government. It has no ditch.

His son, Hamid Khan, built a real Serai in the part of the town which bears his name; that is, he allowed the Betiyaris to build a long straight wide street with their *háts* on each side, while he secured each end with a mud gate. The only other public building of note is a small Imambari in good repair, and a mud building called a Chautera, consisting of three stories gradually decreasing in size, open on all sides, but with a pent roof over each stage. It is a very irregular and sorry structure, but is said to be an exact model of a famous building of the same name at Jaipur. That however is built either of stone or of marble, but unless of a much better design must be a poor thing. Two of the Nawabs have brick monuments near the Imambari, but they are small and rude. The houses are very inferior to those of Gaya, but are almost all built of mud with tiles, and are more comfortable than the lower classes in this country usually possess, although none are fit for persons of any rank.

*12th February.*—I went rather more than eleven miles to Pahaleja.[1] Vast heaps of sand are blown up by the west winds of spring, forming downs along the bank of the Son, as also near the Fulgo. The town extends about two-thirds of a mile from north to south, but much more from east to west. Rather more than four miles from the town, I came to Shumshirganj,[2] a market place and serai formed by a Nawab Shumshir Khan, who is buried in a garden a little south from the village. It is a handsome pretty considerable building of brick, and the garden is surrounded by a brick wall as usual. It has a small endowment, with which a Fakir burns a lamp. The garden supports a mali, but has become wild. The building is in tolerable repair. This Shumshir Khan is commonly called Jubberdost Khan, or the violent Lord, and is said to have married a sister of Joyon Khan. A Borkandaj is stationed in the market as a guard.

About a mile farther on, I came to Aganud Serai, founded by a Mogul of that name. The serai forms a street and is in good repair, being kept up by the Betiyaris, but the gates by which the ends were secured have become ruinous, and one still hangs over the heads of passengers in a very tottering condition. The other has fallen and is no longer dangerous. Here also is

(1) Pallijow, R. and B.A.; **Pahleja.**

(2) Sumseernagur, R.; Sumsernagur, B.A.; **Shamshernagar.**

placed a Burkandaj, as is the case in a village some way farther on at a little distance from the road. Except to act as spies, what good these men can do I know not, and no one of them can, I suspect, be trusted to give information [any] more than he could be expected to fight. Pahaleja is a poor place. Some invalids near, very litigious fellows. This forenoon I felt an earthquake very distinctly. It lasted above a minute, and was accompanied by no noise.

*13th February.*—I went rather more than eight miles by the great road to Arval.[1] The road pretty tolerable for a cart.

*15th February.*—My people brought me a pumice stone from the Son.

*18th February.*—Arval is a poor small bazar, with a ruinous bungalow built by Colonel Hutchinson. I went rather more than eight miles to Mera, and halted on the ruins of a Cheruwan's house. The Atarba Brahmans, who are the owners of the country, say that the Kol and Cheru are the same, that none now remain, but that they are to be found in the southern hills. They were expelled by Mullik Beo, after which the Atarba Brahmans came and occupied the country. Many Musahars here, they are called Bunghiyars.

The ruin at Mera is an oblong heap, perhaps 300 yards in length and 150 in width, and consisting of earth and fragments of bricks. On its middle has been a space of perhaps 150 yards square more elevated than the rest, and there are traces of brick buildings round it, some of the walls still standing. They are not sufficiently thick for a fort, nor do they appear to have been a wall surrounding a court, as there are several hollow angles towards the plain as if there had been separate buildings. I suspect that this building has been erected on a previous ruin. Under a tree are five or six images. One Narasingha; the others all males with four arms, standing between two small

(1) Arval, R. and B.A.; **Arwal.**

figures, but their hands in different positions and [with] different emblems. Under a tree in a village near are two images, one as above, the other Gauri Sangkar. The people say that all around in digging wells they occasionally find images, many of which have been thrown into an old tank at the west end of the heap. About 15 or 16 years ago an English gentleman was persuaded by a Brahman to dig in search of treasure. They found an old well lined with brick, in which was an image, some keys, and human bones.

*19th February.*—I went between twelve and thirteen miles to Vikrampur,[1] called by some, three coses, by others five. About $3\frac{1}{2}$ miles, called one cose, I came to Palli,[2] the first place in Vikram. It is a pretty large bazar, and at one end are the foundations of a brick building.

*21st February.*—I went rather less than four miles to see Raph, which I had passed before. It is a heap extending about 400 yards east and west and 100 north and south, of considerable elevation and very irregular surface. I saw no stones, and the quantity of brick is small. There is no trace of a ditch. On the whole it probably has never been a place of consequence, and owes its size chiefly to the gradual accumulation of clay from the walls of a village situated on its summit. At its east end under a tree is a male image, in the usual form of those called Vasudeva, etc.

*22nd February.*—I went south three coses to Bhorotpur,[3] with a view of seeing some land that produces soda, having previously sent people to dig a well in the place in order to ascertain how far the water might be affected. On coming to the well I found no soda near it; about twenty yards from it a very little could be discerned in one spot of a rice field. The people said that there was plenty there, and would not show me any

(1) **Bikram.**

(2) Pollay, R. and B.A.; **Nirakpur Pali.**

(3) Burdporah, R.; **Bharathpura.**

other place. The Zemindar was busy at the marriage of his daughter, his son-in-law had come from a distance, he had pitched seven or eight tents, two or three of them large, and had three elephants. In short, he seems to be a person of note, and is called a Raja. The house of the zemindar large, and some part of brick.

*24th February.*—I went to Seerpur,[1] and proceeded first to Raph, although I had been told that it was not near the road. Several of the villages that I saw north from thence are situated on similar eminences, which seem to me chiefly owing to the accumulation of mud walls. The boundary between Gaya and Patna at Purnal[2] is about seven miles north from Raph. From thence to the bank of the Ganges is about four and a half miles. I then went east along the Patna road about a mile. I did not keep the road from Vikram to the river, which is a cose round. The road from Patna to Arah is very good, and seems much frequented.

*27th February.*—I went to Moner,[3] passing along the Son the whole way, for it now joins the Ganges at Serpur, and not at Moner as in the time of Mr. Rennell. The country very populous. The huts tolerable. Moner is a large place. At its west end is a fine tank which communicates with the Son by a subterraneous tunnel, but at this season the water is dirty and full of weeds. It is lined all round with brick, and at each side has had a stair of brick with a platform on each side, and on each platform is a small cupola but these buildings have become ruinous, and the bare heaps of earth by which the tank is surrounded must always have spoiled the effect. On its south side is the tomb of the great saint of the place, merely a grave under a tree with a white sheet spread over it, but it is surrounded by a brick wall, and there is a small mosque within this and some cloisters for the reception of Fakirs. Many of the faithful are buried within the enclosure, which

---

(1) Sierpour, R. and B.A.; **Sherpur.**
(2) **Painal.**
(3) Moneah, R. and B.A.; **Maner.**

is as usual slovenly and ruinous.[1] In this simple manner was buried the first propagator of the faith in these parts. His grandson has procured a mausoleum worthy of the increasing power of his sect, and by far the handsomest building that I have yet seen in the course of the survey. On account, however, of the superior sanctity of the grandfather, his tomb is called the great Dorga, while the splendid monument of the grandson is called the little. It is in the usual style of the Muhammadan Mokbaris, consisting of a cubical chamber covered by a dome and at each side ornamented with a portico, while at each corner there is a small chamber surmounted by a cupola. The whole is of stone, but the dome is plastered on the outside to exclude the rain, and has been gaudily painted. The chamber is light within, having windows secured with exceeding neat fretwork in stone. The whole walls, pillars, and roofs of the porticos and small chambers are carved and ornamented with foliages and fretwork, in some places too minute and in too small a relief, but in others in a very good style.

The north side of the enclosure is occupied by a small mosque and a wing of cloisters, both in a very good style and constructed towards the area at least of stone, and the cloister extends along the west face to the principal gate, which has been a very handsome structure of stone. The ascent to it is by the only handsome stair that I have ever seen in a native building. It has steps on three sides, and the steps are of a just proportion, so as to render the ascent easy.

The other parts of the buildings enclosing the area are irregular, but at one of the angles has been a cupola

(1) "In former times, it is said, Maner was the residence of a Brahman chief, but a saint of Arabia named Ahiya, who seems to have been of the military order, arriving in the country smote the infidel and threw his gods into the river. He then took up his abode at the place, and buried on the situation of the temple twelve of his companions, who in the struggle of conquest had obtained martyrdom. When he died, he was buried in the very spot where the idol had stood, and his descendants to this day occupy the palace of the idolatrous chief, or at least a house built where it stood." M. S. Report, pages 144—145.

of stone, the fretwork in the windows of which is remarkably fine. On the whole it is an exceeding handsome building. Its two chief defects are, that it has a kind of castellated embrasure in place of a balustrade, and that under this it is surrounded by a row of sloping flags resembling the eaves of an Italian cottage, in place of a cornice. The stone is from Chandalghur (Chunar) and cuts well, but is not durable, so that much of the carving has suffered from its decay, and the whole is in the most disgusting state. Fakirs have been allowed to boil their pots in the porticos, and have overwhelmed them with soot, to remedy which irregular patches over the pots have been whitewashed. One of the corner chambers is occupied by a beastly ascetic, who has shut up the doors and windows with old pots, clay, and cowdung patched together in the rudest manner, nor are any pains taken to keep the place in repair ; yet the descendant of the saint has 6,000 bighas free of rent, and that of the richest quality. The whole is said to be expended in the feeding in idle squalid mendicants, vagrants who are in this country an intolerable nuisance. That this account is true there is no reason to doubt, as his abode although surrounded by a high brick wall and occupying the seat of former Rajahs bespeaks the most squalid asceticism. The buildings are said to have been erected by a certain Ibrahim Khan, who had been Subah of Gujerat, and who died before they were entirely finished, a circumstance that usually happens, as the completing any work of this nature is considered as unfortunate as immediately to be followed by the death of the founder. Near it has been a handsome monument for the mother of the Nawab. It has become very ruinous. There are no traces of the Rajah's palace except some heaps. The great saint is buried in the place where his God stood, which together with all other objects of idolatry were piously thrown into the river.

*29th February.*—I went to the Golghar,[1] passing through the elegant cantonments of Dhanapur.[2] The

(1) The **Golah** at **Bankipore.**
(2) Dynapour, R. and B.A. ; **Dinapore.**

barracks form an elegant building, and the quarters for European officers are very extensive and also handsome. The grounds of this place are neat, and vastly superior to Bankipore. The bazars extensive. The General [1] has a very good garden, in which he has English apples and Bokhara plums, both of which he says produce excellent fruit. The plums of two kinds, purple and yellow. The grafts of a year old already blossoming. He has also peaches with a depressed fruit, which I have seen nowhere else. Having a taste for cultivation as a florist he has procured some plants from Nepal, especially the fine Porana.

*1st March.*—Went to Futwah by a road already described.

*3rd March.*—Having heard from the Sannyasi of Buddh Gya that the Vazirs of Ava had gone to Champapuri, about eight coses south-east from Patna, I had enquired after the place both at Hilsa and here, and at both places learned that there was a village of this name on the banks of the Ganges[2] about five coses below Futwah, but that no remains of ancient buildings were to be seen. I however sent a man, who told me that near it some children in play had discovered an image, which had been taken by the zemindar and placed under a tree, where it was worshipped by a few persons of the vicinity. I this way went to see it by the route which I had come from Bar. The stone slab is about three feet high, and contains as the principal figure a male standing, with one head and two arms. No traces of weapons, but both hands broken. On each side a flower like what is called the Chokor of Surjo, but there is no horse. On each side, standing, are two male figures, one smaller than the other. Below are some votaries. Above are five Buddhs and the representation of two solid temples. The Buddhs all sitting. The one in the centre has both hands in his lap. The two next have one hand in the lap and one

(1) General Watson. (East India, Vol. I, page 288).

(2) Champapour, R.; Chumperpour, B.A.; **Champapur**, about 1½ miles west of Bakhtiarpur, and twenty-eight miles by road from the Golah.

over the right knee. The extreme one on the right has both hands before the breast. That on the left has one hand on the lap, one raised towards the shoulder. The village where the image is placed is called Gunsur, [1] nor does it contain any traces of buildings, except that it stands on a large elevation of clay and broken pots, as usual in this country.

On the way back, my bearers halted at a tree where some retailers of provisions were placed. These furnished them with copper vessels, out of which even Brahmans will eat. They mixed barley and pease meal together with a little salt and cold water, and ate this with a dry capsicum. Farther on they halted at a hut where a Sannyasi distributed water to the passengers, and each man got a handful of lentils (Cicer Arietinum) on the straw. The Sannyasi said that he has five bigahs of land and an Indera. He seemed to be constantly engaged in pouring water from a brass pot down the throats of the passengers, as from cleanliness he did not allow them to touch it with their mouths. They held their hand under their mouth, and he poured the water upon their hand from whence they drank. In order to compensate for this act of cleanliness, the Sannyasi held the pot with his fingers in the inside and the thumb without, a custom of which it is difficult to break the natives. His fingers were of course in the water. Some passengers gave him a cowrie or two, but his collections in that way cannot amount to above one or two annas a day.

Futwa is a very large village or country town, and some of the houses good in the opinion of the natives, but the clay of the walls is exceedingly rough and unseemly, as usual towards the east. West from Patna they are much neater. On the bank of the river immediately under the town is a stratum of pale yellowish clay, which extends perhaps 200 yards, and is about four or five feet above low-water mark and perhaps 16 or 18 under the surface. It may be about six feet thick, and from the name of the Mauza in which it is found is

(1) Ghoswari.

called Raipur clay.[1] It is used as a wash for the walls of houses and in the distillation of essences, but not by the potters. It is a fine smooth light clay, and contains many cylindrical cavities, as if it had been perforated by the roots of plants, but no remains of vegetables are to be now seen.

*6th March.*—In the morning I went to Rekabgunj, in order to have an interview with Govind Das, one of the chiefs of the sect of Nanak. He is a middle-aged man without any hypocritical cant, but does not seem to be a man of learning, and is exceedingly tiresome from repeating a vast number of Puranic legends. He pretends to be chief of a Bung or division containing 360 Gudis of the Kolasa sect. At Murshedabad and Lucknow are two others, and he calls himself a Fakir. The Fakirs of the Kolasa admit only of Brahmans, Kshatris, and Vaisiyas into their own order, but among their followers they receive every Hindu who is not vile, but they receive no Mlechhas. The Fakirs, like other Hindus, consider that there is one chief God, Parameswor or Para-Brahma, but think that no one, even the Gods, knows his name or anything about him, and that he gives himself no trouble about worldly affairs. He admits that Vishnu, Siva and Brahma are Gods (Iswara), and occasionally makes offerings to them, but says he merely does so in compliance with custom, and that the only object of worship is Parameswar.

They have no private form of prayer, but have a short kind of creed, like that of the Moslems, which they repeat. They have also four forms of prayer for four different times of the day, and when any person gives an entertainment and offerings at the Sangot, one or more of these forms are repeated according to the time when the offering is made. A person of any religion may partake of the entertainment; but is not considered as at all converted by this, nor would any of them admit him to eat at any other time.

---

(1) "Rapura or Gori Mati"; *see* East India, Vol. I, page 274.

The Fakirs sometimes marry, but are somewhat disgraced by this. All Fakirs whatever their caste may eat together, and abstain from many kinds of food and drink. They should give up all connection with Brahmans, but many in compliance with custom employ Purohits to perform their ceremonies. Their pupils not admitted into the priesthood, follow exactly the same customs that they did before, retain their caste customs, Purohits and Gods; they only change their Guru.

Nanak had two sons from whom are descended 1,400 families, called Shahzadas, who are much respected and reside at Dera in the Punjab, where they seem to be dedicated to religion and live on its profits. He appointed as his successor Ungot, who was followed by Amardas, Ramdas, Arjunji, Hara-Govind, Hara Rai, Hur Krishna, Tek Bahadur and Govinda. In his time, the Moslems being exceedingly troublesome, he was obliged to take up arms and the title of Singa, and thus founded the Church militant called Kalisha in order to distinguish it from the spiritual church Kolasa, and there has been since his time no universal head of the sect. In the Punjab every Rajah is at the head of their sect in their own dominions, and they have become persecutors, compelling Moslems and Hindus of all ranks to follow their customs. They admit of the use of all animal food except beef and spirituous liquors; but each caste retains its own customs and worship. He however does not seem well acquainted with the customs of the Singas.

Govinda on assuming the title of Singha appointed four military chiefs, and called them Gurus but made them quite equal. He himself never took to the sword. He was born at the Hari Mondir in Patna, on which account that place is much respected, but the owner is a person of no authority, according to Govind Das, who is evidently very jealous of him and will not allow that he is a Mahanth. Both sects give Kora or entertainments at Harimandir, and the owner has at least the profits of this, but Govinda pretends that he has no authority over inferior Gadis.

Among the 1,400 Shahzadahs, also called Bedis, none it is alleged has produced a daughter. They marry with three other ranks called Sori, Boli and Tihun, whose descent my informant does not know. The daughters, I suspect, are privately murdered.

END OF JOURNAL.

## Patna.

**From Buchanan's MS. Report. Abridged in Eastern India, Vol. I, pages 35—43.**

There is a good deal of difficulty in ascertaining the boundaries of Patna. To exclude what is without the walls would reduce its dimensions to a trifle, while the suburbs are built in a very straggling ill-defined manner. I find it most suitable for my purpose to include in this section the whole of that part of Patna Pergunah, or Haveli Azimabad, that is under the jurisdiction of a Kotwal and 15 Darogahs, who are appointed to superintend the police of the 16 wards (Mahullah), into which the above-mentioned extent is divided. Each ward includes part of the town, but several of them also include an adjacent part of the country, consisting chiefly however of garden land with some low marshy ground that intervenes. The city of Patna, taken in this sense, includes the suburbs of Bakipur and Jafier Khan's garden, an extent nearly of nine miles along the bank of the Ganges. The width from the bank of the Ganges is on an average about two miles, but some part of the channel of the Ganges, and of the islands opposite to the city, must be also considered as belonging to this jurisdiction, so that on the whole I shall allow it an extent of 20 square miles. It must however be observed that among the natives the *gerdnawah* or extent of the city of Patna is usually said to reach along the bank of the Ganges from Sherpur to Baikunthapur, about eleven miles farther west and nine miles farther east than the boundaries which I have assigned.

A plan made by a native assistant will show the subdivisions and explain my meaning. The city within the walls is rather more than a mile and a half from east to west (as may be seen by the plan in the Bengal Atlas, No. 15), extends three-quarters of a mile north and south, and is exceedingly closely built. Many of the houses are built of brick, more however are built of mud with tiled roofs, but very few are thatched. To outward view they are exceedingly unsightly and slovenly, and are rendered peculiarly mean by the lower story towards the street, in even the best of them, being let for shops to low tradesmen or even to artificers, who are very careless. Within, many of them are no doubt neat, and according to the idea of the inhabitants very comfortable, as every one who has means to afford it resides in this part of the town, nor is it fashionable for the wealthy to have country houses. The Nawab Bakur Ali Khan has indeed a house in a suburb, but this was formerly occupied by an European gentleman, and, I believe, has been bought by the Nawab with a view chiefly to receive visits from Europeans, and his family resides in the city. Kasinath, a rich banker, is the only person, so far as I saw, that has a country house, and both the buildings and garden are neat, and of a respectable size; but, I believe, are used very rarely and that only on festivals and entertainments, and his family constantly resides in the town. This predilection for the city would be hard to explain, as it is difficult to imagine a more disgusting place. There is one street tolerably wide that runs from the eastern to the western gate, but it is by no means straight nor regularly built. Every other passage is narrow, crooked, and irregular. The great street, when it breaks into sloughs, is occasionally repaired with earth thrown in by the convicts, the others are left to nature by the police, and the neighbours are too discordant to think of uniting to perform any work. Paving, cleaning, and lighting, considered so essential in every European town in such circumstances, are totally out of the question. In the heats of spring the dust is beyond credibility, and in the rains every place is covered with mud, through which however it is contrived to drag the little one-horse chaises of the natives. In the rainy season there is in the town a considerable pond or lake, which, as it dries up, becomes exceedingly dirty, and in spring is offensive.

East from the city is a very great suburb, the chief part in which, called Marufganj, is situated between the eastern gate and the river, and is the principal market. It contains many store-houses for grain. Most of the buildings, especially the store-houses, are built with wooden posts and walls made of straw-mats, with tiled roofs. Although almost the whole was burned to the ground last year, and although a similar accident usually happens once in five or six years, it has been rebuilt exactly on the same footing. Immediately above the town is a long narrow suburb extending almost four miles in length, but seldom half a mile wide, and there are many short interruptions from gardens, but one great street, lined in most parts on both sides with houses, extends the whole way and near the city divides into two branches, which rejoin at the eastern gate. Many narrow crooked alleys extend on both sides of this road, and are lined with hovels of all kinds, mostly, however, having mud walls and tiled roofs, and some of them have two stories; but there are scarcely any respectable houses occupied by natives. The Nawab Bakur Ali has, however, as said above, a large house; Raja Kalyan Singha, last native governor of Behar, has two or three houses, which, from the caprice of enormous wealth, are now empty; and Raja Mitrajit, of Tikari, has built a house, where he occasionally resides. This part of the town seems to have risen in consequence of the European settlement, and the houses of the Europeans are scattered through it, chiefly along the bank of the river; while, no precautions having been taken, their dependents have huddled along the great road, and formed lanes and crooked passages between it and the gentlemen's premises, so that the access to several of these has become exceedingly disagreeable, and to some of them difficult. Notwithstanding that this is one of the chief European settlements in India, being the seat of a court of appeal, of a city judge and magistrate, of the collector of a very fertile district, of a custom-house, of a commercial resident, of an opium agent, and of a provincial battalion, the number of European houses is trifling, and they are so scattered that they make no show. One of them is a very elegant abode, and had it not been made to consist of two orders, one above the other, and both therefore too small, it might have been a fine piece of architecture; as it is, however, it is undoubtedly the best private dwelling that I have seen in India. The others are indifferent, and some of them very bad. Of the 52,000 houses estimated to be contained in this city it is said that 7,187 are built of brick, 11,639 are of two stories with mud walls and tiled roofs, 53 differ from the last in having thatched roofs, 22,188 are mud-walled huts covered with tiles, and the remainder consists of mud-walled huts covered with thatch. Some of the roads in this quarter are kept in tolerable repair by the labour of the convicts, but the dirt, dust, and mud of the greater part of the suburbs are almost as bad as those of the city.

The town is very indifferently supplied with water. Near the river the supply from thence is abundant, but in the dry season the bringing it from thence is a severe task on the women, and in the rainy season it is very dirty and bad. Near the river the wells are deep, and the water which they contain is generally saline. Farther from the river many wells are good, and some of them not very deep, so that on the whole the people there are best supplied. One magistrate, some time ago, compelled the people to water the street, each person in front of his own house, and this, no doubt, was a general comfort for the whole, but in many particular cases was attended with hardship, so that this has been abandoned. The bank of the Ganges occupied by the town is tolerably high, and in most parts the town might be extended farther south than has been yet done, but all along its northern boundary is a tract of low land deeply inundated in the rainy season; this, however, when the floods subside, is very well cultivated, and I do not believe that it renders the situation of the town unhealthy.

A city nine miles long sounds large; but, when we come to investigate particulars, we shall be a good deal disappointed. It having been last year proposed to levy a tax on houses, the acting collector proceeded to make an enumeration, and the returns procured gave 45,867 houses, exclusive of those occupied by persons dedicated to religion. Two or three houses belonging to one person were often returned as one, which saved trouble, as the tax was to be laid on the value of each property. On account of this and of the religious houses, and a few that may be supposed to have escaped the vigilance of the surveyors, the number must be allowed to be somewhat more than the return given to the collector. The late magistrate had commenced an enumeration of the people, but it was left incomplete, and has not been continued. I am, therefore, under the necessity of proceeding by conjecture concerning the number of people in each house, and the addition that must be allowed to the number of houses returned to the collector. On the first point, the average conjectures of all the Darogahs, each of whom had carried his investigation by actual enumeration to a certain extent, will give an average of six persons for each house, and the total number of houses, according to the conjecture of the Darogahs, amounts to rather more than 52,000. The whole population will, therefore, amount to 312,000, which I do not think liable to any considerable error. There are besides a great many persons, sepoys, camp-followers, travellers, boatmen, etc., whose number fluctuate; but is generally pretty considerable.

The principal road, especially in the city, is very much crowded; but there are no such multitudes of passengers going in and out as are to be seen near the large towns in England. A hundred yards from the southern wall of the city you are completely in the country, and within sight of it I found myself, in looking after the curiosities of the place, just as great a matter of wonder to the women and children as in the most remote parts of Behar. It did not appear that the villagers, at least the women and children, had ever seen an European, and they flocked round my palanquin with great eagerness.

The inside of the town is disagreeable and disgusting and the view of it from a distance is mean. Indeed, at a little distance south from the walls it is not discernible: there is no building that overtops the intervening trees, and no bustle to indicate the approach to a city. The view from the river, owing to the European houses scattered along its bank, is rather better, and is enlivened by a great number of fine-formed native women that frequent the banks to bring water. Still, however, the appearance of the town from thence, especially in the dry season, is very sorry, the predominant feature being an irregular high steep bank of clay without herbage, and covered with all manner of impurities, for it is a favourite retreat of the votaries of Cloacina, accompanied by the swine and curs that devour the offerings.

Major Rennell has given in the Bengal atlas a plan of the poor fortifications by which the city of Patna is surrounded; and, as ever since his survey they have been totally neglected, their condition is now to the last degree wretched. A very little pains would, however, render them a security against predatory horse, and would enable them to preserve the effects of all the vicinity from such a force, which in the present reduced state of the native princes is now more likely to be employed than any other.[1] I have little doubt

(1) These observations had special reference to the conditions in the year in which this Report was written. "The body of Pindarrahs, which lately made an irruption into the Company's territory near Mirzapore, has since created a considerable degree of alarm at Patna and its neighbourhood." (Calcutta Gazette, April 2nd, 1812; *see* Sandeman's Selections, Vol. IV.)

that in case of alarm the inhabitants would willingly undertake the necessary work, were they directed by the Magistrate. The gates are now in a most deplorable state of decay, and are rather alarming to strangers that enter. In order to prevent accidents they should probably be pulled down, as in the present state of the rampart they can be of no use in defending the place. The fort in the north-east corner of the city is now so overrun with modern buildings that its form can be no longer distinguished, nor could I perceive any remains, except some old gates. It is the common idea among the natives that the fort and city were built by Azim, the grandson of Aurungzebe, and that Pataliputra had long been completely destroyed when that prince arrived ; and, as I have before said, it would appear that in A.D. 1266 Patali had become a nest of robbers, and was then punished ; but a fort was built ; nor can I trace anything relating to it in Dow's history until the year 1611, when a convention of Afghan chiefs assembled at the place, which was then the capital of Behar. Further, it would appear that about this time the town was not only fortified, but had within the walls a palace, where the Subah resided. The inscription also on the gate of the fort, dated in the H. 1042, attributes its erection to a Feroz Jung Khan. The vulgar opinion must therefore be a mistake, and takes its rise from the name of Azim having been given to the city. It is alleged that until the Mahratta invasion, the city walls contained all the inhabitants, and its principal increase and prosperity seem to have been owing to the European commercial factories, for at one time the English, Dutch, Danes and French had factories here, and traded to a great extent, especially in cotton cloth. This trade has no doubt suffered, and although that of nitre and opium has increased, yet the parts of the town adjacent to the factories have declined ; but then the city is said to have greatly increased, and the value of the ground in it, within these fifteen years, is said to have doubled, owing to the difficulty of procuring a spot for building a house.

The English Company's original factory is now occupied by the Opium Store-house, a very substantial good building, well fitted for the purpose to which it is applied. Near it is the jail, also a large building, but neither handsome, nor strong enough to confine ruffians. The house at present occupied as the city court is near the jail ; but is a very abominable-looking place. The court of appeal is a handsome modern building, but very small.

At the western extremity of the suburbs is a building called the Golghar, intended as a granary, and perfectly *sui generis.* For the sake of the great man by whose orders this building was erected, the inscriptions should be removed, were they not a beacon to warn governors of the necessity of studying political economy, and were it not of use to mankind to know even the weaknesses of Mr. Hastings.

Immediately above and below the city two native merchants built brick keys, of considerable length, to facilitate the landing and shipping ot goods in the rainy season. Boats can then lay along the key, and deliver and take in goods with ease ; but they never would appear to have been of use in the dry season, when some contrivance to facilitate the conveyance of goods up and down the enormous bank is most wanted. These keys are called Poshta, are private property, and at present are chiefly used for lodging coarse goods, such as timber and bamboos, which in the dry season are deposited on the bank. Parallel to the city, at some distance south from it, and extending some way farther each way is an old bank, which seems to have been intended to exclude the floods, and still answers for that purpose.

These with the roads and a few miserable brick bridges are all the public works that I have seen, except those dedicated to religion. In the middle of the city the Roman Catholics have a church, the best looking building in the place. Near it is the common grave of the English who were treacherously murdered by the orders of Kasem Ali before his final overthrow ; it is covered by a pillar of the most uncouth form, built partly of stone, partly of brick. There are many *musjids*, or mosques, but none of them very large, and many of them are now let as warehouses by their owners. This is the case with the handsomest of them, which is built entirely of stone, and of which a view is annexed. It stands with one end to the street, and the house of a descendant of the prophet, who is styled the *motawoli* of the mosque, is situated in front. This drawing will give an idea of the style of building in Patna, and of the manner in which it is disfigured by the wretched sheds built in front for artificers and petty traders. Although the owner has let his mosque for a warehouse, he is strenuous in his calls on the faithful to pray, and he is the loudest crier and the loudest prayer in the whole town.

The chief place of actual worship among the Moslems of Patna is the monument of Shah Arzani, about the middle of the western suburb. He was a native of the Punjab, and, after a long residence, died here in the year of the Hijri 1032. The proprietors are the *chelas* or disciples of the saint, and not his descendants, and all of these holy persons have abstained from marriage. Kurimbuksh, the present occupant, is the seventh successor in the office. He has considerable endowments, and gives food daily to from 50 to 200 fakirs. Every Thursday night from 100 to 500 pilgrims, Moslems and Hindus, many of them from a distance, come to intercede with the saint for his assistance, and make offerings. In the month Zikad there is an annual fair (Mela), which lasts three days. On the first, people apply to Shah Shujawol ; on the second, to Vasunt ; and on the third, to the great saint ; the two former having been among his successors, and the latter of them, it must be observed, has a Hindu name. About 5,000 votaries attend. Adjacent to the tomb is an *Imamvara*, where 100,000 people assemble with the pageantry used in celebration of the grandsons of the prophet. Near it is a tank dug by the saint, where, once in the year, 10,000 people assemble, and many of them bathe. A public crier calls the people to prayers, but few or none assemble; those who are roused to pray by the crier perform their devotions on the spot where they happen to be at the time. I have not observed among the Moslems of Bengal or Bihar any meetings in their mosques, such as we have in our churches, in order to have public prayers and to hear their scriptures either read or expounded. The only other place of worship among the Moslems at all remarkable is the monument of another saint, named Pir Bahor, which was built about 200 years ago, but it is only attended by a few in its vicinity. It at present belongs to a widow, who, since her husband's death, acts as *Pirzadah* for the families who were wont to require the assistance of the deceased.

The only places of worship at all remarkable among the followers of the Brahmans are the temples of the great and little Patanadevi, Pataneswari, or Goddess of Patana, i.e., the city. The great goddess is said to have been placed in her present situation by Patali, daughter of Raja Sudarsan, who bestowed the town now called Patna on his daughter, and she cherished the city like a mother, on which account it was called Pataliputra, or the son of Patali. The building is small, but avowedly recent, and erected at the expense of the priests. Far from acknowledging the story of Patali, these allege that their deity has existed here from the origin of things. This in India is an usual pretence, but there is a circumstance attending the tutelar deity of this city that in most parts is not so ordinary, although very much so in these districts. The image (see drawing No. 124) called a goddess is a male, and is no doubt a representation of a Boudh, and probably of Gautama, as he has seated by him two disciples as usual in Ava. Near the throne is placed a female deity, but this is not the object of worship, and represents, I have no doubt, Semiramis seated on a lion, and on her knee holding the infant Niniyas (see drawing No. 125). The Pandas or priests are Kanoj Brahmans, and many goats are sacrificed on Saturdays and Tuesdays, but they have no endowment. The little goddess was placed in her present situation by Man Singha, while that noble Hindu had the government of Bihar. The temple is of no great consequence, but is much more frequented than that of the great goddess, and the priest, who is a Kanoj Brahman, is supposed to have very considerable profit.

The Pataneswaris are properly the Gram-devatas of the town, but as the worship of these deities is not fashionable in Behar, this is considered by many as a term too degrading. Still, however, many are aware of the circumstance, but Guriya, Pir Damuriya, Ram Thakur, Damuvir, Sam Sing, Benimadhav, Bhikkari-Kumar, Siriya devata, Karuvir, Patalvir, Jalapa, etc., are also applied to as Gram-devatas. Near the eastern gate in the suburbs is a small temple of Gauri and Sangkar, but the image represents only the generative organs of these deities. Every Monday in Sravan from 1,000 to 5,000 votaries assemble, and make offerings. The priest is a gardener. At the north-east corner of the city, at place where some lady, name unknown, burned with her husband's corpse, 50,000 assemble once a year, and make offerings. In the great days of bathing in the Ganges, most people cross to the junction of the Gandaki; but on a certain day about 10,000 women assemble and bathe at a ghat in the west end of the city.

The followers of Nanak have at Patna a place of worship of great repute. This is called the Hari-Mandir, and owes its celebrity to its having been the birthplace of Govinda Singha, their last great teacher. The Mandir itself is of little consequence, but it is surrounded by pretty large buildings for the accommodation of the owner. The meetings are less frequent and numerous than formerly, the owners applying less of their profits to what are called charitable purposes. The Harimandir, which is in the city, belongs to the Khalesah sect founded by Govinda, and confined in a great measure to the west of India. The Kholasahs or original Sikhs, who prevail in Behar, have in the suburb called Rekabgunj a considerable place of worship, and the owner possesses very considerable authority and income.

Petty causes, even under 50 rupees, must be carried directly before the judge, who appoints a person called Sales to determine each. Four or five persons live by this employment; but the people of the eastern suburb can apply to the commissioner of Phatuha. The same man, however, is also commissioner at Bar, under another judge, so that both duties must be neglected.

The principal Pirzadah among the Moslems is the owner of the monument of Shah Arzani. One Kazi performs the ceremonies for the whole persons of rank, but has deputies who attend the lower ranks, and as usual in this vicinity are called Nekah-Khanis or marriers. Most persons of rank do not employ the Kazi, and their own kinsmen or dependants, having learning sufficient, conduct their ceremonies. Of the Hindus, 2 annas are of the Sakti sect and 3 annas of the sect of Siva. Of these 5 annas, 2 annas follow Brahmans, partly resident in Patna, partly in Tirahut, and a very few in Bengal, but some men of extraordinary virtue from Benares, and called Dandis, intrude on the sacred order; 3 annas follow the Dasnami Sannyasis, most of them strangers. Three annas of the whole are of the sect of Vishnu. By far the greatest part of these follow the Ramawats and Radhaballabhis, nearly in about equal numbers. Part of both classes of these instructors are Brahmans, but most are Sudras. Most of them reside, and there may be 20 houses of both sects, but some of the occupants of these houses have married; and four only of the houses are of considerable note. They have very little endowment, but considerable profits, and the buildings are pretty large, but all modern. The best is in the suburb of Marufganj, and belongs to Ram Krishna Das, a Ramawat. Besides the Ramawats and Radhaballabhis, an Akhara of the Nimawats has a few followers. Four annas of the Hindus are of the Kholasah sect of the Sikhs, mostly following Govinda Das of Rekabgunj, but there are several other inferior Sanggats. Not above 500 houses adhere to the doctrine of the Khalesah sect in the Harimandir, but many strangers frequent this place of worship. Two hundred houses are guided by the Kavirpanthi, of which there is an Akhara. A few weavers are of the Gorakshanathi sect, and have Gurus of their own. All these and a few other trifling castes are considered as orthodox (Astik). Three hundred houses of Jain or Srawaks are considered as heterodox (Nastik), and between 3 and 4 annas, the dregs of impure poverty, are considered altogether unworthy of care.

Most of the few antiquities, that remain, have been already incidentally mentioned. The traces that can be considered as belonging to the Hindu city are exceedingly trifling. Everywhere in digging, broken pots, but very little else, are to be found; and where the river washes away the bank, many old wells are laid open, but nothing has been discovered to indicate large or magnificent buildings. In the Ganges, opposite to the suburbs above the town, I found a stone image lying by the water's edge when the river was at the lowest. It has represented a male standing, with two arms and one head, but the arms and feet have been broken. The face also is much mutilated. It is nearly of a natural size, and very clumsy, and differs from most Hindu images that I have seen in being completely formed, and not carved in relief with its hinder parts adhering to the rock, from whence it has been cut. On the back part of the scarf, which passes round the shoulders, are some letters which I have not been able to have explained, and too much defaced to admit of being copied with absolute precision. Some labourers employed to bring this image to my house informed me that it had been some years ago taken from a field on the south side of the suburbs, and had been intended for an object of worship: but that a great fire having happened on the day when it was removed, the people were afraid, and threw it into the sacred river. They also informed me that in the same field the feet of another image projected from the ground, and that many years ago a Mr. Hawkins had removed a third. On going to the place I could plainly discover that there had been a small building of brick, perhaps fifty or sixty feet in length; but most of the materials have been removed. On digging I found the image to be exactly similar to that which I found on the river but somewhat larger. The feet are entire, and some part of the arms remain, but the head has been removed. On its right shoulder is placed something which seems intended to represent a Thibet bull's tail. This is an insignia of the Yatis, or priests of Jain, but in other respects the images have little resemblance to such persons, one of whom is represented in the Drawing No. 132. I rather suppose that these images have been intended as an ornament to the temple, and to represent the attendants on some god, whose image has been destroyed. In the drawing No. 2 the images have been represented with the inscription on the smaller, that on the larger is totally illegible.

In the suburbs at a little distance from the eastern gate are two heaps called Mathni, which are supposed to be of Hindu origin; but there is no tradition concerning the person by whom they are built, and their size is trifling. South from these heaps about a mile is a very considerable heap, which with some small eminences in the neighbourhood are called the five hills, and are attributed to the five sons of Pandu: but this is probably an idle fable. One is at least 100 feet in perpendicular height, and has no hollow on its top, so that I suspect it to have been a solid temple of the Buddhas. The others are almost level with the soil, and have probably been houses for the accommodation of religious men. It is said by the peasants of the neighbourhood that they consist entirely of brick, but the owner of the larger obstinately refused his consent to allow me to dig for its examination.

I cannot learn any tradition concerning the island Sambalpur, opposite to Patna, having ever been a town;

nor, so far as I can learn, are any ceremonies performed there, as Major Wilford had heard.

It need not be wondered, that so little traces of the Hindu city should remain, as the occupancy of men totally regardless of the monuments of antiquity soon obliterates every trace; and it is only in remote and wild parts of the country, that the ruins of buildings are allowed to remain undisturbed; or among nations very far civilized, that any attention is bestowed on the preservation of the monuments of art. Chehelsutoon, the palace of the viceroys of Behar, which has accommodated many personages of royal birth, and which fifty years ago was in perfect preservation, and occupied by the king's son, can now be scarcely traced in a few detached portions retaining no marks of grandeur; and the only remain of a court of justice, that had been erected in the year of the Hijri 1142, is a stone commemorating the erection, which was dug up in the (year) 1221 (A.D. 1807), when a police office was about to be erected on the spot where the other had formerly stood, and which in 79 years from its foundation had been completely obliterated.

# Appendix.

## The Collection of Mineral Specimens.

Buchanan's report on the Minerals of Patna and Gaya has been reproduced without abridgment in Eastern India, Volume I, pages 241 to 274. He classified the hills in which most of the specimens were found into three main groups, as follows :—

(A) The Southern range of Hills, consisting of two main ridges, approximately parallel to each other—(1), hills which he considered to be pure granite, forming the southern boundary of the district from the Gurpa Hill to Durvasarikh and Sringgirikh near Rajauli, this granite further to the east and south of Rajauli becoming much modified in the neighbourhood of the mica mines of Belam and Dubaur ; and (2), hills of quartz, jasper, or hornstone, stretching from Ektara and Mahabhar in the neighbourhood of Akbarpur, in a north-easterly direction as far as the hills of Gidhaur in western Monghyr. He also thought that he could trace (3), a series of small isolated hills of granite, lying north of the latter ridge, and likewise running north-easterly from the neighbourhood of Fatehpur through Sitamarhi as far as the group of hills close to Lakhi Sarai and Kiul.

(B) The Rajgir Hills, which he also subdivided into two principal portions—(1), the hills traceable, in most parts as a double ridge, from a small heap north of Bakraur close to Bodh Gaya in a north-easterly direction past Tapoban, Hanria, Rajgir itself, and Giriak, as far as the Sheikhpura hills, but including also the isolated hill at Bihar ; all of these being almost entirely silicious and very little modified by contact action ; and (2), the subsidiary range of small isolated hills which lie close to the northern ridge of the main group, commencing from Narawat and continuing through Majhauli and Saran to the confused heap of low hills north of Chakra Ghat in the main ridge, and called Dukri Ghat or Belsara. These he considered to be mainly silicious, but much more metamorphosed.

(C) The Barabar Hills, which he regarded as (1), a central nucleus, the Barabar hills proper, including Kawa Dol, all pure granite; (2) an eastern wing, comprising the series of isolated hills such as Dhermpur or Charbigha (mis-spelt Tarbigha in Martin's edition), Patharkati, and Bathani, all of these being granitic in their nature, but with the exception of the last-named hill more or less modified; and (3), a southern wing, consisting of the hills close to the town of Gaya, some of these being of granite, some of quartzite, and the rest a mixture of these natures in varying degrees, modified by contact action.

The principal omissions in this classification are the numerous low hills in the strip of country lying between his route of December 13th, 1811, past the north of the Maher and Sobhnath hills as far as Sitamarhi, and that taken on January 14th to 16th, 1812, skirting the southern boundary of the Rajgir Hills from Hanria to Tapoban and Amethi. The Journal shows that he did not examine the nature of the hills in this area, amongst which the quartzite ridge about five miles long ending on the east at Reula, and the isolated hill at Tungi near Jamuawan, are the most prominent. If he had done so, and particularly if he had examined the small hills close to the present Gaya-Nawada road near Wazirganj, the four easternmost of which are of granite exactly similar to that of the Barabar Hills, it is not unlikely that he would have modified his classification to some extent, and that he would not have associated the isolated granite hills south of the Rajgir Hills so closely with his Southern division.

The list of minerals which follows has been compiled from the numbers given to them in the Journal, as shown in the various footnotes. It seems that while it can hardly be regarded as anything more than a temporary classification, pending the more detailed examination which Buchanan made during his stay at Patna after his tour had been completed, it is as regards numbers fairly complete.

Judging from the Report, the collection of minerals from the hills of Patna and Gaya consisted of either 111 or 112 specimens, and at least three or four so-called Minerals of the Plains were probably also included. The highest number definitely assigned to any specimen in the Journal is 115, but there are seventeen blanks in the list. Amongst the specimens collected from the hills, fourteen of these omissions can be explained, for in at least three cases Buchanan has assigned the same number in the Journal to two quite different minerals, and in eleven other cases has not written down any number at all.

In this list the brief description of each specimen follows that of the Report rather than the Journal, as the former represents Buchanan's matured views. The hill at which each specimen was found is mentioned in the Journal, but in the list its locality is shown according to Buchanan's classification described above.

| Number. | Description. | Where found. | Reference. |
|---|---|---|---|
| 1 | Grey silicious nodules, immersed in marl (No. 101), and like No. 68. | C. 2. | 23 |
| 2 | Quartz, imperfectly glassy, with some reddish matter intermixed. See Nos. 46 and 85. | A. 2. | 79 |
| 3 | Porphyritic argillaceous cement, strongly impregnated with iron, and containing concretions of hornstone and Khari. | B. 2. | 124 |
| 4 | Jasper, granular, variegated red and white, takes good polish ornamental. | B. 1. | 120 |
| 5 | Khari (indurated clay), uniform white in colour and apparently approaching pipeclay. | B. 2. | 124 |
| 6 | No record. | | |
| 7 | Jasper, variegated red and white, in places covered with irregular crystals of white quartz. | A. 2. | 79 |
| 8 | Silicious hornstone, dark-coloured, with small fragments of felspar. | C. 3. | 32 |
| 9 | Silicious hornstone, grey, very fine-grained and tough ... | B. 2. | 127 |
| 10 | Black potstone (Kalapathar), hornstone impregnated with hornblende, like No. 96, but much harder. | C. 2. | 23 |

| Number. | Description. | Where found. | Reference. |
|---|---|---|---|
| 11 | Rock intermediate between granite and hornstone ... | C. 3. | 29 |
| 12 | Jasper, reddish with white veins ... ... ... | B. 1. | 140 |
| 13 | Jasper, blotched red and white, exactly like No. 33 .. | B. 1. | 86 |
| 14 | Gneiss, anomalous, materials very powdery ... ... | A. 3. | 81 |
| 15A | Stone, very strange, fracture conchoidal, and very difficult to break, on the whole most resembling jasper. | C. 3. | 55 |
| 15B | Crumbling sandstone, in which rock crystal is found, surrounded by silicious rock. See also No. 29. | B. 1. | 140 |
| 16 | Granite, small-grained ... ... ... | C. 1. | 11 |
| 17 | Khari, surrounded by imperfect reddle ... ... | B. 2. | 123 |
| 18 | Khari, imperfect, bad quality ... ... ... | B. 1. | 62 |
| 19 | No record. | | |
| 20 | Granite, appearance somewhat uncommon, but tolerably perfect, looks well when polished. See also No. 45. | A. 3. | 81 |
| 21 | Rock showing transition from hornstone to indurated clay (Khari). | B. 2. | 124 |
| 22A | Granite, imperfect, approaching hornstone ... ... | C. 3. | 49 |
| 22B | Gneiss, the black micaceous matter perhaps hornblende ... | A. 1. | 67 |
| 23 | Granite and hornstone, both imperfect, and degenerated into a uniform white sandstone. | C. 3. | 49 |
| 24 | Hornstone, red ... ... ... ... | B. 1. | 118 |
| 25 | Gneiss, the black micaceous matter perhaps an iron ore, as very heavy. See also No. 112. | A. 1. | 67 |
| 26 | Granito, fine grained, in bed of river and decaying into thin vertical plates owing to the action of water. | A. 1. | 69 |
| 27 | Hornstone, found imbedded in a rock of granite (No. 41) ... | C. 3. | 50 |
| 28 | No record. | | |
| 29 | Rock, the matrix of rock crystal. (See also No. 15A) ... | B. 1. | 140 |
| 30 | Quartz or hornstone, white, granular ... ... | A. 2. | 76 |
| 31 | No record. | | |

| Number. | Description. | Where found. | Reference. |
|---|---|---|---|
| 32 | Silicious nodules, opaque, resembling indurated Khari ... | A. 2. | 74 |
| 33 | Jasper, blotched red and white, exactly like No. 13 ... | B. 1. | 80 |
| 34 | Granite, imperfect, approaching hornstone. (See also No. 22A.) | C. 3. | 49 |
| 35 | Hornstone, grey, very fine-grained ... ... | B. 1. | 140 |
| 36 | Gneiss, with the quartz entirely changed or destroyed ... | A. 1. | 67 |
| 37 | No record. | | |
| 38 | Granite, with glassy quartz, takes good polish, very fine. (Like Nos. 63 and 66.) | C. 1. | 18 |
| 39 | Granite, bleached, appearance very anomalous ... | A. 3. | 81 |
| 40 | Hornstone, greyish, in places stained red ... ... | B. 1. | 115 |
| 41 | Granite, grey, perfect ... ... ... ... | C. 3. | 49 |
| 42 | Hornstone, grey and granular, in places stained red ... | B. 1 | 91 |
| 43 | No record. | | |
| 44A | Quartz, white, glassy, etc. ... ... ... | C. 3. | 50 |
| 44B | Quartz, fine opaque white, with some black dots ... | A. 1. | 71 |
| 45 | Granite, appearance somewhat uncommon, but tolerably perfect. felspar yellowish, and quartz glassy, takes good polish. See also No. 20. | A. 3. | 81 |
| 46 | Quartz, fine white grains, with black dots and some mica. | A. 2. | 79 |
| 47 | Hornstone, impregnated with iron, in waved layers of various shades of colour, like some Kharis, but very hard. | B 2. | 126 |
| 48 | Granite, imperfectly fused, the quartz remaining unchanged. | A. 3. | 85 |
| 49 | Sandstone, partly white, partly ferruginous, inclining to red. (Like No. 29.) | B. 1. | 140 |
| 50 | Granite, quite perfect ... ... ... | C. 3. | 152 |
| 51 | No record. | | |
| 52 | No record | | |

| Number. | Description. | Where found. | Reference. |
|---|---|---|---|
| 53 | Schistose substance, intermediate between jasper and indurated clay (Khari). | B. 2. | 124 |
| 54 | Khari, white, like No. 5 ... ... ... | B. 2. | 124 |
| 55 | Jasper, red, with veins of white quartz, ornamental, but red parts do not polish so well as No. 4. | B. 1. | 121 |
| 56 | Jasper, variegated red and grey, changing into Khari ... | B. 1. | 137 |
| 57A | Hornstone, grey, stained red in some places. (Not described in Report.) | B. 2. | 125 |
| 57B | Quartz, white opaque, in large grains mixed with dark dots. | A. 2. | 75 |
| 58 | Mica, in veins or bed ... ... ... ... | A. 1. | 71 |
| 59 | Granitel, much black micaceous matter, with a little white quartz, very ornamental if procurable in large blocks. | A. 2. | 79 |
| 60 | No record. | | |
| 61 | No record. | | |
| 62 | Gneiss, usually called schistose mica ... ... | A. 1. | 71 |
| 63 | Granite, quite perfect, like No. 38. ... ... | C. 1. | 14 |
| 64 | Granite, grey, appearance uncommon, white felspar predominating, admits of good polish. (See also No. 97.) | A. 3. | 81 |
| 65 | No record. | | |
| 66 | Granite, quite perfect, like No. 38 ... ... | C. 2. | 126 |
| 67 | No record. | | |
| 68 | Silicious nodules, like No. 1, and similarly immersed in marl (No. 103). | C. 2. | 152 |
| 69 | Quartz, white and opaque, with white felspar, like No. 110. | A. 1. | 68 |
| 70A | Quartzose, approaching to jasper or hornstone, white, red, or blackish. | B. 1. | 81 |
| 70B | Hornstone or imperfect quartz, like 70B, but with silky fibres of amianthus. | B. 1. | 82 |
| 71 | Mica (Abarak), brownish in thick masses ... ... | A. 1. | 68 |
| 72 | Petrosilex, grey, like No. 35. | B. 1. | 140 |

| Number. | Description. | Where found. | Reference. |
|---|---|---|---|
| 73 | Quartz, glassy and mealy aggregate, with red and black specks. | B. 1. | 62 |
| 74 | Quartz or hornstone, red, granular. See also No. 30 ... | A. 2. | 76 |
| 75 | No record. | | |
| 76 | Granite, fracture rather conchoidal, consisting of white quartz and felspar, and granular hornblende, rather like No. 104. | C. 2. | 23 |
| 77 | No record. | | |
| 78 | Granite, imperfect, very dark and difficult to break, apparently impregnated with hornblende. | C. 3. | 49 |
| 79 | Quartz or Jasper, with red stains ... ... ... | B. 1. | 62 |
| 80 | No record. | | |
| 81 | Masses in decay, white, red, or greenish, perhaps approaching to cornelian, with greasy appearance, and can be polished. | C. 3. | 50 |
| 82 | Granite (called Urdiya) like No. 38 ... ... | C. 2. | 25 |
| 83 | Quartz, small opaque masses united by a greyish powdery substance, which does not take a polish, into very solid rock. | A. 3. | 85 |
| 84 | Rock Crystal (called Phatik) ... ... ... | B. 1. | 141 |
| 85 | Quartz, glassy ... ... ... ... | A. 2. | 79 |
| 86 | Iron ore in loose nodules ... ... ... | C. 2. | 152 |
| 87 | Hornblende, in large masses, blackish and exceedingly heavy, ornamental for building purposes. | A. 2. | 76 |
| 88 | Schistose mica, quartz reddish, mica silvery ... ... | A. 2. | 79 |
| 89 | Iron ore, like No. 86 ... ... ... ... | C. 2. | 28 |
| 90 | No record. | | |
| 91 | Hornstone, grey, containing many small masses of felspar, and clusters of black dots. | C. 2. | 151 |
| 92 | No record. | | |
| 93 | Reddle, imperfect, mixed with hornstone or quartz ... | B. 2. | 123 |
| 94 | Khari, more or less perfect ... ... ... | B. 2. | 126 |
| 95 | Hornstone, imperfect, white, degenerated into a kind of sandstone. | C. 3. | 50 |

| Number. | Description. | Where found. | Reference. |
|---|---|---|---|
| 96 | Potstone, blackish, very heavy, softer than hornblende, takes a polish but inferior to marble in lustre. (Called Sungmusa.) | C. 2. | 22 |
| 97 | Granite, grey. appearance uncommon, powdery black micaceous matter predominating, does not take good polish. (See also No. 64.) | A. 3. | 81 |
| 98 | Quartz, glassy red and white, larger-grained than No. 106, and not at all schistose. | A. 3. | 74 |
| 99 | Indurated reddle, called Geru ... ... ... | B. 2. | 126 |
| 100 | Marl, white, calcareous, rather harsher than Nos. 101 and 103. | C. 2. | 22 |
| 101 | Marl, white, exactly like No. 103 ... ... ... | C. 2. | 23 |
| 102 | Slag, ferruginous, very heavy, containing nodules of quartz and Khari, but in appearance resembles No. 3. | B. 2. | 126 |
| 103 | Marl, white, harsher but more friable than chalk, will not mark wood, used for white-washing houses. | C. 2. | 152 |
| 104 | Hornstone, grey, similar to No. 91, but proportion of quartz, felspar and black matter reversed. Admits of tolerable polish. | C. 2. | 152 |
| 105 | Iron ore, called Losinghana, fracture resembling granite, except in colour. | C. 1. | 19 |
| 106 | Quartz, glassy red and white, fine-grained and splitting into vertical plates. | A. 3. | 74 |
| 107 | Rock consisting of large grains of quartz and felspar intermixed. | A. 1. | 68 |
| 108 | Granite, reddish, exceedingly ornamental ... ... | A. 1. | 70 |
| 109 | Hornstone, white, with small masses of white felspar, and blackish or dark green micaceous matter in large irregular blotches, very ornamental, as it takes a fine polish. | C. 2. | 22 |
| 110 | Felspar, white, very beautiful, sometimes mixed with white or glassy quartz. | A. 1. | 71 |
| 111 | Quartz, granular, white, grey and red ... ... | B. 1. | 114 |
| 112 | Gneiss, perhaps an iron ore. See also No. 25 ... ... | A. 1. | 67 |
| 113 | Hornblende, very fine, crystals large and distinct, does not take a fine polish. | C. 2. | 23 |

| Number. | Description. | Where found. | Reference. |
|---|---|---|---|
| 114 | Hornstone, strange, whitish, livid, and red, in parts evidently a slag. | A. 3. | 81 |
| 115 | Hornstone, greenish, decaying into an imperfect steatite, called Khungtà. | C. 2. | 152 |
| | **Minerals of the Hills.** | | |
| | Described in the Report, but not numbered in the Journal. | | |
| 1 | Granite, very fine, middle-sized grains ... ... | C. 1. | 13 |
| 2 | Silicious stone, white, stained dirty red in irregular specks, fracture intermediate between flint and quartz. | B. 1. | 30 |
| 3 | Granite, grey and fine-grained, but much decayed, found in river bed. | A. 3. | 31 |
| 4 | Granite, grey and large-grained, very fine, would be highly ornamental in building. | A. 1. | 32 |
| 5 | Granite, grey and solid, very fine ... ... ... | A. 3. | 63 |
| 6 | Jasper, rude, red and white ... ... ... | B. 1. | 54 |
| 7 | Quartz, strange, glassy and intermixed with brownish matter. | A. 3. | 81 |
| 8 | Quartz or hornstone, imbedded in white Khari. (Probably rather like No. 3.) | B. 1. | 115 |
| 9 | Silajit ... ... ... ... ... | B. 1. | 116 |
| 10 | Yellow clay, unctuous, called Pilla Mati ... ... | B. 2. | 125 |
| 11 | Indurated clay, schistose, in red, white and yellow layers ... | B. 2. | 125 |
| | **Minerals of the Plains.** | | |
| | Described in the Report, but not numbered in the Journal. | | |
| 1 | Sone pebbles, silicious, chiefly quartz, opaque or diaphanous, take a high polish. | ... | 7 |
| 2 | Pumice, found in bed of Sone ... ... .. | ... | 162 |
| 3 | Mus, small detached masses like slag from iron furnaces of the Kols. | ... | 159 |
| 4 | Yellow clay, called Kaputa or Gori Mati, from furnaces of Ganges at Fatuha. | ... | 168 |

# Appendix 2.

## Two New Inscriptions from the Barabar Hills, and an Identification of Gorathagiri.

### By V. H. Jackson, M. A.

*From the Journal of the Bihar and Orissa Research Society, Vol. I, Part II, 1915, pages 159-171.*

## I.

In his account of the country between Pataliputra and Gaya, Hiuen Tsang mentions a great mountain, inhabited by the divine Ṛishis, poisonous snakes and savage dragons, fierce beasts and birds of prey. On its top a stūpa about ten feet high had been built of gold, silver and precious stones by the Devas, but so long ago that the precious substances had turned into stone, while no one had visited the spot for ages. He then says [1] "*On the eastern summit of the mountain there is a stupa. Here Tathagata formerly stood for a time beholding the country of Magadha.*"

There is little, if any, room for doubt regarding the true position of this mountain. If Telārha, Dharāwat, and Kauwādol are to be identified with the sites of the monasteries of Tilādaka, Gunamati, and Silabhadra, respectively, as seems practically certain, their bearings and distances from the Barābar Hills correspond sufficiently closely to those stated by Hiuen Tsang to show that these hills are the mountain to which he referred, and that the temple of Siddheswarnath now occupies the site from which Buḍdha was said to have contemplated the country of Magadha. These identifications were first suggested by Mr. Beglar in

---

[1] Beal's translation, Vol. II, p. 104.

1872-73.[2] For some years General Cunningham, probably misled by an error in Julien's translation,[3] considered that Hiuen Tsang's mountain was in the southern range of the hills lying between Giriak and Gayā, "somewhere about three miles to the north-west of Wazirganj".[4] During his third tour in Bihar in 1877-78 he altered his opinion,[5] and the reports of his two last tours in 1879-80[6] and 1880-81[7] show that no doubt was left in his mind regarding the correctness of Mr. Beglar's identification. This is accepted by all later observers.[8]

In the Mahā-bhārata, Sabhā Parva, Ch. XX, v. 30, a reference is made to another hill, named Gorathagiri, from which the country of Magadha was surveyed by Kṛishṇa, Bhīma and Arjuna, on their way eastwards to Girivraja (Rājagriha) to fight against Jarāsandha. This passage, with Dr. Wenger's translation, was quoted by Broadley in his account of the Buddhistic Remains of Bihar,[9] but I am indebted to Prof. Ramavatar Sarma, M.A., of Patna College, for the following extract from and strictly literal translation of the Madras edition text :—

उत्तीर्य सरयूं रम्यां दृष्ट्वा पूर्वांश्चकोशलान् ।
अतीत्य जग्मु मिथिलां मालां चमण्वतो नदीम् ॥२८॥
अतीत्य गङ्गां शोणं च त्रयस्तेप्राङ्मुखास्तदा ।
कुशचीरच्छदा जग्मुर्मागधं क्षेत्रमच्युताः ॥२९॥
ते शश्वद्गोधनाकीर्णमम्बु मन्तं शुभद्रुमम् ।
गोरथंगिरिमासाद्य ददृशुर्मागधं पुरम् ॥३०॥

---

[2] Arch. Survey Reports, 1872-73, Vol. VIII, pp. 35-37, 1878.

[3] Watters, Vol. II, page 105.

[4] Ancient Geography of India, Map XII and p. 457, 1871.

[5] Arch. Survey Reports, 1877-78, Vol. XI, p. 165, 1880.

[6] Arch. Survey Reports, 1879-80, Vol. XV, preface, p. iv, 1882.

[7] Arch. Survey Reports, 1880-81, Vol. XVI, pp. 40, 48, 49, 1883.

[8] *E.g.*, Grierson, Notes on the district of Gaya, page 42; Stein, Indian Antiquary, Vol. XXX, p. 96, March 1901; Keith, Bengal: Past and Present, Vol. VII, p. 74, 1911.

[9] *J.A.S.B.*, Vol. XLI, Part 1, p. 308.

वासुदेव उवाच—

एषपार्थं महान्भाति पशुमान्नित्यमम्बुमान् ।
निरामयः सुवेश्माढ्यो निवेशोमागधः शुभः ॥१॥
वैहारो विपुलः शैलो वाराहोवृषभस्तथा ।
तथाऋषिगिरिस्तात शुभाश्चैत्यकपञ्चमाः ॥२॥
एतेपञ्च महाश्रृङ्गाः पर्वताः शीतलद्रुमाः ।
रक्षन्तोवाभिसंहत्य संताङ्गा गिरिव्रजम् ॥३॥

XX, v. 28 " Crossing the charming Sarayu and seeing the eastern Kośalas, going beyond Mithilā, they crossed the rivers Mālā and Charmanvatī.

29. And crossing the Ganges and the Sono, proceeding eastward, the three infallible ones, clad in sacrificial grass and rags, went to the Magadha *field*.

30. *Getting to (or on) the Goratha hill they saw the Magadha city*, ever full of cattle wealth, possessed of water and having beautiful trees.

Said the son of Vasudeva—

XXI, v. 1. O son of Pṛithā (Kuntī), thus shines the great, beautiful Magadha *settlement*, possessed of cattle, ever full of water, free from diseases and rich in good houses;

2 and 3. The great hill Vaihāra, the Vāraha, the Vṛishabha and the Ṛishi hill, with the fifth Chaityaka, these beautiful five lofty-peaked, cool planted mountains, closely constituted, are unitedly guarding, as it were, Girivraja."

I have been unable to trace any other reference in Sanskrit literature to this hill called Goratha, and as far as I can ascertain, Mr. Beglar is the only archæologist who has attempted to identify it with any particular hill in Bihar. He says that as " the names ' Goratha ' and ' Bathan ' are both connected with cattle, and as there is no hill near enough to Rājgir besides the Bathan hill, the inference is obvious that the hill named Goratha in the Mahā-bhārata is the same as the present Bathāni hill ".[10]

---

Arch. Survey Reports, Vol. VIII, pp. 46-47, 1872-73.

In this case, Mr. Beglar's attempt at identification cannot possibly be regarded as successful. The connection between the names of the hills is so slight that it could scarcely be taken into account even if there were any other better reasons for selecting Bathāni as a possible site of Goratha, but of these there appear to be none whatever. The distance from the Siddheswar peak of Barābar to the northern gap in the hills at Rājgir is about 23 miles in a straight line. The hill called Bathāni is merely a low ridge of large granite boulders lying approximately on this line and at a point about two-thirds of the way from Barābar to Rājgir. Quite close on the south there are higher hills, some of which are nearer to Rājgir than Bathāni itself, but all are low compared with the hills in the Rājgir range and none would naturally be selected as hills from which a comprehensive view of the surrounding country could be obtained.

If there were no other clues for ascertaining the true position of Gorathagiri it would be unprofitable to suggest any other site, but the object of this paper is to show that during the last two years additional facts have been discovered which appear to establish beyond any reasonable doubt the conclusion that when this part of the Mahā-bhārata was composed Gorathagiri was a name given to the Barābar hills. The new evidence which is brought forward is that of inscriptions, for the name itself has been found cut on rocks in two separate places, both of which are not far from the well-known caves dedicated by Aśoka to the Ājīvikas.

It is an interesting fact that both these new inscriptions are in Brāhmī characters of the same type as those used in the dedicatory inscriptions of the caves, and that in the opinion of Babu R. D. Banerji of the Archæological Department they belong to the third century B.C. It is therefore probable that they are contemporary with the cave inscriptions themselves, which date from 257 and 250 B.C., and possible that they may have been cut by the same workmen. According to Vincent Smith, "no extant inscription, in either the north or south, can be referred with confidence to a date earlier than that of Asoka."[11] Hence the epigraphic evidence for the identification of Gorathagiri is for India one of unusually great antiquity.

Again, if this identification is accepted, it becomes practically certain that the references in the Mahā-bhārata and in Hiuen Tsang's account to a hill from which the country of Magadha was surveyed are both to be applied to the Siddheswar peak of the Barābar hills, on which an ancient temple of Śiva now stands, shaded by tamarind trees. Hiuen Tsang's story thus becomes a Buddhist version of the Hindu legend regarding this hill. No more suitable choice could have been made, as the view on all sides from the level and artificially raised platform round this temple is remarkably fine. On a clear day at the end of the rains the whole of the northern range of the Rājgir Hills stands out sharply defined and appears quite close, while hills like Gurpā and Sringirikh are perfectly distinct on the horizon, although twenty or thirty miles further away.

## II.

An estampage of the first and larger of these new inscriptions is reproduced in Figure 1. This was discovered by Mr. C. Russell and myself on March 5th, 1913. The weather at the time was dull and rainy. It will be seen later on that these conditions, though very unusual for March, are exceptionally favourable when searching for or endeavouring to decipher inscriptions which have become weatherworn and indistinct. As is shown in Figures 2 and 3, the inscription has been cut on a large isolated boulder, and is now about 8½ feet from the ground. The rock itself can best be found by going about 100 yards along the ordinary path which leads north-west of the long low ridge in which three of the four caves have been excavated, to a part of the valley where the general level rises distinctly, and an ancient dam has recently been repaired for irrigation. The rock is close to the dam, on the south side of the path. The inscription faces west-north-west. As it is quite exposed, it has become rather indistinct even under the

[11] Early History of India, 3rd edition, 1914, p. 16.

most favourable conditions. When first found, the word Goratha could be read at once, but the remainder was not clear until an estampage was taken by the Archæological Department six months later (Figure 1*a*). On this, Babu R.D. Banerji has kindly reported as follows : " The impression which I find in this office is not complete. It omits the last letter. I read the inscription as follows : *Gorathāgiro.*—There is no doubt about the reading of the last syllable, it is *giro* = (?) *girau*, 'in the hill'. Goratha may be an *apabhraṃśa* form of Gorata, which is a form of the acacia, or it may be simply the *ratha* or chariot drawn by oxen."

Since receiving this report I have examined the inscription carefully on several occasions, and have taken the estampage shown in Figure 1. It seems certain that no letter has been omitted, and that there are no signs that a final letter ever existed.

The second inscription, shown in Figure 4, was discovered by me on December 27th, 1914, while making a systematic search of the whole of the western face of the long ridge which contains the Sudāma and Lomaśa Ṛishi caves. The photograph reproduced in Figure 5 shows that it is to be found about 20 feet south of the centre of the doorway in the latter cave. It is about seven feet above the level of the lintel of this door, but except along the face of the rock, where a ditch was cut in 1847 by Captain Kittoe in order to drain the water out of the caves, earth has accumulated to a depth of about three feet. Figure 4 shows that with the exception of the letter *tha* this inscription is practically identical with the first. Babu R. D. Banerji informs me that the reading is *Gorathagiri*, and that while the form of the *tha* is unusual it could not possibly be anything else. ▲

This inscription is only about half the size of the first, and though deeply cut is if anything more worn, owing to the fact that there is a slight depression in the rock just above it, down which a stream of water runs during rain. A little distance from the final character there is some evidence of the existence of another, perhaps *va*, but this is very doubtful and the letter could not in any case belong to the same word.

▲ See note added, February 1925.

Figure No. 1.

Figure No. 1*a*.

Figure No. 2.

Figure No. 8.

Figure No. '4.

Figure No. 5.

The existence of at least two inscriptions of exactly the same type is probably sufficient to remove most of the doubts regarding the identification with Barābar which might remain if only a single record of the name Goratha had been found there, but it is necessary to discuss two possible objections.

The first is one which depends on the meaning to be attached in the extract from the Mahā-bhārata already quoted, to मागध॰ पुरम् Māghadhapuram or "City of Magadha", which Kṛishṇa and the two Pāṇḍavas are said to have seen from the Goratha hill. If the definite fortified city of Old Rājagṛiha or Girivraja is referred to, as might naturally be supposed, it is impossible to see this city from the highest point of the Barābar hills. It is however just as impossible to see it from any hill outside the Rajgir range itself, and it does not appear necessary to assume that in the text anything more than the country of Magadha is intended. In his translation Professor Sarma has called attention to the fact that in this extract Magadha is associated with three different terms—क्षेत्रम्—field, पुरम् city and निवेश settlement—although in each case the idea conveyed seems to be the same.

The Hon'ble Mr. Oldham, to whom I am much indebted for advice and criticism on this paper, has suggested to me a very interesting explanation which is not inconsistent with a literal interpretation of the word Māgadhapuram. He writes—"It is just possible that Māgadhapuram may have been a town close to the east of the Barābar hills, on the site of what is now known as Ibrahimpur."

It is certain that a large settlement formerly existed on this site, in the southern portion of the triangular area between the two branches of the Phalgu, which bifurcates at this point, with the granite ridge named Jibhiya on the north as its base. The foundations of the houses in the villages of Ibrahimpur and Jaru contain a large number of granite blocks, all of which have been cut and some carved or otherwise ornamented, while in the fields surrounding the villages similar blocks and large quantities of bricks are constantly unearthed by the cultivators.

This town may have extended as far as the hill, at the foot of which there are many similar remains, but there are no signs that it was of such great antiquity as a reference to it in the Mahā-bhārata would imply. Though a careful watch was kept during a survey of Old Rājagṛiha or Girivraja, which I was recently enabled to carry out by the kind assistance of Sir John Marshall, Director-General of Archæology in India, no artificially shaped stones were noticed in the foundations of the numerous buildings which can still be traced, and hardly any amongst the large quantities of loose stones scattered over the area of the ancient city, so that it seems certain that the original builders were not acquainted with the use of dressed stone. Moreover, there are no signs in the Ibrahimpur area of the artificial elevations with flat tops which seem to have been used as forts, or of the massive walls and roads of gentle gradient leading up the neighbouring hills, which are characteristic features of Old Rājagṛiha.

At the very foot of Siddheswarnath, however, there is a site which includes all these features. This is, on the south, the natural enclosure within the hills, which contains the four caves of Aśoka, and on the east, the extensive plain stretching as far as the western branch of the Phalgu, which was described by Buchanan as follows :—"The people of this division have a contention with those of Gaya, and pretend that Rama performed the offerings to the gigantic Asur on that part of his body which extends to the north-east corner of the Barābar hills, and they contend that, much inconvenience in attending on the pilgrims to such a distance having been experienced by the Gayawals, these priests set up a new Ram-Gaya of their own, which I have mentioned in my account of the sacred places that are their property. This account is far from improbable, and on the Vishuwa-Sangkranti from 10,000 to 15,000 assemble on the west bank of the Sungr river, where there is a plain above a mile in diameter surrounded by small hills and rocks, and called Ram-Gaya. In the middle of this plain is a round hill named Murli, to the summit of which a road has formerly been made, probably to some building, of which a few traces remain. Throughout the plain are heaps of bricks and stones, but whether the remains of a town or temples it is impossible to say: the former, from the extent, is the most probable opinion." [12]

A more careful examination of this site has shown that Buchanan's opinion is correct, as will be seen from the following extract from a description of some little known features of interest in the Barābar hills,[13] which was written [by me] shortly after the first of the two inscriptions described in this paper had been found :—"Inside the Barābar enclosure the stone foundations of buildings can be seen in various places, notably upon and to the east of the artificially raised area at the foot of the Siddheswarnath Hill, due north of the caves, and in the jungle towards the south-western end of the valley. The whole enclosure is too small to have been the site of any large town, but the natural strength of the position and the fact that the defences are strengthened at all vulnerable places by stone walls render it reasonable to suppose that it formed a refuge, used in times of danger by the people who ordinarily lived in the plains and valleys outside. Apparently the main town was at the foot of the artificial road leading down from the strongly fortified eastern gate of the enclosure. In this part of the plain, now called Ram-Gaya, there are numerous rectangular heaps of rocks marking the site of ancient buildings, and it is interesting to observe that the buildings here and also inside the enclosure were considerably larger than the majority of those which can be traced in Old Rājagriha. The town seems to have extended over the Ram-Gaya plain as far as the little hill called Murāli, which is noteworthy for its artificially flattened top, approached from the north and south by roads of gentle gradient, evidently intended for wheeled vehicles."

The inference that the town on this site was contemporary with Old Rājagṛiha is supported by other evidence. On the

---

[12] *Eastern India*, Vol. I, p. 100.

[13] *Patna College Magazine*, Vol. VI, No. 3, pp. 97-104; or *Hindustan Review*, Vol. 28, September 1913, pp. 683-688.

crest of the southern range of the hills which surround the Barābar enclosure there is a flat-topped stone fort exactly like the numerous examples which can be seen on the Rājgir hills. This fort was approached from the interior of the enclosure only, by a road up the hill which was defended by a stone wall. At the western end of the hill Murāli in the Ram-Gaya plain there is a similar but much larger rectangular structure, which is now called, together with the hill itself, the *Ākharā* or wrestling-ground of Banasura.[14] Structures like this, though less regular in shape, can be seen to the north-east and south-west of the Maniyar Math, the most prominent feature in the centre of Old Rājāgṛiha.

The second possible objection to the identification is that in one at least of the three dedicatory cave-inscriptions the Barābar hills are called by a different name—खलतिक Khalatika. The Viśvāmitra cave has been excavated in a ridge of rocks some distance to the south of the ridge which contains the other three caves. Its own inscription has been cut on the polished side of the entrance, so that it has been protected from the action of rain and, with the exception of the reference to the Ājīvikas which has been intentionally defaced, it is still almost as sharp as when first cut. It reads as follows:—

Lajina piyadasina duva- | dasavasabhisitena iyam
Kubha Khalatika pavatasi | dina Ajivikehi

or, as translated by Senart—[15] "This cave situated on Mount Khalatika has been given to the Ajīvikas by King Piyadasi in the thirteenth year after his coronation."

The only other reference to a hill named Khalatika pavata which can be traced occurs in the fourth Vārttika to Pāṇini I, 2, 52. Here the obscure reference in the text to the word Khalatika is explained by indicating the proper gender of the adjective which must be used to denote forests near this hill.

---

[14] "Ram-Gaya and its remains," by K. P. Sen Sinha, *Patna College Magazine*, Vol. III, 1910, pp. 49-51.

[15] Indian Antiquary, Vol. XX, p. 169, 1891.

Again, Cunningham has stated that in the dedicatory inscription on the north side of the entrance to the Karna Chaupar cave he was able to recover the words Khalati (or Khalanti) pavata. [16] His version of this inscription is given in Arch. Survey Reports, Vol. I, Plate XX, and in Corp. Inscr. Ind., Vol. I, Plate XVI. Before this restoration can be accepted, further evidence seems to be required. Senart has commented on the absence of a locative in this, and neither Burnouf who worked on Kittoe's record of this inscription, [17] nor Bühler who used a later impression obtained by Fleet, [18] were able to make out anything beyond the first letter *kha*.

The meaning of the word Khalatika itself appears to have given some trouble to Sanskrit scholars. Burnouf proposed to substitute for it स्खलतिक Skhalatika or "slippery", [19] and Bühler, assuming it to be equivalent to Khalati, translated it as "bald" or "bare". Both slippery and bare are suitable adjectives to apply to portions of these hills.

If it were not for philological objections which are apparently insuperable, I would have ventured to suggest that Khalati or Khalatika, and Goratha or Gorathaka, were different versions of a still older name given to the Barābar Hills. It is however quite safe to conclude that these hills are called, in inscriptions of a more or less contemporary nature, by two different names, owing to the example of Rājagṛiha or Girivraja. The names of both these localities were changed at a later date. Old Rājagṛiha was known as Kusāgārapura in the time of Hiuen Tsang. Buchanan in 1811 recorded its name as "Hangsapurnagar", and Kittoe in 1847 as "Hansu Tanr", but at the present time both these interesting names seem to have been forgotten. Similarly, the Lomaśa Ṛishi cave is called "Pravaragiri-guha" in the Sanskrit inscription over its entrance, which although undated appears to belong to the 7th century A.D. From

---

[16] Corp. Inscr. Ind., Vol. I, p. 133.

[17] Le Lotus de la Bonne Loi, Appendix X, p. 781.

[18] Indian Antiquary, Vol. XX, p. 364, 1891.

[19] Burnouf, Le Lotus, p. 779.

Pravaragiri or "excellent hill" the modern name Barābar appears to have been derived.[20]

## III.

In a paper to which reference has already been made,[12] I mentioned that other inscriptions of Aśoka's time are possibly still awaiting discovery in the Barābar hills, and that a search under favourable conditions might be successful. As this anticipation has already been justified, other visitors may perhaps be sufficiently interested to make searches, so that a few remarks on the conditions which have been shown by experience to be especially favourable may be useful.

In order to detect or decipher indistinct inscriptions, any contrast which exists between the different parts of the surface of a rock must be developed as much as possible. Occasions should therefore be selected when (*a*) the incident light is oblique and not too strong; (*b*) the general illumination due to glare from the sky or clouds is small; and (*c*) the natural reflecting power of the rock itself is reduced. It is easy to see that observations made in the early morning or evening are suitable in most cases, but it is not so obvious that a remarkable improvement in visibility can be effected even in a strong light by thoroughly wetting the rock-surface and thus diminishing its reflecting power. During showers of rain, the conditions (*b*) and (*c*) stated above are obtained by natural agency, but rain seldom falls during the cold weather, which is the only suitable season for examining bare and slippery rocks, and would probably damp enthusiasm as well as rocks if it did occur. Its most important effect, however, can be produced at any time by drenching the rocks with water by means of a garden syringe.

The remarks of different observers on the Karna Chaupar inscription already mentioned show how much its visibility varies at different times. Apparently it was not noticed by Sir William Jones and Mr. Harington in 1784,[21] or by

---

[20] Fleet, Inscriptions of the Early Gupta Kings, Corp. Inscr. Ind., Vol. III, pp. 221-223. I have to thank Babu R. D. Banerji for this reference.

[21] Asiatic Researches, Vol. I, pp. 276-278.

Dr. Buchanan in 1811.[22] It was first recorded in 1847 by Captain Kittoe, who was compelled to spend a night in the cave—"bears having been graciously pleased to forego their visits"—and thus was able to observe that the inscription was "best seen by clear moonlight, standing beneath".[23] This is likely enough, for a comparatively weak light like that of the moon produces no appreciable glare, so that if it is sufficiently oblique the reflecting power of the surface is comparatively unimportant. Kittoe also remarked that sunrise and sunset were favourable, and he noticed a sentence which seemed to have been cut over the door, though this had become illegible. Mr. Caddy also noticed a figure resembling a fish on the inscription.[24] On the other hand, Dr. Grierson who had seen the inscription many times when he was Collector of Gaya, considered that it would be useless to attempt to obtain a satisfactory impression, as "the face of the inscription has been chiselled away by some Musalman fanatic".[25] It is quite possible that any reference to the Ājivikas has been purposely obliterated, as in four of the other five Barābar and Nagarjuni dedications, but it does not appear necessary to assume that the damage to the rest of the inscription is due to anything except exposure. I have on occasions seen enough to enable me to confirm the accuracy of the observations of Kittoe and Caddy, and I believe that with careful attention to the conditions for visibility it will be possible, if not to agree with General Cunningham's version, at any rate to make out more than is shown in Fleet's impression, from which Bühler was unable to satisfy himself regarding more than sixteen or at most twenty-one out of the first forty characters given by Cunningham. [B]

---

[22] Eastern India, Vol. I, pp. 103-104; and M. S. Journal, pp. 21-22.

[23] *J. A. S. B.*, Vol. XVI, Part I, pp. 401-416, 1847.

[24] Proceedings, A. S. B., 1895, pp. 152-168.

[25] Indian Antiquary, Vol. XX, p. 170, footnote, 1881.

*B. See* note added, February 1925.

*Notes added, February* 1925.

**(A) The Lomasa Ṛishi Cave.**

Two years after this identification of Gorathagiri with the Barābar Hills was published, Mr. R. D. Banerji detected the word *Goradhagiri* in his impression of the Hāthi-gumphā inscription of Khāra-vela (in the Khaṇḍagiri hills near Bhubaneswar) at the end of the seventh line. It is now clear from the editions of this inscription published by himself [1] and by Mr. K. P. Jayaswal [2] that in the eighth year of Khāravela's reign (about 165 B.C.) his army was at the Barābar hills, and four years afterwards at Pāṭaliputra. The Hāthi-gumphā itself and its inscription date from the following year.

This new fact regarding the relations between Bihar and Orissa in the second century B.C., together with the similarity of the second of the two inscriptions described in Part II of the preceding paper to Mr. Banerji's discovery, and its close proximity to the entrance of that curiously anomalous cave called the Lomaśa Ṛishi, render it quite probable, in my opinion, not only that much of the remains of buildings, fortifications, etc., still traceable in the neighbourhood are those of Khāra-vela's army of occupation, but also that the excavation of the Lomaśa Ṛishi cave itself was commenced under his orders, and left unfinished because for some reason or other which is not yet known his occupation of Gorathagiri was suddenly abandoned. This cave, which was evidently intended to resemble its immediate neighbour, the Sudāma cave, in every respect internally, is the only one of the seven Barābar or Nagarjuni caves which is unfinished or which bears no dedicatory inscription. The polish of its walls, in the places where these are polished at all, is

[1] *J. B. O. R. S.*, Vol. III, Part IV, December 1917, pp. 486-507.

*Ibid*, pp. 425-485.

distinctly less perfect. On the other hand, it is the only one of these caves which possesses a well-finished and polished *chaitya* porch, with a frieze of crocodiles and elephants. I believe that this is the only example in Northern India of the horse-shoe gabled type of porch, which is not uncommon in the caves found in Southern and Western India. There are examples in the Orissa caves, e.g., the Rāni-gumphā; and the striking resemblance of the Lomaśa Ṛishi entrance to that of the Guntupalle cave-temple in the Kistna district, and to the facade of a modern Toda dwelling, has been noticed by Longhurst in the Madras Archaeological Report for 1916-17, page 31.

**(B) The Karna Chaupar dedicatory inscription.**

On the 30th December 1921, I examined this inscription on a dark night, using a syringe to drench the rock as suggested in Part III of the preceding paper, and also employing a new idea, namely, a petrol lantern to throw a bright light at different angles upon the inscription. Under these conditions the improvement in visibility was remarkable, and it became evident that the inscription had been cut on a flat and polished surface, though this is now much weather-worn; that in certain places damage to the surface was perhaps accidental, but that in one place at least it was undoubtedly intentional.

Each of the first four lines originally contained ten letters. In the third line the first letter has been badly damaged and is now undecipherable, and the second is not much better. In the fourth line all the letters after the fourth, *kha*, have been intentionally and completely obliterated, and the chiselling extends upwards, probably accidentally, to include the sixth letter of the third line, and downwards into a small portion of the polished surface on which no inscription has ever existed.

The remaining letters agree generally with Cunningham's transcript, except the last two letters of the second line, which are certainly not *meta*; the fourth letter of this line is *tha* instead of *ta*, and the eighth letter of the third line is undoubtedly *yam* instead of *ya*. The first letter of the fifth line, which is followed by a *svastika* and a sign resembling an upright dagger, which may be a *trisula,* though like *si* is really *nā*. The fish mentioned by Caddy is below these symbols and is quite distinct. It possesses a well-marked dorsal fin, and appeared to be headless, but closer examination has recently shown that the stone surface within the outline of the head, which can be traced, has either chipped off or crumbled away.

I found no signs definitely confirming Kittoe's idea that a sentence had been cut over the doorway of this cave, but the rock in this region is much more weather-worn, and parts may have broken away. Polish acts as a preservative.

Two facts are therefore clear. First, that the name of the hill in this inscription began with *kha* and that nothing else can possibly be deciphered now. Second, that this inscription differs from those of the other five in the Barābar and Nagarjuni hills in that it omits the name of the sect to which the cave was dedicated ; unless indeed the combination of a *svastika* followed by an inverted *trisula* or dagger can be regarded as a symbol of the sect of the Ājīvikas, who are definitely named in the other inscriptions.

## Hiuen Tsang's Route in South Bihar. An identification of the Buddhavana Mountain and a discussion of the most probable site of the Kukkutapadagiri.

**By V. H. Jackson, M.A.**

*From the Journal of the Bihar and Orissa Research Society, Vol. III, Part III, 1917, pages 293-316*

The Eighth Book of Hiuen Tsang's Records of the Western World, which contains the first part of his account of the country of Magadha, concludes with a long and detailed account of Bodh Gayā. The Ninth Book opens with a description of the places of interest to Buddhist pilgrims in South Bihār, starting from Bodh Gayā and reaching Kuśāgārapura or Old Rājagṛiha. About this part of the itinerary there are difficulties which have been much debated by archæologists, but not yet finally settled. From Bodh Gayā itself, across the Nairanjana (Nilājan) river to Bakraur and thence to the east bank of the Mahi (Mohāna) river, the route is clear enough. Later on, the Yashṭivana, or "forest of the staff," was reached, in the midst of which was a stūpa built by Aśoka, and in which the "exceedingly simple-minded and moderate" Jayasena read with his pupils, and "amused himself amid the forests and hills, dwelling in a sort of fairyland, whilst his mind wandered amid the limits of truth".[1] This must undoubtedly have been, as General Cunningham first suggested,[2] somewhere in the neighbourhood

[1] Beal's translation, Vol. II, p. 146.

[2] Arch. Survey Reports, 1871-72, Vol. III, p. 139, 1873.

of the modern village of Jeṭhian, in the valley between the parallel ranges of hills which run up with scarcely a break to Rājgir and terminate at Giriak. This is clear from the fact that the "two warm springs" in which the water was "very hot", which can only be the well-known hot springs at Tapoban, were, according to Hiuen Tsang, "south-west of the Yashtivana about ten li (two miles) or so, on the south side of a great mountain". Moreover, Sir Aurel Stein, the only archæologist who has published a detailed account of Jeṭhian and its neighbourhood, has drawn attention to the fact that the name Yashṭivana itself still survives as Jeshṭiban, "a small undulating plateau, partly grassy, partly covered with low jungle, at the west foot of the hill which is the last offshoot of the Haṇḍia ridge in this direction".[3] I hope to be able to discuss Stein's identification of this site, and of the others mentioned by Hiuen Tsang as far as Old Rājagṛiha, in a future paper dealing with the antiquities of Jeṭhian and its neighbourhood. All that need be said at present is that the Yashṭivana must have been either on this site, an ancient settlement about ¾ mile east of the village of Jeṭhian, said by the villagers to have been the residence of a Raja of Bhaluahi, or between this site and Jeṭhian itself.

**Unsolved Problems—Kukkutapadagiri, Buddhavana.**

Before arriving at the Yashṭivana, however, Hiuen Tsang describes two hills, neither of which has as yet been conclusively identified. These are the Kukkuṭapādagiri, or Cock's-foot Mountain, also called Guru-pādāh, and the Buddhavana Mountain. Dr. D. B. Spooner has kindly supplied me with the following strictly literal translations of the data given by Hiuen Tsang for ascertaining the position of these hills, and has drawn attention to the fact that there is no important variation in these data in any of the numerous Chinese manuscripts which have

[3] Stein, Tour in South Bihār and Hazāribāgh; Indian Antiquary, Vol. XXX, p. 62, February 1901.

been collated in the preparation of the standard text of the Si-yu-ki :—

(1) "Mahi river east enter large forest wild, go hundred and more li, reach Cock-foot mountain,"

(2) "Cock-foot mountain east north go hundred and more li, reach Buddhavana mountain,"

(3) "Buddhavana mountain empty valleys midst east go three tens and more li, reach Yashti-grove."

The attention of archæologists has been hitherto mainly directed to the fascinating problem involved in the determination of the true site of the Kukkuṭapādagiri. This is only natural, because not only are its position and physical features described with apparently considerable definiteness, but also because the great Kāśyapa, the president of the First Council held after Buddha's death at the Sattapaṇṇi stone house near Rājgir, is associated by Hiuen Tsang with this hill, and with the remarkable legend that he still lies covered over by the three peaks which "rise up into the air"

"In future ages, when Maitreya shall have come and declared the threefold law, finding the countless persons opposed to him by pride, he will lead them to this mountain, and coming to the place where Kāśyapa is, in a moment Maitreya will cause it to open of itself, and all those people having seen Kāśyapa, will only be more proud and obstinate. Then Kāśyapa, delivering the robe, and having paid profound reverence, will ascend into the air and exhibit all sorts of spiritual changes, emitting fire and vapour from his body. Then he will enter Nirvāna. At this time the people, witnessing these miracles, will dismiss their pride, and opening their minds, will obtain the fruit (*of holiness*). Now, therefore, on the top of the mountain is a stūpa built. On quiet evenings those looking from a distance see sometimes a bright light as it were of a torch; but if they ascend the mountain there is nothing to be observed."[4]

[4] Beal, Vol. II, page 144.

**Kukkutapadagiri either Sobhnath or Gurpa.**

Of the three different sites which have been suggested as a possible site of the Kukkuṭapādagiri the earliest, namely, General Cunningham's identification with the low Pathraura ridge about a mile N.N.E. of the large village of Kurkihār, [5] must be dismissed as impossible, as Stein has already remarked. There remain therefore Stein's own identification with the Sōbhnāth Hill about four miles S.S.W. of Wazirganj,[6] and Babu Śrī Gopāl Bose's identification with the Gurpā Hill, about a mile south of the station of that name on the Grand Chord Railway, which was supported by Babu Rakhal Das Banerji and Dr. Bloch.[7] The arguments for and against these sites have been summed up with much fairness by A. W. Keith, [8] who after careful inspection of both hills came to the conclusion that "Sōbhnāth and not Gurpā was the site shown to Hiuen Tsang", although it was "quite possible that in late Buddhist time Gurpā may have been a rival site, shown to pilgrims, among others Ma Tuan-li, [9] as the resting place of Kāśyapa". In coming to this conclusion, however, Keith appears to have been much impressed by the fact that all the Buddhist remains, etc., at Gurpā, were small and portable :—

"The inscriptions at Gurpā are all on pieces of stone easily carried. None have been found cut on the rock itself, so they are useless in indicating the age of Gurpā as a sacred place. The bricks and stones of the two shrines (on the summit of the hill) obviously belonged to some other building, and there are no signs of any stūpa ever having existed on the peak itself."

---

[5] Archæological Survey reports, 1861-62, Vol. I, pp. 15-16; and 1879-80, Vol. XV, pp. 4-6.

[6] Stein, loc. cit., pp. 86-89.

[7] An account of the Gurpā Hill, by R. D. Banerji, *J.A.S.B.*, Vol. II, New Series, 1906, pp. 77-83.

[8] Keith: Notes on some Buddhist Remains in Magadha; Bengal: Past and Present, Vol. VI, July-September 1910, pp. 57-68. The reference to Ma Tuan-li is corrected in the next number.

[9] Watters, Vol, II, p. 147.

This makes it evident that he did not notice the ruins of a stūpa on the peak, to the north-west of the two small shrines which he mentioned, but quite close. The foundations are, as R. D. Banerji says, quite distinct and are composed of large bricks, like the other Buddhist stūpas on the hills in the neighbourhood of Jeṭhian which will be described and illustrated in another paper. In this important respect, therefore, the remains on the Gurpā Hill are at least as distinctively Buddhistic as those on Sōbhnāth, which as Keith admits may have been "adapted in later years to serve as a Brahmanical temple".

Until quite recently, the opinion which I had formed after independent consideration of the problem for eight years and after several visits to the localities concerned was that, on the whole, the balance of probabilities inclined in favour of the Gurpā Hill. The close correspondence of the remarkable fissures in the rocks, by which alone access to the eastern summit of Gurpā can be obtained, with the passages which Kāśyapa is said to have opened by striking the rocks with his staff in order to enable him to reach the mountain peak, seemed almost decisive, especially because there is nothing remotely resembling these narrow passages on Sōbhnāth. For reasons mentioned later on in this paper, it now seems to me probable that Hiuen Tsang intended to describe Sōbhnāth when he wrote his account of the Kukkuṭapādagiri. A rival site for this mountain may have existed at Gurpā even in his time, and the confusion thus caused would explain why he seems to have mixed up the characteristic features of Gurpā with his description.

## The Data for the Buddhavana Mountain.

The real reason why the opinions of experienced observers differ in this manner is that, somewhere or other, the bearings and distances between Bodh Gayā and the Yashṭivana given by Hiuen Tsang are wrong, and must be modified, and that until a satisfactory site can be proposed for the Buddhavana Mountain little or no help in the task of discriminating between Sōbhnāth and Gurpā can be obtained by working backwards along his route, from the Yashṭivana to the Kukkuṭapādagiri. A study of the map will show that the Yashṭivana is only 30° north-east of Sōbhnāth, and practically due north of Gurpā, while the corresponding distances in a bee-line are about 12½ and 25 miles respectively. How then could the Yashṭivana (Jeṭhian) be reached from the Kukkuṭapādagiri (Sōbhnāth or Gurpā) by going first of all about 20 miles to the north-east and then another six miles or so in an easterly direction? Such a course from either hill must lead a long way to the east of Jeṭhian, and in fact to the south-east of the Bawanganga-Giriak ridge, the most easterly portion of the whole range; and deductions from the distances mentioned, such as "one-fourth required to compensate for the excess measurement on ordinary roads from village to village"[10] would only make matters worse. As it is quite certain from the account given by Hiuen Tsang that the Buddhavana Mountain was somewhere in the Jeṭhian-Rājgir-Giriak range, all that can be inferred is that a pilgrim following Hiuen Tsang's directions from Sōbhnāth would not go so far astray as he would from Gurpā.

I now believe that the Buddhavana Mountain can be satisfactorily identified, and that Hiuen Tsang's account only needs a simple and not unnatural correction in order to clear up all the difficulties. Before discussing this in connexion with previous attempts at identification, his description of this mountain must be quoted in full[11] :—

"Going to the north-east of the Cock's-foot Mountain about 100 li, we come to the mountain called Buddhavana, with its peaks and cliffs lofty and precipitous. Among its steep mountain cliffs is a stone chamber where Buddha once descending stayed; by its side is a large stone where Sakra, king of Devas, and Brahma-rājā pounded some ox-head sandal-wood and anointed Tathāgata with the same. The scent is still to be perceived on the stone. Here also five hundred Arhats secretly dwell in a spiritual manner, and here those who are influenced

---

[10] Stein, loc. cit., p. 89.

[11] Beal, Vol. II, p. 145.

by religious desire to meet with them sometimes see them, on one occasion under the form of Samanēras just entering the village to beg food, at other times as withdrawing (*to their cells*), on some occasions manifesting traces of their spiritual power in ways difficult to describe in detail.

"Going about 30 li to the east, amongst wild valleys of the Buddhavana mountain, we come to the wood called Yashṭivana."

It is important to notice that almost immediately afterwards Hiuen Tsang gives a very similar description of another "stone chamber" in the side of a hill [12]:—

"To the north-east of the solitary hill [of the Ṛishi Vyāsa] there is a small hill, also standing alone. In the side of this hill (*has been excavated*) a stone chamber. In length and breadth it is enough to seat 1,000 persons or so. In this place Tathāgata, when living in the world, repeated the law for three months. Above the stone chamber is a great and remarkable rock, on which Sakra, king of Devas, and Brahma-rājā pounded some *ox-head* sandal-wood, and with the dust sprinkled the body of Tathāgata. The surface of the stone still emits the scent of the perfume."

Now this second stone chamber has already been identified by Stein as the well-known Rājpiṇḍ cave, high up on the precipitous north face of the hill called Chaṇḍu in the Jeṭhian valley, and rather less than two miles north-east of Jeṭhian itself.[13] Although this hill can hardly be described as "small" and "standing alone" (being in fact a portion of the high and almost level ridge which runs up transversely for several miles to connect with the hill called Chhatagiri which separates this valley from that of Old Rājagṛiha) Stein's identification is placed beyond all possible doubt by the existence of a road nearly a mile long, which has been constructed to lead with an easy gradient up to the cave from the plain below. This road is also described by Hiuen Tsang, and attributed by him to King Bimbiṣāra of Rājagṛiha. This being so, it may

[12] Beal, Vol. II p. 148.

[13] Stein, loc. cit., pp. 82-83.

reasonably be assumed that the "stone chamber" in Buddhavana was also a cave similar to the Rājpiṇḍ, even if perhaps not so large, and similarly situated amongst "steep mountain cliffs"

**Buddhavana not Budhain.**

The first site for the Buddhavana Mountain was suggested by General Cunningham.[14] Led almost entirely by the resemblance between the names, which is certainly remarkable, he considered that it was Budhain, "one of the stations of the Indian Survey, 28 miles to the north-east of Buddha-Gayā and 8 miles to the south-west of Rājagṛiha."[15] But as he himself indicated in his "Map of Magadha showing the Routes of Fa Hian and Hiuen Tsang"[16]. Budhain is several miles east or north-east, i.e., on the wrong side, of Jeṭhian, and he made no attempt to explain this discrepancy. Since he never visited either Budhain or Jeṭhian, his knowledge of the locality was vague, as his map itself shows. And such evidence as he could collect did not tell in favour of his site—"I could hear nothing ...........of the cave in the northern (?) face of the Buddhavana Mountain. There are several holes or recesses on Budhain, but no cavern, either natural or artificial. This may have fallen in".

At the end of the account of Rājagṛiha in his paper on the Buddhistic Remains of Bihar,[17] Mr. A. M. Broadley mentioned that he had visited "the rugged valley of Jetiban" and the hot springs of Tapoban, and he closed his third paper in the *Indian Antiquary* for 1872 with the words "I propose in the next part to trace the route of Hiuen Tsang amongst the hills and valleys to the west of Rājagṛiha".[18] He was evidently on the track followed twenty-seven years later by Sir Aurel Stein, but unfortunately the further instalment of his explorations which he promised did not make its appearance, and he seems to have left nothing on record.

[14] Ancient Geography of India, 1871, p. 461.
[15] Archaeological Survey Reports, 1871-72, Vol. III, p. 139, 1873.
[16] Archaeological Survey Reports, Vol. III, Plate XL.
[17] *J. A. S. B.*: Vol. XLI, Part 1, 1872, p. 250.
[18] *Indian Antiquary*, Vol. I., April 1872, p. 110.

If, in the autumn of the same year, Mr. Beglar had been able to carry out General Cunningham's instructions to explore the valley west of the old city of Rājagṛiha, he could not have failed to obtain valuable information. But he was deterred by the "pathless jangal" in the valley, and after making two unsuccessful attempts to penetrate it, confined his observations to the top of Baibhārgiri, whence with "a powerful binocular" —a rather unsatisfactory instrument for archæological research at the best of times—he worked out a series of identifications, which are quite erroneous and need not be discussed here.[19]

In his Notes on the District of Gaya, published in 1893, Sir George Grierson described several interesting features of the Jeṭhian valley, but he did not criticize Cunningham's identification of the Buddhavana Mountain, owing apparently to a misreading of Hiuen Tsang's route; for he says that "after leaving *Yashtivana* he came to the Buddhavana, the modern Budhain, four miles north of Jeṭhian. Thence he descended into the Rājgir valley".[20]

Thus it was not until October 1899, when Stein made his tour in South Bihār and Hazāribagh, which remains the standard and almost the only authoritative account of this part of the country, that Cunningham's identification seems to have been seriously questioned. Going on an elephant through the valley south-west of Old Rājagṛiha, he notes[21] :—

"After a march of close on three hours I reached a rocky ridge which traverses the valley in the direction from north-east to south-west and culminates in the Haṇḍia Hill, marked as a Trigonometrical station (elevation 1,472 feet) on the Survey Map. The pass by which I crossed this ridge near its northern end, where it joins the main northern range of the valley, was called Budhain by the Ahīrs who accompanied me. This name may possibly apply also to the high rocky eminence of the main range, which rises to the north of the pass. But a glance at

[19] Archæological Survey Reports, 1872-73, Vol. VIII, pp. 86-87.

[20] Notes on the District of Gaya, p. 23.

[21] Stein, loc. cit., pp. 61-62.

the map will show that its *identification with Buddhavana of Hiuen Tsang is manifestly impossible.* The pilgrim tells us that he reached Yashṭivana by going to the *east,* whereas *Jeṭhian and the neighbouring Jeshṭiban, which, as we shall see, corresponds undoubtedly to Yashṭivana,* lie to the south-west of Budhain."

Stein thus does not mention what seems to be a conclusive argument against Cunningham's identification. After finishing his description of the neighbourhood of Jeṭhian, and reaching the stone chamber and Bimbisāra road identified with the Rājpiṇḍ cave, Hiuen Tsang continues : "From this spot, proceeding eastward through the mountains about 60 li, we arrive at the city Kusāgārapura . . . High mountains surround it on each side, and form as it were its external walls. *On the west it is approached through a narrow pass."* This is undoubtedly the pass now called Budhain, and it cannot be imagined that a traveller of Hiuen Tsang's calibre would describe the same place twice over, first as the Buddhavana Mountain and last as the neighbourhood of a pass leading away from the locality.

In two minor respects Stein's statement quoted above requires correction. Although, as he says, this pass and the hill to the north of it are called Budhain by the people of the district, the Survey station called Budhain is to the south of the pass, on the transverse hill which they call Chhatagiri. Also, this hill does not culminate in the Haṇḍia (Haṇṛia) Hill as he supposed, and as a study of the maps available would indicate. The two are quite distinct, and are separated throughout by a narrow, but deep valley choked with dense jungle, which provides an alternative though difficult route from Rājagṛiha to Jeṭhian.

It is much to be regretted that when the Cadastral Survey of this neighbourhood was carried out in 1907-08 and 1913-15 this range of hills was not resurveyed. In archæological interest and importance these hills can scarcely have their equal in India, but with the exception of the portion between Rājgir and Giriak which was resurveyed by the Archæological Department under

Sir John Marshall's orders between 1905 and 1908, they are almost unknown. Though, thanks to the Hon. Mr. Oldham, the form lines of these hills from the old Survey have been inserted in the Standard Sheets, they are hopelessly inaccurate in many respects, and contrast very unfavourably with the new maps of the Kharakpur Hills.

**Buddhavana probably not west of Jethian.**

The identification which Stein himself suggested for the Buddhavana Mountain is as follows [22] :—

"It appears to me highly probable that the Buddhavana Mountain, 'with its peaks and cliffs lofty and precipitous,' must be looked for in that portion of the southern range which lies to the south-east of Jeṭhian, near the point marked by the entry 'Shahpoor' in the Revenue Survey Map. Here the hills rise once more to a fair height, and project small transverse spurs all covered with jungle. The central and apparently highest point of this portion of the range is at a direct distance of about five miles from Jeṭhian. My enquiries in the neighbourhood did not bring to my notice any local name that could be connected with Buddhavana, nor could I hear anything of the cave which Hiuen Tsang mentions on this mountain . . . . . . . In view of the vagueness of the topographical information here furnished, a personal search for the cave offered little hope of success within the limited time available. I accordingly decided to proceed from Jeṭhian direct to Kurkihār, where a far more important question concerning the position of Hiuen Tsang's 'Cock's-foot Mountain' required close examination."

After identifying this with the Sōbhnāth Hill, Stein became emboldened, for he says [23] :—

"It only remains to point out that the distances and bearings given by Hiuen Tsang with reference to the 'Cock's-foot Mountain' are in full agreement with the position now ascertained for it . . . . After leaving the 'Cock's-foot Mountain' Hiuen Tsang counts about 100 li in a north-

[22] Stein, loc. cit., p. 83.

[23] Stein, loc. cit., p. 89.

easterly direction to Buddhavana. Accepting the position I have above approximately marked for the latter locality, we find it a little over eleven miles and the bearing north-east. The slight difference here noticed in the two map values of Hiuen Tsang's '100 li' is easily accounted for by the fact that in proceeding to Buddhavana the pilgrim had to cross the southern Rājgir range at a point where it is comparatively high and rugged, as his own reference to 'peaks and cliffs lofty and precipitous' clearly indicates."

This cannot be regarded as a satisfactory explanation, as Stein would no doubt have seen if he had been able to visit the locality which he proposed. Shahpur is close to the place where the great Tapoban ridge commences, and is not *south-east* of Jeṭhian, but *south-west*, Stein having evidently written *east* for *west* by inadvertence. Shahpur is not "north-east" of Sōbhnāth, but only 16° to the east of north. The direct distance from Sōbhnāth is not eleven miles, but only nine, and there is too great a discrepancy between this and "a hundred and more li"—especially when there is, as a matter of fact, no "comparatively high and rugged" range between Sōbhnāth and Shahpur—to be accounted for by any allowance like "one-fourth required to compensate for the excess measurement on ordinary roads from village to village". Between Shahpur and Jeṭhian there certainly is a "wild valley" two or three miles long (not shown on the maps), but although I have not yet actually traversed it, the most careful enquiries have failed to give any information regarding any cave or other feature of interest in its vicinity.

Between Majhāuli and Chiriāwān Ghāts, two low gaps in the northern range, there is a large and prominent hill usually called Tetua from the large village of that name close to its northern foot. The highest part of this hill is about three miles north-west of Shahpur, and about six or seven miles west of Jeṭhian, while it is about eleven miles from Sōbhnāth, though naturally its bearing is still nearer due north than that of Shahpur. In spite of the obvious discrepancies, it appeared to me for several years that this hill was a more likely site of Buddhavana. Its southern face especially is very precipitous, and the valley between it and Jeṭhian, though now fully cultivated, might have been "wild" 1,300 years ago. Its alternative name, Ghordaur, suggests that it is associated with local legend. But closer examination has brought to light no feature of interest. In December 1908 I searched it on all sides for a cave, but without success, and I have recently found that even on the top, which seemed to be a most likely site for an old Buddhist stūpa, there is nothing to be seen.

### Buddhavana as the Hanria Hill.

These observations lead to the conclusion that there is no hill west of Jeṭhian which answers to Hiuen Tsang's description of the Buddhavana Mountain, either in physical features or in distance and direction from the two possible sites of the Kukkuṭapādagiri. It will now be shown that if a single correction is made in Hiuen Tsang's account, making the Yashṭivana about 30 li, or six miles, to the *west* of Buddhavana instead of *east* as he wrote, this mountain can be readily identified as Hāṇṛiā, the highest hill in the whole range, and a station of the Survey as mentioned by Stein in a passage already quoted.

This leads to the conclusion that, as the survey station marked Budhain in the map is only just over a mile W. N. W. of the station on Hāṇṛiā on the other side of the valley, the name Buddhavana still lingers not far from the immediate neighbourhood of the mountain itself; and that Cunningham's suggestion was not far wrong after all.

It also follows, if this identification be accepted, that the probabilities are in favour of Sōbhnāth rather than Gurpā as the site of the Kukkuṭapādagiri, as described by Hiuen Tsang, because the direct distance from Sōbhnāth to Hāṇṛiā is about 17 miles and the bearing just under 40° to the east of north, thus corresponding remarkably closely to Hiuen Tsang's distance, 100 li, and direction, north-east. From Gurpā the indications are less accurate, the direct distance being about 27 miles and the bearing only about 11° to the east of north.

This identification first suggested itself early in March 1916, whilst I was engaged in tracing the footsteps of Dr. Buchanan, as described in his hitherto unpublished Journal for 1811-12. I had previously assumed that the large cave described in Buchanan's Report, about six miles "east and north from Tapoban, and in the same ridge of the Rajagriha Hills, at a place called Hangriyo"[24] could be no other than the Rājpiṇḍ cave in the Jeṭhian valley, and that the discrepancy in distance could be accounted for by supposing that he had approached it from Tapoban *via* Saffi Ghāt, which would involve a considerable detour. With the exception of a small cave high up on the south face of the Makariwān Hill just above Jeṭhian I had failed to discover or hear of any cave on these hills except the Rājpiṇḍ; and this cave closely corresponded in its main features with Buchanan's description, although it seemed difficult to account for the fact that he did not mention the artificial platform in front, or the Bimbisāra road leading up to it. A closer study of the Journal revealed the fact that Buchanan never entered the Jeṭhian valley, and that he had described an altogether different cave, in the Hāṇṛiā Hill. On 13th January, 1812, he says: "I went [from Giriak] 6 coses to Hariya but the road or path is very circuitous." On the next day his Journal begins: "In the first place, I went about a mile northerly to see the rock from whence *Silajit* proceeds. I ascended the hill to about its middle by an exceeding steep rugged path . . . I then came to an abrupt rock of white quartz. . . . Scrambling along the foot of this perpendicular rock some way I reached the mouth of a considerable cave which has a wide mouth and may be 50 or 60 feet in diameter and 10 or 12 feet high where highest."[25] Then follows an

[24] Eastern India, Vol. I, p. 254.

[25] M. S. Journal, p.150.

account of the cave, etc., which has been incorporated without substantial alteration in the published Report [26] :—

"Immediately below this was a mass consisting of small fragments of quartz or hornstone, imbedded in a white harsh indurated clay like some of the kharis described in Bhagalpur . . . . . . . . . The floor rises inwards with a very steep ascent; and the cave has no doubt been formed by large masses of the rock having decayed, or having been changed into the imperfect Khari above mentioned, and having then tumbled down the slope. The roof looks very threatening, and in its crevices shelters wild pigeons; while the cave is said to be an usual haunt of bears and tigers. It is perfectly dry, and near the mouth is cool and airy, but at its further side an aperture, twelve feet wide and four or five high, leads into another smaller cave, the heat and stench in which was so great, that I merely looked in, to satisfy myself that there was no farther opening. On approaching the mouth of this, on a cold morning in January, I was instantly thrown into a most profuse perspiration; but unfortunately I had not heard of any such circumstance, and I had no thermometer with me. The heat, I have no doubt, is subterraneous, the stench appeared to me to proceed from bats. I did not see any, but thought I heard them chattering among the crevices of the rock. The rock, in which the cave is, consists of a greyish siliceous hornstone, in some places stained red. The rock of imperfect Khari lying under this cave, and which has evidently fallen from it, confirms strongly the opinion mentioned in the Bhagalpur papers, of Khari owing its change from siliceous rock to the action of heat."

After descending the hill, the Journal shows that Buchanan went towards the west about six miles to Tapoban, passing on the way "a deep recess in the hill like a broken crater, as it is funnel shaped," and the gaps in the ridge now called Saffi and Jethian Ghāts. By an obvious slip, exactly similar to that made by Stein as regards Shahpur and to that attributed in this paper to Hiuen Tsang, the Journal states that this crater-like recess, easily

[26] Eastern India, pp. 254-255.

recognizable at the place called Sarsu Ghāt, was *east* instead of *west* of Hāṇṛiā. This has been corrected in the Report.

**The Hanria Cave and Hill.**

The southern slopes of the Hāṇṛiā Hill are so far from any roads that they are perhaps the least easily accessible portion of the whole range. From the foot of the hill Buchanan's cave is hardly visible, and no information can be obtained from the people of the locality. This is on account of the fact that, just as Buchanan described, *silajit* is still collected from the steep rocks around the cave during the months of Paus and Magh, by the Musahars living in or near the village of Hāṇṛiā, and is a valuable commodity, said to sell in the neighbourhood for medicinal purposes at one rupee a tola. Not unnaturally, therefore, the exact localities and the method of collecting the *silajit* are kept as secret as possible.

The ordinary path mentioned by Buchanan which leads up the hill is easily found, and though very rough, shows signs of considerable traffic. About halfway up the hillside it skirts the westernmost of the precipices at the foot of which Buchanan's cave, or the cave of the five hundred Arhats, is to be found. A side track much overgrown with jungle leads eastwards and upwards to the cave itself. There are in reality three caves here, close together, of which the centre and much the largest one is evidently Buchanan's. Very little remains to be added to his description. Immediately in front of the caves the slope is extremely steep, and the general appearance cannot but suggest his theory that portions of the hillside have slipped out from underneath and fallen down precipitous slopes. It is singular that all caves in the neighbourhood of Jeṭhian show this family resemblance. Though Buchanan did not associate the formation with the effect of water, the "mass of small fragments of quartz or hornstone imbedded in a white (or red) indurated clay" in front of the cave so strongly resembles the curious concrete-like masses found in Old Rājagṛiha, where water is present, as immediately to suggest that the long-continued percolation of water has been the cause.

The upward slope of Buchanan's cave is not remarkably steep, and though its roof is lower, it is on the whole considerably larger than the Rājpiṇḍ cave. Immediately on entering it, one is impressed by the sensation of hidden life and movement due to the swallows, pigeons, owls, and especially bats, which with an occasional jackal, hyaena, or bear inhabit this cave in large numbers. It is easy to account for the effect produced on the mind of a superstitious pilgrim more than a thousand years ago which led him to ascribe these things to the supernatural agency of Arhats, particularly if he, as Fa Hien mentions regarding the Kukkuṭapādagiri, paid his religious worship in the evening—" if any should happen to be distressed with doubts, directly the sun goes down the Arhats arrive and begin to discuss with (*the pilgrims*) and explain their doubts and difficulties ; and, having done so, forthwith they disappear. " [27]

Though no definite foundations of ancient buildings can be traced, it is noteworthy that both inside the cave and on the steep slopes underneath it there are large bricks about ten inches square, of the type usually seen in the ruined stūpas on these hills. These are not apparently to be found in other places on the Hāṇṛiā Hill itself.

Buchanan ascribed the " most profuse perspiration " into which he was thrown when he explored the inner recesses of this cave to subterranean heat. This, if correct, would be an observation of considerable importance in connection with the nature of the rocks in these hills, and with the origin of the hot springs which issue in three localities at their foot. It is quite true that at the back of this cave, as also at the back of the Rājpiṇḍ cave and the Gidhadwār cave near Giriak, a sensation of most oppressive warmth is felt, which causes an immediate outburst of profuse and prickly perspiration at all seasons of the year. This sensation is, however, not due to any physical cause, such as high temperature, but merely to physiological causes, owing to the fact that the air is stagnant and extremely foul. On 3rd March 1916, the temperature in the shade at the mouth of the

[27] Beal, Vol. I, p. lxvii.

Hāṇṛiā cave was 80·8° Fahr., but the air seemed quite cool and pleasant. At the farthest end of the cave, where the sensation of oppressive heat was almost intolerable, the temperature was only 82·0°. Without a thermometer I would have guessed that the temperature was at least ten or even twenty degrees higher than this, and that Buchanan's theory was correct.

Returning to the ordinary track, this winds over the precipices to the crest of the ridge. Here it joins an ancient road more than a mile long, which does not appear to have been noticed by any previous observer. This road was evidently constructed in order to provide easy means of communication between the valley of Old Rājagṛiha and the system of fortifications on the top of Hāṇṛiā Hill. From the valley the road ascends the northern side of the ridge in a westerly direction. On the ridge it turns sharply to the east, continuing to ascend until it joins a large flat-topped stone fort, of the type common in all the hills surrounding Old Rājagṛiha, built on the south side of the more or less level summit of the hill. The platform containing the Survey mark is about fifty or sixty yards north of this *garh*. From the fort, which commands a fine view of the plains of South Bihar, a massive stone wall evidently intended to guard the summit proceeds first to the west and thence to the north until it drops to a precipice so steep that evidently no further defence to this hill—the farthest outwork of the defences of Old Rājagṛiha on the south-west—was considered necessary.

The ancient road from the valley to the top of the Hāṇṛiā Hill is quite broad and still comparatively level. It is of course much overgrown with jungle, but the gradient throughout is very gentle and uniform, and there is no difficulty in tracing it on account of the stability of the massive stone foundations resembling walls on which it has been carried. In all essential respects it resembles the other roads ascending hills from the valleys of Rājgir and Jeṭhian, which were ascribed by Hiuen Tsang, whenever he saw them, to King Bimbisāra of Rājagṛiha. I now know at least ten roads of this kind.

## An explanation of "ox-head sandal-wood."

So far, no theory of any kind has been advanced by Stein or other archæologists in order to explain the scent of the "ox-head sandal-wood" which Hiuen Tsang describes as still lingering on the rocks by the side of or above the "stone-chambers" now identified with the caves in the Hāṇṛiā and Chaṇḍu Hills, where it had been pounded by Sakra and Brahma-rājā in order to sprinkle the body of Tathāgata. The observations of Dr. Buchanan suggest a very probable explanation, namely, that Hiuen Tsang was describing the *silajit* which still undoubtedly exudes from the rock above the mouth of Hāṇṛiā cave during the cold weather months, and probably also under favourable conditions from the rocks above the Rājpiṇḍ cave. Buchanan's object in visiting the Hāṇṛiā cave was "to see the rock from whence *silajit* proceeds" and his account of this is as follows [28] :—

"Looking up from before the cave, I saw, about 30 feet above my head, the *silājit* besmearing the face of the rock, and proceeding from the edge of a small ledge, in which, I am told, it issues from a crevice in the hornstone. It was impossible for me to inspect the place, which is only visited by one old man of the Musahar tribe. Before venturing on the peril, he fortified himself with some spirituous liquor, having previously made a libation to the ghosts (vira) of the vicinity. An active young man in my service attempted to follow him. Going along the foot of the rock, they found a projecting ledge, along which, supporting themselves by the roots of trees, they advanced, until they had reached about 40 or 50 feet above the place from whence the *silajit* exudes. Here the young man's heart failed, while the old Musahar descended the naked rock by little crevices and projections with which he was well acquainted, and having collected as much of the *silajit* as he could scrape from the rock in a leaf, he returned by the same way. A very moderate ladder, placed where I stood, would have saved all this

---

[28] Eastern India, Vol. I, pp. 255-256.

danger; but the old Musahar perhaps considered that such a means of facilitating the route might interfere with his gain. I was told that the old man generally ascends three times a month during *Paus* and *Magh*, and visits as often another place about a quarter of a mile farther east, which I did not see. He says, that in the season he does not collect above two pounds weight, and perhaps gives no more to the owner, Ray Khosal Singha of Patna, who sends it in presents, as it is considered a valuable medicine. When fresh from the rock, *silajit* is of a dirty earth colour, and is always mixed with impurities, that crumble into it from the precipice above. It is then about the consistence of new honey, and has a strong rather disagreeable smell [somewhat like that of cows' urine, but stronger] although it cannot be called very offensive. When kept in a bottle with a glass stopper for some months, it acquires a deeper brown colour, and becomes thicker; and, exposed to the air, it may soon be made into pills. It seems to be very different from a substance which, in Nepal, is called by the same name. From the hot springs in the vicinity and the heat of the cave below, I suspect that it exudes from the action of subterraneous fire. The natives pretend that monkies eat it, and attribute the small quantity procured to their depredations; but I think that the circumstance is doubtful, and have no doubt that, with care and a ladder, several pounds might be procured, should it be found useful; but it owes its celebrity among the natives to its being supposed to possess the imaginary quality of an aphrodisiac. When placed on burning charcoal, it swells a little and smokes, and when heated red, is reduced to white ashes, without emitting flames. It cannot, I presume, therefore be considered as a bituminous or inflammable substance, the only class of minerals to which it has any resemblance."

In March 1916 nothing resembling Buchanan's description could be seen. Parts of the precipice above the mouth of the Hāṇṛiā cave were stained black or brown, but these patches were all quite dry and dusty, and the interior and roof of the cave were also quite dry. This tallies with the statements made to Buchanan, and also by a Musahar from Jeṭhian who accompanied me, to the effect that *silajit* always dries up after the month of *Magh*. In December 1916 the appearance was quite different, and resembled Buchanan's account. The *silajit* was readily distinguishable as a black glistening exudation, spreading over several square feet of the rock, including the ledge which he mentioned. Unfortunately a sample could not be obtained for analysis, as the place where it occurs is quite inaccessible from below without a ladder, or from above without a rope. The whole of the roof at the back of the cave was found to be wet, and drops of water were falling from several places. Even in the month of December I have never seen anything so definite as this at the Rājpiṇḍ cave, but portions of the perpendicular rock above the mouth of this cave are also stained in exactly the same way, and I believe that *silajit* is also collected in the immediate neighbourhood, if not at the cave itself.

**Summary.**

It is clear, therefore, that in all important respects except one the Hāṇṛiā Hill corresponds to the Buddhavana Mountain. It fits in most accurately with one of the two possible sites of Kukkuṭapādagiri. It contains "among its steep mountain cliffs a stone chamber" so similar to the other "stone chamber" now known as the Rājpiṇḍ cave that Buchanan, in describing it, was until recently supposed to have described the latter. The fortification on the top of Hāṇṛiā and the great road constructed up to it show that considerable importance was attached to the hill. And lastly, the valley underneath, between the Makariwān-Hāṇṛiā-Sonagiri range on the south and the transverse Chaṇḍu-Budhain-Chhātagiri ridge is still an altogether wild and jungle-covered valley which may easily be identified as the "wild valleys of the Buddhavana Mountain". This valley ends five or six miles W.S.W. of the foot of the ancient road, just opposite the ruined stūpa near Saffi Ghāt known as Sahudrasthān, identified by Stein, and within two or three hundred yards of the site known as Jeshṭiban, or Yashṭivan, itself.

Thus the only discrepancy is that the Yashṭivana is about as far west of Hāṇṛiā as according to Hiuen Tsang it was east of the Buddhavana Mountain. In order to establish the identification of Hāṇṛiā with Buddhavana, it must be assumed that Hiuen Tsang wrote " east " instead of " west " by mistake, for as Dr. Spooner has pointed out, this cannot be accounted for by any error in the Chinese manuscripts used for the translation. It has been shown that both Buchanan and Stein have made exactly the same kind of error in their accounts of this neighbourhood.

# Appendix.

## The Nature of Silajit.

Buchanan, who was acquainted with both varieties, considered that this Bihar *silajit* was very different from the *silajit* which is still exported from Nepal. The latter, according to the descriptions of J. Stevenson [29] and A. Campbell, [30] consists almost entirely of crude aluminium sulphate. The same kind of *silajit* was reported by Sherwill to be produced in small quantities from alum slate in the neighbourhood of the river Sone near Rohtas. [31] Buchanan's description of the Hāṇṛiā *silajit*, and the manner of its formation, suggest an altogether different explanation, which must, however, remain merely a hypothesis until a detailed chemical analysis can be made. This kind of *silajit* seems to appear some months after the close of the monsoon, and at a time when, as numerous recent observations not yet published have shown, the flow of the hot springs in the Rājgir Hills is at a maximum in normal years, and when water is penetrating through the rocks at the back of the cave. Though these rocks are not stratified, they are split at intervals into horizontal layers, with a general downward slope roughly corresponding to that of the roof or floor of the cave. Should communication exist through these layers between crevices at the back of the cave and the outer face of the rock, as is probable, the water which accumulates behind would have to trickle through deposits of the excrement of bats, etc., before it could reach the surface. It would thus take up large quantities of organic and nitrogenous matter, and probably dissolve out some of the silica and other constituents of the rocks themselves, and it would in this manner acquire the general characteristics of the substance which Buchanan describes.

*Postscript.*—Early in April, 1917, shortly after the explanation given above was written, the Hon. Mr. Oldham, who had been kind enough to interest himself in the matter, sent

---

29 *J. A. S. B.*, Vol. II, p. 321, 1830.

30 *J. A. S. B.*, Vol. II, pp. 482-484.

31 On the Geological Features of Zillah Bihar, p. 17.

me a small quantity of *silajit*, obtained from the Hāṇṛiā Hill through the Sub-Inspector of Hisua at the rate of two rupees a tola, which he had received from the Subdivisional Officer of Nawādah. This has been chemically analysed by Dr. K. S. Caldwell, Professor of Chemistry, Patna College. It will be seen from Dr. Caldwell's analysis, which is printed in this number of the Journal, that the theory that this Hāṇṛiā *silajit* is of animal origin is fully confirmed. The peculiar and very persistent musky odour of small traces of this substance can hardly be said to resemble sandal-wood, but it is characteristic of the rocks in the Hāṇṛiā and Rājpiṇḍ caves.

PORTION OF A MAP, DRAWN IN 1812, SHOWING BUILDINGS, ETC., ON THE RIVER-BANK AT PATNA FROM THE GOLA TO THE FORT.

[FROM THE ORIGINAL IN THE RECORD-ROOM OF THE DISTRICT JUDGE'S COURT.]

Reg. No. 1164 E.. 25.

HELIO. S. I. O., CALCUTTA.

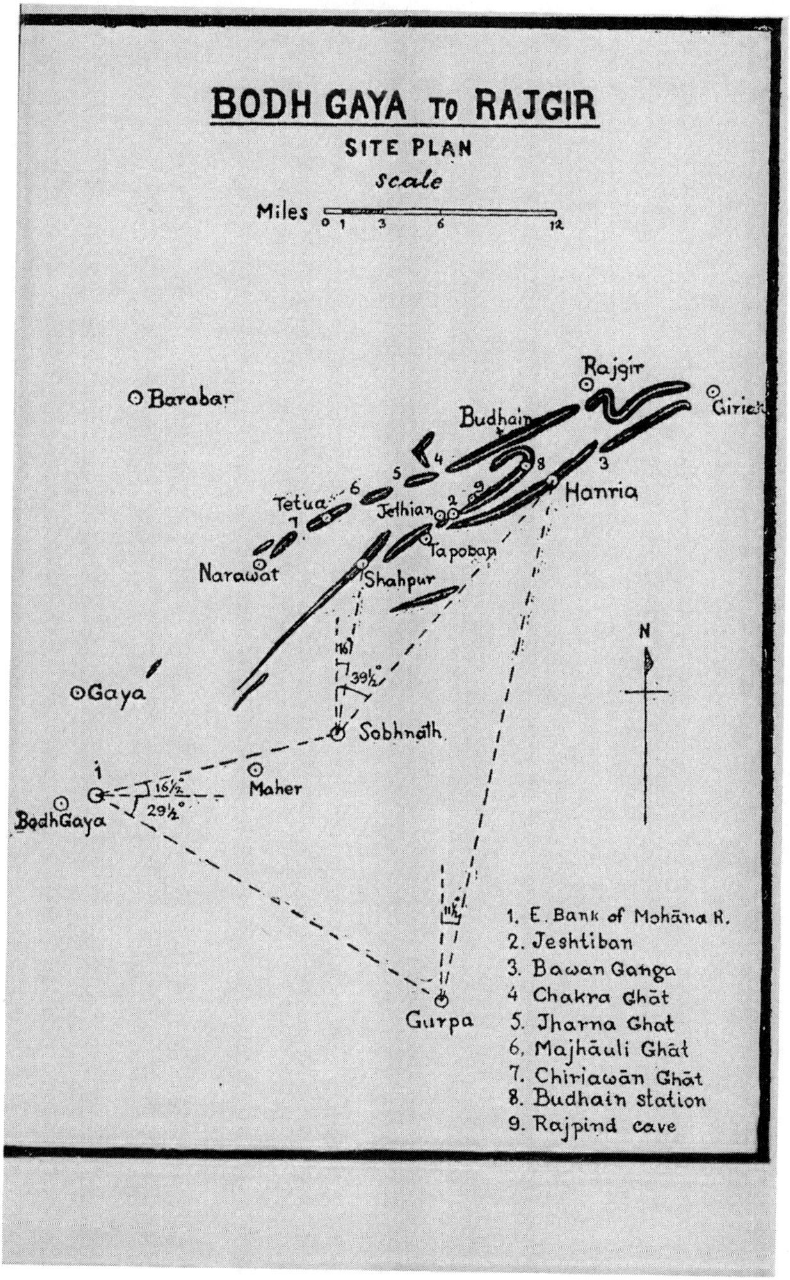
BODH GAYA TO RAJGIR
SITE PLAN
scale
Miles
0 1 3 6 12
Rajgir
Barabar
Giriek
Budhain
Hanria
Tetua
Jethian
Tapoban
Narawat
Shahpur
Gaya
Sobhnath
Maher
BodhGaya
Gurpa
16½°
29½°
39½°
N
1. E. Bank of Mohāna R.
2. Jeshtiban
3. Bawan Ganga
4 Chakra Ghāt
5. Jharna Ghat
6. Majhāuli Ghāt
7. Chiriawān Ghāt
8. Budhain station
9. Rajpind cave

## Chemical Analysis of Silajit from the Hanria Hill.

By K. S. Caldwell, Ph. D., F.I.C.

*From J.B.O.R.S. Vol. III, Part III, pp. 317-318, 1917.*

The specimen received for analysis was a semi-liquid viscous substance of a dark brown colour with a smell reminiscent of wet guano. It is, as will be seen below, mainly organic in nature, gives off ammonia readily on warming with alkalis, and contains an organic acid soluble in alkalis and reprecipitated by hydrochloric acid. This acid contains nitrogen and is probably uric acid, though with the small quantity available I was unable to free it from the accompanying brown colouring matter which interfered with the usual colour reactions.

On ignition a nearly colourless residue is obtained which contained phosphate (about 13%), silica and calcium, together with some magnesium and alkalis. The substance is mainly of animal origin, and the results of the analysis support the explanation of its formation suggested by Mr. Jackson in the previous paper.

*Analysis.*

| | | |
|---|---|---|
| Water ... ... | ... = | 20·4% |
| Inorganic residue on ignition | ... = | 13·5% |
| Organic matter ... | ... = | 66·1% |
| | | 100·0 |

8·24% of the organic matter is nitrogen, 1·36% being in the form of free ammonia and ammonium salts.

*Composition of the inorganic residue.*

Silica ... = 13·4%

Phosphoric acid ($PO_4$) ... = 13·1% (=1·8% of original substance.)

The remainder being mainly calcium with some magnesium and potassium with small quantities of sulphate and chloride.

*Alkalinity of the Inorganic Residue.*

100 grms. of ash = 1969 ccs. of normal NaOH.

= 98·5 gm. $CaCO_3$.

As far as I am aware, no previous chemical analysis has been published. Dr. P. C. Roy in his History of Hindu Chemistry gives the following quotation from Rasaratnasamuchchaya :—"Silajatu (Bitumen) is of two kinds, one having the smell of cow's urine, the other resembling camphor. It oozes out in the heat of the sun at the foot of the Himalayas from the bowels of gold, silver and copper respectively"—and remarks that "the resin of Styrax Benzoicum and also a variety of bitumen, especially the latter, are referred to."[1] The substance obtained from Hānriā Hill may well be that described as having the smell of cow's urine but, as the analysis shows, it is neither a resin nor a bitumen.

Campbell[2] mentions a Black Silajit—"a bituminous substance used in Nepal said to be exuded from rocks." He says it resembles shale, but has much vegetable matter in it. He apparently made no detailed examination of it, and remarks that he is ignorant of its nature. This substance may be similar to that analysed above, but evidently contained less water.

---

[1] History of Hindu Chemistry, p. 47.

[2] *J.A.S.B.* 1831, Volume II, p. 321.

## Notes on Old Rajagriha.[1]

**By V. H. Jackson, M.A.**

*From Annual Report, Archæological Survey of India, 1913-14, pp. 265-271.*

Very little is known about Old Rājagṛiha, *i.e.*, the ancient city in the valley enclosed by the Five Hills. It seems to have been abandoned as a royal residence by the kings of Magadha about 500 B.C. When Fa Hien visited it about 400 A.D., he noted that it was entirely deserted.[2] Both Fa Hien and Hiuen Tsang, however, considered this area to be the old city of King Bimbisāra, and inside it, or at any rate very closely connected with it they saw four stūpas commemorating certain incidents in the life of Buddha. Briefly, these were as follows: (1) Outside the north gate of the Palace City (or "north face of the royal precinct") a stūpa where Ajātaśatru liberated the drunken elephant; (2) north-east of this, a stūpa where Śāriputra heard Aśvajita declare the law; (3) north of this, "not far off," a stūpa by a very deep hollow or ditch where Śrīgupta's fire-pit was; and (4) north-east of this, at a "bend of the mountain city wall," a stūpa marking the site of Jīvaka's preaching hall, with the foundations of the house of Jīvaka and "the hollow of an old well" still visible.

None of these sites have as yet been identified. The walls which surrounded the old city are still fairly complete, but the area inside these walls is now covered with jungle, in many parts exceedingly dense, and nothing stands out prominently, except the Maṇiyār Maṭh in the centre of the enclosure.

---

[1] For an account of "Rajagṛiha and its remains," accompanied by plans of the site, photographs, bibliographical references, etc., see Sir John Marshall's article in A.S.R., 1905-06, pp. 86-106.

[2] Legge's translation, p. 82.

With one remarkable exception, all modern travellers, including the Jain Pandit employed by Colonel Colin Mackenzie in 1821, [1] have recognized that an ancient city actually existed on this site, but only in very vague terms. Dr. Buchanan visited Rājgīr from the 18th to the 20th January, 1812, in the course of his survey of Bengal and Bihar. It is a great pity that practically the whole of his account of this portion of the survey has been overlooked, owing to the fact that Montgomery Martin, who edited the Reports for publication in 1838, cut out no less than 22 pages of the MS. at this point, so that the fragments referring to Rājgīr, which appear in Vol. I of his Eastern India, are limited to a description of the hot springs and of New Rājagṛiha. The complete Report, which is still in the India Office Library, shows that in Buchanan's time the people of the neighbourhood called the portion of the valley enclosed by the walls "Haugsapurnagar," and that they considered it to be the site of an ancient city. Nevertheless, after receiving the reports of the assistants whom he sent to examine the Maṇiyar Maṭh, Buchanan came to the conclusion that there was not "the smallest trace of anything resembling a city, nor indeed is the situation at all fitted for the purpose. It is surrounded on every side by arid rocks, which would render the heat intolerable, and it is well known that all such situations in India are to the last degree insalubrious."[2]

If Buchanan had investigated the matter personally, he would undoubtedly have changed his mind; for the stone foundations of ancient buildings can still be traced in many places, and are particularly numerous in the neighbourhood of the northern entrance close to the road leading from the modern village of Rājgīr. Buchanan's own Journal, however, which has never been published and still remains in the India Office Library, makes it quite clear that he did not enter the enclosure, but with the exception of a visit to the Sonbhaṇḍār Cave confined

[1] Indian Antiquary, Vol. XXXI, 1902, pp. 68-70.

[2] MS. Report, pp. 363-364.

his own observations to the portion of the Vipula and Vaibhār Hills in the immediate neighbourhood of the hot springs.[1]

In the year 1847 Capt. Kittoe mentioned that the name given to the locality was Hansu Taur (Tanr ?),[2] but at the present day this name as well as Buchanan's "Hangsapur-nagar," both of which are interesting in connection with General Cunningham's identification of the stūpa on the hill at Giriak with the Goose Monastery of Hiuen Tsang,[3] seem to have been forgotten. The late Dr. T. Bloch was of opinion that this city in the valley was not used for permanent habitation, but only as a last resort for purposes of defence.

Though the map published by Sir John Marshall in 1905-06 gives a very accurate representation of the hills, etc., surrounding Old Rājagṛiha, the difficulty of surveying an area covered with dense jungle has stood in the way of any attempt to show the interior of the ancient city in any detail. For several years I have endeavoured to make myself as familiar with this area as the jungle permitted, and during the Christmas holidays of 1912-13 and 1913-14 I was enabled, by the kind assistance of Sir John Marshall, to complete a survey of it. The plan now shown represents with very considerable accuracy practically all the important features of the old city which are visible without excavation. Whether any of the foundations of walls, etc., which can be traced on the surface, belong to the ancient city or are comparatively modern is of course uncertain. On the other hand, it is evident that on the higher levels, especially those in the south of the area surveyed, the accumulation of soil in this valley has not proceeded with anything like the same rapidity as it has in the plains outside the hills, for the natural rock in many places is still close to the surface, and occasionally crops out over considerable areas.

For the loan of the necessary surveying apparatus I am indebted to Mr. F. Walford, Principal, Bihar School of Engineering.

---

[1] MS. Journal, pp. 167-186.

[2] *J.A.S.B.*, Vol. XVI, Part II, p. 958.

[3] Rep. Archæological Survey, Vol. I, pp. 18-19.

Most of the measurements were carried out by Babus Chandi Prasad Misra and Ram Lall, Student-Overseers of the School. I can confirm the accuracy of their work in many respects, but the portion of the work for which I am specially responsible is the preliminary survey of all the details shown in the plan, and the supervision of the men employed to clear the jungle along the lines of measurement, etc., during the survey.

The reference table on the plan will probably be sufficient to explain the results which have been obtained, but a few notes on some of the main features may be of interest.

(1) *External walls and gates.*—The north wall of the city has practically disappeared, having been carried away by the torrent which runs down from the ravine between Ratna-giri and Vipula-giri during the monsoon. A few fragments still remain, but these are rapidly vanishing The unusually heavy rainfall of 1913 made considerable changes, especially in the longest portion of the wall which still exists. The eastern end of this, on which a survey mark was built in December 1912, was carried away, and at its western end enough subsided into the bed of the stream to conceal one of the two sāl posts which were visible during the cold weather of 1912-13. These posts are stumps embedded in a kind of white cement, and appear to be very old.

The original north gate was probably in the gap about 50 feet wide immediately east of the temple mound in the north-west corner of the city.

The west wall, as far as the Son Bhāṇḍār Cave, has also disappeared, owing to the branch of the Sarasvatī stream which runs from the south. There is now no sign of a west gate. The remainder of this wall, as well as the whole of the south and east walls, are still practically complete.

The south wall is the highest, rising 30-40 feet above the level of the valley inside. In this there are three well-marked gaps, through which ancient roads can be traced. The pilgrims' road from Sona-giri to the Son Bhāṇḍār Cave now passes through one (No. 5 on plan) which probably represents a South-

West gate leading towards Jethiān. Near the middle of this wall there is another gap which seems undoubtedly to have been the principal gate of the city on the south. From the Bangaṅgā opening in the hills a road can be distinctly traced, which turns to the west round a spur of Sona-giri, part of which has been cut away to make room for it, and then after some distance again turns sharply through this gap to enter the old city. This road can then be traced through the city as far as the north gate. It runs close to the eastern wall of the Maṇiyār Math compound, as is shown by the dotted line in the plan, and was almost certainly the ancient main road.

Still further to the east is the gap (No. 4 in plan) through which the modern road from Rājgīr now passes. Until recently, I was under the impression that this gap, like the road itself, was comparatively modern. A closer examination, however, leads to the conclusion that this gap represents an ancient gate, and that the original road through it corresponds very closely with the track still taken by the pilgrims who descend from Ratna-giri and cross the valley to Udaya-giri.

There is still another gap in this wall near the centre (No. 6 in plan) through which a torrent from Sona-giri now runs. Probably this was not a gate, but immediately to the south of it there is a "Bimbisāra road" leading some way up the hill, with artificial mounds or forts in the plain below.

The details connected with the section of the wall at the extreme east of the city are of much interest, and have been surveyed very carefully after much of the jungle was cut down. It is evident that the great embankment from Udaya-giri, called the Nākve Band, originally joined the city wall, and that the whole of the drainage from the Giriak valley on the western side of the watershed was diverted to the north through a moat on the outer side of the wall. For the first 300 yards or so of its length this moat has been cut out of solid rock, and is 15 to 20 feet deep. Floods have, however, broken through the Nākve Band in quite recent times, so that the main stream now runs to the south, and has commenced to cut away the city wall.

It is also clear that in ancient times the chief, if not the only communication, with the Giriak valley was maintained by a bridge which crossed the moat, in connection with the gap in the city wall marked (5) in the plan. The foundation, for the columns which supported this bridge are still visible.

Another interesting feature in this neighbourhood is the embankment which runs to the east for more than a mile in a straight line as far as the Gṛidhrakūṭa Hill, where it joins a similar structure which leads across the valley up to the hill, and connects with the "Bimbisāra road" which can be clearly identified from Hiuen Tsaug's account. This embankment seems to have been intended partly as a road and partly as a protection for the portion of the Giriak valley on its north. This area, though lying outside the city wall, appears to have been the site of a considerable settlement.

The remainder of the east wall has not been surveyed accurately, as time did not permit me to clear the dense jungle with which it is covered. There must have been a gate in this wall communicating with the remarkable zigzag road which runs up Ratna-giri and ends in a flat-topped structure close to the Jain temple on the top of the hill. It is possible that this gate is represented by the gap through which the pilgrims now pass, but close to this gap is another narrower one, the sides of which are faced with stone, sufficiently wide to allow a palanquin to pass. A similar gap can be seen in the south wall of New Rājagṛiha, close to the Dāk bungalow, and immediately west of the large gap in this wall through which the modern road passes.

The only other feature of the eastern wall which may be mentioned is the curious bend near its north end, with a tank close to it outside the wall. This is possibly the site of the garden of Jīvaka mentioned by the Chinese pilgrims.

(2) *High areas inside the city.*—The plan shows that the interior of the city is by no means so uniform as a casual observer unfamiliar with the locality might suppose. On the contrary, a sharp distinction can be drawn between relatively high areas, on which, as a rule, stones and the foundations of

PLAN OF OLD RAJAGRIHA

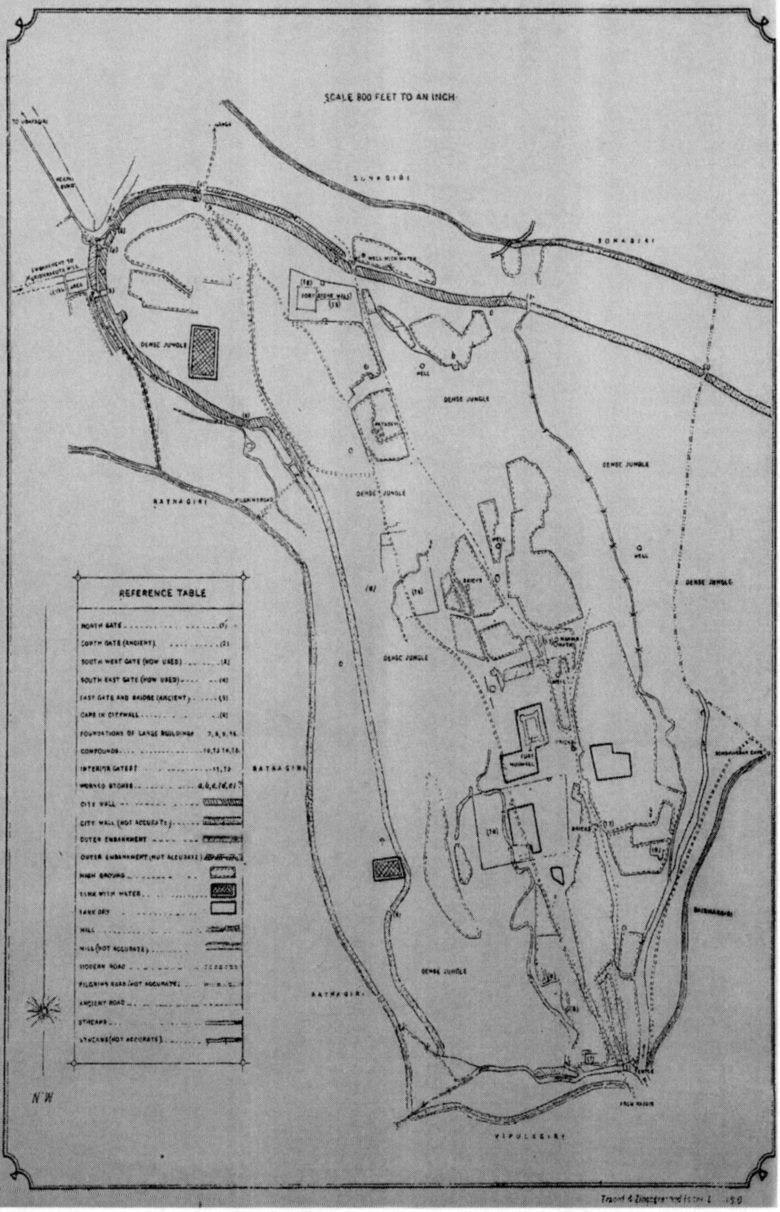


Traced & Zincographed ...

buildings exist in abundance, and lower areas, in which few if any signs of previous inhabitation can be traced. Most of the portions of the city marked in the plan as covered with "dense jungle" are low-lying, and it is practically impossible to trace anything of interest in these, owing to the accumulations of soil and the changes caused by the sluggish streams which wind through them.

The irregularity of the boundaries of the higher areas shown in the plan is to some extent due to the fact that the survey lines have been taken along their bases, so that the appearance is complicated by débris fallen from above. In many cases the tops of these areas are defined by boundary walls. Some of them have obviously been built up artificially with level tops, and thus resemble in all respects the numerous forts which can be seen on the hills which surround Old Rājagṛiha. Others, which are less definite, have probably been built up in the usual manner from the débris of a succession of buildings on the site. Notable amongst the former are (*a*) the area on the north-west of the Maṅiyār Maṭh, which is about 1,500 feet long and 500 feet broad with a tank, now usually dry, in its centre; (*b*) the approximately rectangular area lying about 800 yards south-east of the Maniyār Maṭh with the shrine of Patadeví on it, which is worshipped by Ahirs as a protection against wild animals; this stands quite 30 feet above the level of the old main road which runs past it on the west, and on the north and east is connected with similar, though lower, areas; (*c*) the area to the south of this close to the south city wall (No. 15 in plan), on which stands a square fort with stone walls 8½ feet thick and circular bastions at the corners. This fort was altogether concealed by jungle, so thick that sixty wood-cutters took more than four hours to clear the foundations of the walls sufficiently to allow measurements to be made. It appears to be of great antiquity, and as it lies in the very limited portion of Old Rājagṛiha from which the Gṛidhṛakūṭa Hill is visible, it may be of interest in connection with the tradition that when King Bimbisāra was shut up in prison by his son Ajātaśatru, he was able to see Buddha on that hill.[1]

(3) *Roads.*—Two considerations are of assistance in tracing the ancient roads through the city. The first is that these roads do not cross old foundations, and are comparatively free from stones. The second is that they run along comparatively low lands, with higher areas on either side. The roads which traversed the level country outside the city itself seem to have been protected by walls on either side. In 1812 Buchanan was able to trace "the foundations of a double wall leading to the gap" all the way from the South Gate of New Rājagṛiha to the entrance to the valley. Though these traces are no longer obvious, a similar arrangement can be seen along portions of the road which leads from Old Rājagṛiha to the Bāngaṅgā gap.

The ancient main road through the city has already been described. At two places (Nos. 11 and 12 on plan) it passes through narrow gaps between embankments which project from the high areas on each side. These may possibly represent gates within the city itself, and one of them may be the "north gate of the palace city". It seems certain that the road on the east of this, which is now used, is comparatively modern, as throughout its length it crosses the foundations of walls and buildings, some of the more important of which are shown in the plan. Still further to the east there are signs of another main road, which probably ran from the north gate to the portions of the city on the east. Other roads seem to have run by the side of the city walls, usually on the inside, but there is a well-marked road on the outside, which extends from the centre of the south wall as far as the moat on the east. This road is protected externally with a similar though lower wall.

(4) *Wells.*—The Nirmāyal well close to the Maṇiyār Maṭh on its north is well known, and a tradition still exists that treasure was formerly concealed in it. This well is of the ordinary circular type, and has been excavated in a mass of brick-

[1] *Life of Buddha.* Rockhill, p. 90

work. It is now dry, and about 25 feet deep. The similar well by the side of the old road near the Baṅgaṅgā gap from which Beglar obtained two inscriptions[1] still contains water.

There are several other wells which seem to have escaped the notice of previous observers, and indeed are known to very few of the villagers. These wells are all square, and have been cut out of solid rock. Just outside the old south gate there is one which still contains water, apparently stagnant. Its sides are about 10 feet square and 20 feet deep. The well north-west of this one and inside the city resembles it in all respects, except that it is choked with earth and is only about 12 feet deep. A third lies between this well and the Maṇiyār Maṭh, which is almost filled up. About 500 feet to the west of this is a fourth, about 30 feet deep. The lower part of this is square, but the upper third is built up in circular courses of stones. As it is surrounded by dense bamboo jungle which made observations impossible, its position shown in the plan is only approximate. A similar well is said to exist close to the south-west gate outside the walls, but I have not yet seen it.

(5) *Foundations of walls.*—All the walls which are shown in the plan were from 4′ to 4½′ thick. They are composed of large stones, and at present are in most cases practically flush with the ground. As already mentioned, walls of this type can frequently be traced along the edges of high areas. Others form the boundaries of rectangular compounds. The enclosure surrounding the Maṇiyār Maṭh is about 90 yards long and 62 broad. The area of the compound north-east of this (No. 10) is about 10½ acres. The stream which runs through the similar compound further south (No. 14) has carried away large portions of the boundary walls, but enough remains to give an idea of its size. Though all these walls run approximately north and south, or east and west, the direction is not accurate, the error varying from 2 to 14 degrees.

(6) *Buildings.*—No attempt has been made to show the foundations of these in any detail. As a general rule, the houses

1. Rep. Archæological Survey, Vol. VIII, pp. 85-86.

must have been very small, not more than ten feet square. In a few places the foundations are circular.

In addition to the stone fort on the south which has already been mentioned, another strong building or fort (No. 9) stood close to the western wall, about half way between the Rājgīr entrance and the Son Bhaṇḍār Cave. The foundations are about five feet thick and it seems to have been about 110 feet square. At its north-west corner was a semi-circular tower about 36 feet in diameter.

Another large building (No. 7) ran parallel to the north wall of the city. Its breadth was about 72 feet, and its northern wall can be traced for 160 feet.

(7) *Dressed stones.*—Though a careful watch was kept, very few dressed stones were found. It seems certain that the original inhabitants of the valley were not acquainted with the use of dressed stone for buildings. At several places in the valley to the south of the Maṇiyār Maṭh, fragments of the curious low grind stools which are worshipped in Patna under the name of *gorayā* were found. The flat tops of these are polished.[1]

(8) *Identification of sites.*—Before sites can be assigned to the four stūpas which both Fa Hien and Hiuen Tsang associated with the north gate of the Palace City, the position of either this city itself or of the Garden of Jīvaka must be definitely ascertained. In Plate XLI of Volume III of the Archæological Reports, General Cunningham marked on the map of Rājgīr what he called the "probable position" of these two sites. He placed the north gate of the Palace City (calling it Hastināpur Gate for some reason not mentioned) at a point on the modern road through the old city about 800 yards S.-S.-E., of the small temple which stands on the mound in the north-west corner of the city wall; and he marked the garden of Ambapāli or Jīvaka outside the north wall and at the foot of Vipula-giri, with its centre about 400 yards east of this temple.

---

1 "Smooth" in A. S. R.

Although the present survey has shown that there is no evidence of the existence of either the gate or the garden in or very near the positions assigned to them by Cunningham, there are distinct signs of a gate on the ancient main road about 600 yards south of the temple, with brick remains close to it. This gap or gate stands at the north-east corner of the largest of the artificially raised areas found inside Old Rājagṛiha.

It seems quite possible that this area represents the site of the Palace City. Apart from the probability that the royal residence was a well-protected area inside the city, and at a considerable distance from any of the gates in the outer wall, the Chinese pilgrims' account shows that its north gate was so far from the north gate of the mountain City that they found it convenient to describe the Gṛidhrakūṭa Hill after mentioning the four stūpas, and before describing the remainder of the notable places, such as the Karaṇda venuvana, associated with the north gate of the mountain city.

Still farther to the south, however, there is a similar though less distinct gap or gate across the main road close to the north-east corner of the small walled compound which surrounded the Maṇiyār Maṭh, so that the identification cannot be regarded as certain.

Similarly, there seem to be two possible sites for the Garden of Jīvaka. Hiuen Tsang stated that this was north-east of the north gate of the palace city, and close to a bend in the mountain city wall. According to another Chinese account cited by Watters, [1] it was apparantly "in the enclosure between the city proper and the hills which form its outer defence on the east side". Both accounts would be correct, if the garden were either near the north-east corner of the city wall, which has been partially washed away by the torrents from Ratna-giri, or near the small tank just outside the wall at the place where this makes a very distinct bend.

It is impossible to decide between these sites, which are both concealed by dense jungle. The probabilities seem to be in

[1] *Yuan Chwang*, Vol. II, p. 151.

favour of the neighbourhood of the tank, but this, while north-east of the Maṇiyār Maṭh, is only slightly to the north of due east from the northern gap or gate on the old main road.

Between the sites suggested for the gate and the garden it is necessary to cross a stream shown in the plan. The bed of this lies low, and the stūpa by the very deep hollow or ditch marking the site of Śrigupta's fire-pit was probably at some point along its ancient course, in or close to the large compound (No. 10).

B. & O. G. P. (Rev.) no. 39—1,000—26-5-1925—H. P. G

# INDEX TO JOURNAL.

(*For references to minerals, see Appendix, pages 190-196.*)

## H

## R